Spares, Repairs and Intellectual Property Rights

To Spyros,

In friendship, in work and play.

Anselm

IEEM and International Intellectual Property Law

The involvement of the Institute of European Studies of Macau (IEEM) in matters of intellectual property is based on annual conferences that take up topical issues of intellectual property from a comparative perspective with a particular focus on Asia and Europe. The first of these conferences was held back in 2000, and has meanwhile become an annual event complemented by an Intellectual Property School and IP Master Classes. All three venues serve as a platform for academic teaching and discussion on intellectual property awareness and the proper place and function of intellectual property law in the context of society and public interest.

From the very start, the intellectual property conferences, the IP Law School and the Master Classes have enjoyed the support, assistance and commitment of Mr Gonçalo Cabral, who is an advisor to the Government of Macau, of Ms. Maria do Céu Esteves, past president of the IEEM, and the IEEM's current president Dr José Luís de Sales Marques. The latter was also instrumental in setting up an IEEM chair for intellectual property law at the University of Maastricht, currently held by Anselm Kamperman Sanders, thereby further contributing to IEEM's academic commitment to the field of intellectual property law.

The conference papers, as revised and updated, are edited by Christopher Heath and Anselm Kamperman Sanders as an IEEM Intellectual Property Series the volumes of which are listed at the end of this book.

KLUWER LAW INTERNATIONAL

Spares, Repairs and Intellectual Property Rights

IEEM International Intellectual Property Programmes

Christopher Heath and Anselm Kamperman Sanders (eds.)

INSTITUTE OF EUROPEAN STUDIES OF MACAU
澳 門 歐 洲 研 究 學 會
INSTITUTO DE ESTUDOS EUROPEUS DE MACAU

Wolters Kluwer
Law & Business

AUSTIN   BOSTON   CHICAGO   NEW YORK   THE NETHERLANDS

Published by:
Kluwer Law International
PO Box 316
2400 AH Alphen aan den Rijn
The Netherlands
Website: www.kluwerlaw.com

Sold and distributed in North, Central and South America by:
Aspen Publishers, Inc.
7201 McKinney Circle
Frederick, MD 21704
United States of America
Email: customer.service@aspenpublishers.com

Sold and distributed in all other countries by:
Turpin Distribution Services Ltd.
Stratton Business Park
Pegasus Drive, Biggleswade
Bedfordshire SG18 8TQ
United Kingdom
Email: kluwerlaw@turpin-distribution.com

Printed on acid-free paper.

ISBN 978-90-411-3136-2

© 2009 Kluwer Law International BV, The Netherlands

Printed in Great Britain.

Abstract

Intellectual Property rights have obtained an unprecedented significance in devising business strategies of enterprises. Scope and exercise of such rights often conflicts with the interests of consumers and society at large. While on the one hand refill, recycle, and replacement of spare parts have become an ecological and economic necessity, this may run counter to attempts of manufacturers to monopolize the spare parts market or prohibit a recycle outright by the use of intellectual property rights. This book sheds light on the different interests involved, the different intellectual property rights that are used, and the competition issues to be considered in this respect.

Summary of Contents

Table of Contents

Preface

The editors hereby present papers of the Seventh Intellectual Property Conference organized by the Macau Institute of European Studies (IEEM) on intellectual property (IP) law and the economic challenges for Asia.

The objective of the conferences is to provide up-to-date information on developments in global intellectual property law and policy and their impact on regional economic and cultural development. The conference on Spares, Repairs, and Intellectual Property Rights, whose papers are presented in this volume in updated form, took a holistic approach on the attempts of manufacturers to prevent the refill/recycle or exchange of spare parts as part of a business strategy that allows a competitive advantage at the market stage of selling the main product – and a subsequent recuperation of costs – by monopolising the market for spares, repairs and refills. While the first two chapters analyse the issue against the conflicting interests of manufacturers, consumers, spare parts makers, and the general public, the following Chapters three to seven answer the question to what extent such a business strategy can be more or less successful with respect to the different rights involved, and in different jurisdictions. The last chapter deals with the competition issues of the business strategy. The book thereby tries to answer two related questions: to what extent is it *desirable* to use intellectual property rights and contract in order to shift competition from the stage of the main product to the spare parts market; and to what extent can and does such a strategy work in markets such as Europe, the US, and, to some extent, China and Japan.

The success of the past IEEM intellectual property law seminars has turned the venue into an annual event that since the year 2005 has been coupled with the IP Law School and the IP Law Master Classes. The IP Law School is a unique initiative in Asia offering a taught programme in international intellectual property law and its relevance for Asian, European, and global economic development and innovation policy. The master classes are much more topical and are taught jointly by the regular IP Law School team and expert speakers at the IP Seminar. The IP Law School and Master Classes form a seamless companion programme to the Annual Intellectual Property Seminar. The eighth conference in 2007, whose proceedings are forthcoming, analysed the issues of intellectual property and the pharmaceutical industry, while the ninth conference in 2008 looked at the tension between territorial IP rights and international trade. The tenth conference in 2009 highlights a number of landmark IP cases from various jurisdictions, and traces how these cases have shaped the international IP system today and how they may still affect future discussion and policy.

The editors would specifically like to thank Mr Gonçalo Cabral, who has been instrumental in organising both the IEEM annual seminars and the intellectual property summer school, and José Luís de Sales Marques, President of the IEEM, for his continuing support for both venues. Moreover, the seminars would not have happened without the tireless commitment of Bentham Fong, Beatrice Lam, and the other staff members of IEEM in Macao. Last but not least, the editors would like to thank Christine Robben of Kluwer Law International for having agreed to publish the proceedings of this and future conferences in a series on international intellectual property law.

Christopher Heath and Anselm Kamperman Sanders

About the Authors and Editors

Veronica Barresi is Research Fellow in Intellectual Property at University College London. She worked in the *cabinet* of the Italian judge at the European Court of Justice from 1997 to 2000 and as an associate at international law firm White & Case in its Rome and London offices between 2002 and 2007. She obtained an LLM degree from University College London in 2001.

She can be reached by email at v.barresi@ucl.ac.uk.

Estelle Derclaye, Lic. Droit, LL.M., D.E.S., Ph.D., PGCAP is associate professor and reader at the University of Nottingham, teaching and researching in intellectual property law. Prior to joining the University of Nottingham, Estelle was an associate specialising in intellectual property law in an international law firm in Brussels and was previously a lecturer at the Universities of Leicester and London (Queen Mary). She also spent time as a scholar at the Max-Planck Institute for Intellectual Property and Competition Law (Munich). In November 2005, she successfully defended her doctoral thesis on the legal protection of databases at the University of London (Queen Mary). A list of publications is available at: http://www.nottingham.ac.uk/law/lookup/lookup_az.php

She can be reached at estelle.derclaye@nottingham.ac.uk

Alison Firth is professor of law at the University of Surrey. From 2005-2009 she held a chair in commercial law at Newcastle University, England. She originally studied physics at Oxford University and later read for the English Bar, where she practised in intellectual property chambers. From 1987 to 2004 she taught at Queen Mary, University of London, specialising in intellectual property. In January 2005 she was January term visiting professor at the University of Western Ontario, Canada.

She can be reached by email at alison.firth@surrey.ac.uk

Christopher Heath (1964) studied at the Universities of Konstanz, Edinburgh and the LSE. He lived and worked in Japan for three years, and between 1992 and 2005 headed the Asian Department of the Max Planck Institute for Patent, Copyright and Competition Law in Munich. Christopher Heath, who wrote his PhD thesis on Japanese unfair competition prevention law, is a Member of the Boards of Appeal at the European Patent Office in Munich, co-editor of IIC and editor of the Max Planck Institute's Asian Intellectual Property Series published by Kluwer Law International.

He can be reached by e-mail at cheath@epo.org

Anselm Kamperman Sanders (1968), PhD (Lond.), is Professor in European and International Intellectual Property Law at Maastricht University, The Netherlands. He was Marie Curie Research Fellow at Queen Mary and Westfield College, University of London and has held a research grant from the VSB fund and a Chevening Scholarship. Further research, teaching and advisory affiliations comprise the International Institute of Infonomics, the ETH in Zürich, Switzerland and the Institute of European Studies of Macau SAR, China. In 2003 he was adjunct professor at the Queensland University of Technology, Brisbane, Australia. He has acted as Rapporteur to an EC Commission DG Research working group on Strategic Use and Adaptation of Intellectual Property Rights Systems in Information and Communications Technologies-based Research. Anselm has worked in developing countries on WTO accession assistance projects for the EC/GTZ. His editorial and advisory board memberships comprise the Maastricht Journal of European and Comparative Law, Intellectuele Eigendom en Reclamerecht, International Journal of Intellectual Property Management, and the Intellectual Property Quarterly.

He can be reached by e-mail at A.KampermanSanders@pr.unimaas.nl

Valentine Korah is a barrister who advises on competition, an emeritus professor of competition law, University College London, still teaching parts of LL.M. courses part time. She was visiting professor, responsible for dominant course on EC competition law at the College of Europe, Bruges 1985-2004, and is currently honorary professor of the College. She was a visiting professor at Fordham Law School spring semesters from 1991-2004. Valentine Korah is a member of the joint Bars and Law Societies of the UK, Working Party on Competition Law Reform, a member of the Foreign Advisory Board of the Antitrust Bulletin, on the editorial board of the World Competition Law and Economics and of Competition Law Insight. She is author to numerous articles, case notes and books, the best-known being *EC Competition Law and Practice*, 9th. ed., Hart Publishing, Oxford, September 2007.

She can be reached by e-mail at valentine.korah@ucl.ac.uk

David Llewelyn is External Director of the IP Academy Singapore; Professor of Intellectual Property Law at King's College London; and a partner of international law firm White & Case in its London office. He is joint author of Cornish & Llewelyn *Intellectual Property: Patents, Copyright, Trade Marks & Allied Rights*

(6th ed., 2007) and one of the authors of *Kerly's Law of Trade Marks and Trade Names* (14th ed., 2005).

He can be reached at david.llewelyn@kcl.ac.uk

Mineko Mohri is a Japanese attorney-at-law and also admitted in the New York State. Mineko earned her LL.M. degree from Stanford Law School (California), and is currently pursuing her PhD degree at Ludwig Maximilians University of Munich granted a scholarship from the Max Planck Institute for Patent, Copyright and Competition Law. She worked at Yuasa and Hara (Tokyo), Fross, Zelnick, Lehman and Zissu (New York), and Duane Morris (New York). She was a visiting scholar at the Max-Planck Institute (Munich) in 2004 and 2005.

She can be reached by e-mail at minekomo@stanfordalumni.org

Michael Pendleton (1953) taught at the Faculties of Law at Sydney University, University of Hong Kong Kong and Murdoch University. He presently teaches at the School of Law of Chinese University of Kong Kong. He practised law with Blake Dawson Waldron and Deacons Australia, Bird & Bird, UK and with Deacons, Hong Kong. He currently practises law with Baker & Mckenzie Hong Kong. According to Stephen Stewart QC LLD, writing in the *International and Comparative Law Quarterly* in 1985, Michael Pendleton's 1984 book on IP in Hong Kong was only the second book on IP as a whole subject after WR Cornish's seminal IP text in 1980. He wrote several books and many articles with the late Prof Zheng Chengsi. He was Chairman of the Law Reform Commission of Western Australia (1993) and member of two Copyright Law Review Committees.

He can be reached at mpendleton@cuhk.edu.hk

Andy Sun M.C.L., the George Washington University Law School, J.D., University of Maryland School of Law. The author is an Associate Professor at the Graduate Institute of Intellectual Property and the Graduate Institute of Interdisciplinary Laws, National Chengchi University, Taipei, Taiwan. He is also the Executive Director of the Asia Pacific Legal Institute, a non-profit organization chartered in Washington, D.C. and dedicated to the legal cooperation and exchange between the U.S. and East Asia.

E-mail: asun@apli.org and asun@ncu.edu.tw

Part 1

General Overview: Balancing Interests of IP Owners and the General Public

Chapter 1

Right Holders' Control over Repair and Reconditioning

David Llewelyn and Veronica Barresi

I.   INTRODUCTION

Spare parts are component parts of a complex product, namely a product made of different components, used to repair or restore the original appearance of that product. Examples generally refer to car body panels, bumpers, and windscreens, as a motor vehicle is certainly the most important complex product. Spare parts, however, also include components of household devices, electronic goods, as well as cartridges, pen refills, blades of razors, and so on.

Spare parts may be merely functional when they only have to fit the original product without reproducing the appearance of it ('must fit' spares). On the other hand, spare parts which instead are effectively a copy of the original, except that they do not bear the original equipment manufacturer's (OEM) trademark, must be such that the design of their visible parts exactly matches the appearance or 'design' of the original component ('must match' spares). The latter kind of spares are also called 'pattern' parts (or spares), that is *replicas of the original parts, made deliberately so, to look as close as possible to the original parts.*[1]

---

1. This is the expression used by Jacob LJ in *Dyson v. Qualtex* [2005] RPC 19 and [2006] RPC 769 (refer to 'The UK Regime' below).

Christopher Heath, Anselm Kamperman Sanders (eds.), *Spares, Repairs and Intellectual Property Rights*, pp. 3-19.
© 2009 Kluwer Law International BV, The Netherlands.

Unlike the market for 'single-unit' products, the market for complex products (also called the 'primary market') is intimately related to the market for the components used to repair such products or replace their parts (the 'secondary market' or 'aftermarket').

In Europe, as elsewhere, the policy debate concerning the manufacture and sale of spare parts focuses on whether spares made by independent manufacturers should or should not be allowed to fully compete with products made by the OEM. As for other intellectual property areas, the question is therefore where the line should be drawn between exclusive or 'monopoly-like' intellectual property rights (i.e. the right holder's right to control competition) and freedom to copy without infringing (i.e. freedom to compete).

This paper will provide an overview of the scope of protection available and the limits to it in the European Union (EU) and the United Kingdom (UK) under registered and unregistered design law, copyright, trademark, and patent law.

II.   THE EU REGIME: REGISTERED AND UNREGISTERED DESIGN

The process of harmonizing national legislation on the protection of designs began in the EU with Design Directive 98/71/EC[2] ('Design Directive'). In the absence of harmonization of copyright law, the Design Directive established the principle of 'cumulative protection', on the basis of which a product or an article can enjoy both the protection of registered design law and copyright law, whilst leaving the Member States[3] free to establish the extent of copyright protection and the conditions under which such protection is conferred. At the same time the Design Directive does not exclude the application to designs of national or Community law providing protection other than that conferred by registration or publication as a design. This includes the law relating to unregistered design rights (UDR), trademarks, patent and utility models, as well as unfair competition ('passing off' in the UK) and other civil law liability.[4]

Only with the 2001 Community Design Regulation (CDR)[5] was a Community-wide system introduced according to which a 'Community Design' having

---

2.   Design Directive 98/71/EC of the European Parliament and of the Council of 13 Oct. 1998 on the legal protection of designs, OJ L 289, 28 Oct. 1998, 28. For a general description of the area, see Cornish & Llewelyn, *Intellectual Property: Patents, Copyright, Trade Marks and Allied Rights*, 6th edn (2007), Ch. 15.
3.   The EU includes the following twenty-seven Member States: Austria, Belgium, Bulgaria, the Czech Republic, Cyprus, Denmark, Estonia, Finland, France, Germany, Greece, Hungary, Ireland, Italy, Latvia, Lithuania, Luxembourg, Malta, The Netherlands, Rumania, Slovakia, Slovenia, Spain, Sweden, Poland, Portugal, and the United Kingdom.
4.   Cf. Recitals 7 and 8 and Art. 17 ('Relationship to copyright') of the Design Directive.
5.   Council Regulation (EC) No. 6/2002 of 12 Dec. 2001 on Community Designs, OJ L 3, 5 Jan. 2002, 1.

unitary character and equal effect throughout the EU was created, thereby eliminating the need to register designs separately in individual Member States.

Most of the provisions of the Design Directive are reproduced both in the CDR and the UK Registered Design Act 1949, as subsequently amended (RDA). Therefore the provisions of the CDR and the RDA will be examined together with the provisions of the Design Directive.

A.   THE DESIGN DIRECTIVE

The Design Directive is applicable to national registered designs and design rights registered under international arrangements that have effect in the Member States.

For its purposes (and for the purposes of the CDR and the RDA), 'design' means:

> the appearance of the whole or a part of a product resulting from the features of, in particular, the lines, contours, colours, shape, texture and/or materials of the product itself and/or its ornamentation;

'product' means:

> any industrial or handicraft item, including inter alia parts intended to be assembled into a complex product, packaging, get-up, graphic symbols and typographic typefaces, but excluding computer programs; and

'complex product' means:

> a product which is composed of multiple components which can be replaced, permitting disassembly and re-assembly of the product.[6]

According to Article 3 of the Design Directive, design protection of (registered) designs confers exclusive rights in the appearance of an individual product, to the extent it is new and has individual character. In order for a design to be new and capable of individual character, it must, respectively, materially differ from earlier designs made available to the public before the date of application for its registration, and it must produce on the public an overall impression that is different from the one produced by any design existing before such date.[7]

As regards spare parts, Article 3(3) of the Design Directive states that component parts of complex products shall only be considered to be new and to have individual character if (a) the component part, once it has been incorporated into the complex product, remains visible during normal use of the latter; and (b) the visible features of the component part fulfil in themselves the requirements as to novelty and individual character. 'Normal use' is defined as use by the end user, excluding maintenance, servicing or repair work.[8] Therefore, (internal) spare

---

6. Article 1 of the Design Directive and Art. 3 of the CDR which is the equivalent provision.
7. Article 3(1) and (2) of the Design Directive.
8. Article 3(3) and (4) of the Design Directive.

parts that are visible only during servicing or repair (but not in normal use) are excluded from design protection.

Article 4(2) and (3) of the CDR and sections 1(3), 1B(8) and 1B(9) of the UK RDA are the equivalent provisions.

The Design Directive clarifies, with respect to disclosure, that a design shall be deemed to have been made available to the public if it has been published following registration or exhibited, used in trade, or otherwise disclosed – except where these events could not reasonably have become known in the normal course of business having regard to the sector concerned – all before the date of filing of the application for registration (or, if priority was claimed, the date of priority).[9]

Under the 'must fit' exclusion, the Design Directive excludes from design protection any article the shape or design of which is dictated solely by its function and those which have to be copied to enable an interface with another product. Accordingly, Articles 7(1) and (2), respectively, provide that a design right shall not subsist:

> in features of appearance of a product which are solely dictated by its technical function

and

> in features of appearance of a product which must necessarily be reproduced in their exact form and dimensions in order to permit the product in which the design is incorporated or to which it is applied to be mechanically connected to or placed in, around or against another product so that either product may perform its function.[10]

The policy considerations underlying this provision are that technological innovation should not be hampered by granting design protection to features dictated solely by a technical function and that, likewise, extending protection to the design of mechanical fittings would hinder the interoperability of products of different makes. Apparently, the exclusion applies only where no other shape would achieve the technical result.[11]

It is to be noted, however, that the Design Directive provides an exception (to this exclusion) for mechanical fittings of modular products. According to the European legislator, these fittings may constitute an important element of the innovative character of the products in question and represent a commercial asset which deserves to be protected. Thus, the Directive (as well as the CDR and the RDA) states that, providing it is new and has individual character, a design right shall subsist in a design that serves the purpose of allowing multiple assembly

---

9. Article 6 of the Design Directive.
10. Article 8(1) and (2) of the CDR and Art. 1C(1) and (2) of the RDA are the equivalent provisions.
11. *Per A.G. Ruiz-Jarabo Colomer in Philips v. Remington* [2001] RPC 745 at paras 33-34; also HH Judge Fysh in *Landor & Hawa v. Azure Designs* [2006] FSR 427.

or connection of mutually interchangeable products within a 'modular system'.[12] Many products are modular – that is, mass-produced, and made from standardized, mass-produced parts to fit together in a standardized way – although as noted by Cornish & Llewelyn '[Why this] should constitute some difference in kind from connective elements in other products (often excluded for their technical character) goes unexplained. The concession does show how determined lobbying can squeeze special concessions into legislation.'[13]

Upon registration, a design is protected for one or more periods of five years from the date of filing of the application, renewable for one or more periods of five years up to a maximum of twenty-five years from such date.[14] A design right confers on its holder the exclusive right to use and to prevent its use by third parties not having his consent. Third party use includes the making, offering, putting on the market, importing, exporting, stocking (for those purposes), or using of a product in or to which the design is, respectively, incorporated or applied.[15] This means that notwithstanding the fact that a design right concerns, like copyright, the appearance or shape of an article or (more grandly) the creativity which has been put into it, it is in fact a 'monopoly' right granting exclusivity (as in the case of a trademark or a patent) and differs from copyright in that a work protected by the latter can be infringed only by copying the whole or a substantial part of that work.

Also, it should be borne in mind that, as for trademarks, the principle of exhaustion applies to registered design rights. According to this principle, such rights are 'exhausted' once the product in which the design is included or to which it is applied has been put on the market in the European Economic Area (EEA)[16] by the rights holder himself or with his consent. At this stage, in other words, the design rights holder has no further power to control – in the EU – the (legitimate) use by third parties of products originally protected by such right.

Finally, and more important, the issue of spare parts used to repair a complex product and restore its original appearance remained outstanding in the Design Directive because an agreement could not be reached on the correct approach to be taken, in particular with regard to the inclusion of a 'repair clause' excluding design protection for spares destined to repair. Article 14 of the Design Directive states that until amendments are adopted on a proposal from the European Commission ('Commission'), Member States shall maintain in force their existing relevant legal provisions and shall introduce changes to those provisions only where

---

12. See Recitals 11, 14 and 15 and Art. 7(3) of the Design Directive. See also Recital 10 and Art. 8(3) of the CDR and Art. 1C(3) of the RDA.
13. Cornish & Llewelyn, *Intellectual Property: Patents, Copyright, Trade Marks and Allied Rights*, 6th edn (2007), 15 marginal note 20.
14. See Art. 10 of the Design Directive.
15. See Art. 12 of the Design Directive and the equivalent provisions in the CDR and the UK RDA, which are, respectively, Art. 19 and s. 7.
16. The EEA includes the twenty-seven Member States of the EU (cf. above, fn. 4) and Norway, Iceland and Liechtenstein.

such provisions liberalize the aftermarket. This is known as the 'freeze-plus' option adopted to mitigate the consequences of the failure to provide a repair clause.

B.   THE COMMUNITY DESIGN REGULATION

As mentioned, the CDR mirrors the provisions of the Design Directive. It provides for unitary design right protection throughout the EU, although not precluding concurrent national rights, and has several similarities to the Community Trade Mark Regulation,[17] including the office responsible for registration, namely the Office for Harmonization of the Internal Market (OHIM), in Alicante, Spain.

The CDR creates two distinct Community design rights that are directly applicable in the twenty-seven Member States of the EU: (1) a right obtained by registration at the OHIM, which has a maximum duration of twenty-five years from filing the relevant application (initial period of five years renewable for one or more periods of five years each) and (2) an unregistered right which has a duration of three years from the date on which the design was first made available to the public within the EU.[18]

C.   THE PROPOSAL FOR AMENDING THE DESIGN DIRECTIVE

Neither the Design Directive nor the CDR achieved full harmonization in the EU on the use of protected designs for the purpose of permitting the repair of a complex product so as to restore its original appearance where the design is applied to or incorporated in a product that constitutes a component part of a complex product upon whose appearance the protected design is dependent ('must match' spares). Both the Design Directive and the CDR provide that it is for the European legislature to decide its policy on the issue, on the basis of a Commission proposal.

The Commission proposal ('Proposal') was eventually published in September 2004[19] and was then considered by the European Parliament. Its only purpose is to harmonize the position in respect of spare parts by including the 'right to repair' clause, which could not be agreed at the time of the freeze-plus option. Until an amended Design Directive comes into force, however, protection for spare parts in the EU remains governed by different regimes: where nine Member States have liberalized systems (which do not allow the OEM to register the design of replacement visible parts) and eighteen Member States extend design protection to spare parts. Notwithstanding the fact that the Design Directive has now been implemented by all Member States, the situation is as follows: Austria, Denmark, Finland, France, Germany, Portugal, and Sweden still have design protection for spare parts. In Belgium, Ireland, Italy, Luxembourg, the Netherlands, Spain, and the

---

17. Council Regulation (EC) No. 40/94 on the Community trademark, OJ L 11, 14 Jan. 1994, 1.
18. See Arts 1(2), 11 and 12 of the CDR.
19. COM (2004) 582 final.

United Kingdom a repair clause is provided allowing design protection on new products but leaving the possibility for alternative parts in repair or replacement in the aftermarket. Greece provides for a repair clause combined with a term of protection of five years and fair and reasonable remuneration thereafter. As far as the new Member States are concerned, Bulgaria, Cyprus, Czech Republic, Estonia, Lithuania, Malta, Poland, Rumania, Slovakia, and Slovenia have not adopted special provisions for spare parts, thus these enjoy de jure protection. Hungary and Latvia have a repair clause in their legislation.

Recital 1 of the Proposal states that:

> Whereas the sole purpose of design protection is to grant exclusive rights to the appearance of a product, but not a monopoly over the product as such; whereas protecting designs for which there is no practical alternative would lead in fact to a product monopoly; whereas such protection would come close to an abuse of the design regime; whereas if thirds parties are allowed to produce and distribute spare parts, competition is maintained; whereas if design protection is extended to spare parts, such third parties infringe those right [sic] competition is eliminated and the holder of the design right is de facto given a product monopoly.

The proposed repair clause provides that:

> Protection as a design shall not exist for a design which constitutes a component part of a complex product used within the meaning of Article 12(1) of this Design Directive, for the purpose of the repair of that complex product so as to restore its original appearance.[20]

The amendment's objective is to ensure the right of independent spare parts producers and distributors to operate in the market alongside the OEM in the twenty-seven EU countries. As prices of replacement (visible) parts in the car sector appear to be higher in EU countries that provide design protection for such parts, the amendment is intended to increase competition and lower prices to the benefit of consumers. Also, as a result of fostering competition mainly from (and between) small and medium enterprises, the proposed repair clause is meant to increase employment opportunities in the EU.

However, the Proposal has been strongly criticized, in particular by the car industry, the sector that would be affected most by the removal of design protection (although it would apply to any sector where the replacement and repair of visible components of complex products is relevant). OEMs perceive the proposed amendment as an interference with their intellectual property rights and argue that the revenues derived from the sale of spares are an essential financial incentive for investments into design innovation, as well as research and development. They also object that the Proposal to liberalize the aftermarket can be challenged on safety grounds as independent spares manufacturers may not be able to meet the appropriate quality and safety standards. The main issue for OEMs in fact

---

20. See the Proposal at above fn. 19.

remains that of fearing competition from new entrants and above all from Asian manufacturers.

An amended version of the Design Directive remains to be adopted.

III.   THE UK REGIME

A.   THE UK REGISTERED DESIGN ACT

The UK currently has a liberal regime which will not be affected much by the Proposal if and when it enters into force. However, it should be highlighted that the wording of the Proposal differs from that in UK law. As will be discussed below, UK law states that the design rights are 'not infringed' by use of must match parts for repair, but the Proposal's construction is that protection 'shall not exist'.

As seen above, the provisions of the RDA mostly reproduce those of the Design Directive, including the definitions of design, product, and complex product as well as the provisions on novelty and individual character.

The UK Intellectual Property Office's (IPO) Designs Practice Notice[21] clarifies how the requirements of novelty and individual character should be interpreted. As to novelty, designs examiners will not consider a design as new if they are aware of a prior publication of the same design and have some documentary evidence on which to base their objection to registration. As far as individual character is concerned, the relevant test is, according to the IPO, 'much broader' and 'more difficult' than the simple novelty test, which only considers whether or not a design has been published previously. In practice, when considering whether or not a design would create a different overall impression from that produced by an earlier design (from the point of view of the 'informed user'), the examiner must bear in mind the 'degree of freedom' that the designer has in creating the design. The question to answer is therefore: *'Is it a design applied to a "narrow field" of goods where there is little room for manoeuvre in terms of product design? If so, relatively small differences may be more significant'*. The earlier design may in fact have several features which are different from the one applied for, but it is only the 'overall impression' that counts. To stick to IPO examples: *'[A] tall narrow drinking mug with a small round handle may be compared with a tall narrow mug with a slightly larger round handle. The differences in the handles may be quite apparent when viewed side by side, but the overall impression of the two mugs (tall, narrow, round handle) may be the same'*.

Like the Design Directive (and the CDR), the RDA provides exclusions from registration for: (1) products that are dictated solely by their function; and (2) products that have to be reproduced to enable an interface with another product ('must fit' exception).[22]

---

21.   See Designs Practice Notice 4/03 ('Requirements of Novelty and Individual Character', 24 Jun. 2003 available at <www.ipo.gov.uk>.
22.   Refer to 'The Design Directive' above.

In addition, section 7A(5) of the RDA dealing with infringement provides a repair clause under which the right, in a registered design of a component part that may be used for repairing a complex product so as to restore its original appearance, is not infringed by the use for that purpose of any design protected by the registration.

B.   UNREGISTERED DESIGNS

As far as UK unregistered design is concerned, the Copyright, Designs, and Patents Act 1988 (CDPA) provides that this covers 'the design of any aspect of the shape or configuration (whether internal or external) of the whole or any part of the article'.[23] This includes only three-dimensional features and excludes methods or principles of construction, as well as surface decoration.[24]

The duration of (unregistered) design rights in the UK is ten years from the end of the calendar year in which an article was first made from the design. The original date the design was first fixed in a tangible form is also taken into account, and the duration should not exceed fifteen years from the end of the calendar year in which the design was first recorded. The UK ten-year duration is split into two five-year periods. Exclusive rights are granted for the first five years, but during the second five years other parties are allowed to apply for licenses as of right to the design (for which the owner may require royalties).[25]

The CDPA itself provides exclusions from protection. Along with the 'must fit' and 'must match' exclusions,[26] the CDPA provides that a design right does not subsist: (1) in a method or principle of construction (i.e. a design that is concerned only with how a product works); and (2) in surface decoration.[27] Designs contrary to law or morality and in parts which are invisible in normal use are also excluded.

It is interesting to note that before the CDPA, OEMs who produced design drawings of an original part could claim copyright in those drawings. They could therefore prevent the production of spare parts by competitors by asserting that in making the parts the drawings had been copied. Moreover, because copyright was then protected for fifty years after the death of the author, the OEM obtained protection for the spares for the lifetime of the product and could effectively control the secondary market.

The 'must fit' and 'must match' exceptions were created by the English judiciary in order to solve this issue of 'overprotection'. In *British Leyland Motor Corporation v. Armstrong Patent Co. Ltd*[28] the House of Lords considered whether Armstrong had infringed British Leyland's copyright in the latter's original design drawings of

---

23. CDPA, s. 213(1).
24. CDPA s. 213(1) and (3).
25. CDPA ss 216 and 237.
26. See, respectively, CDPA s. 213(b)(i) and (ii).
27. See, respectively, s. 213(3)(a) and (c) of the CDPA.
28. [1986] RPC 279.

exhaust pipes. Expressing sympathy for independent spares manufacturers and favouring competition in the after-sales market, the court held that consumers are entitled to keep a product in working order and that they must be free to obtain spare parts from whomever they like. Aspects of designs which merely allow a mechanical connection or a product to fit with another product to allow the original product to perform its function should be therefore excluded from protection. The court found that the same applied to articles whose appearance (shape and configuration) was dependent on the appearance of another article.

However, the scope of the *British Leyland* repair defence has been subsequently narrowed. In *Canon Kabushiki Kaisha v. Green Cartridge Co. (Hong Kong) Ltd*[29] the Privy Council allowed an appeal from the Hong Kong Court of Appeal that had reversed the trial judge's finding that the defendant's manufacture of replacement toner cartridges to fit Canon's photocopiers and laser printers had infringed the latter's copyright in the drawings of forty-eight parts of its own toner cartridges. In Hong Kong and before the Privy Council, the defendant had relied on *British Leyland*. Lord Hoffmann, however, held that for the repair defence to apply, it must be obvious that the circumstances are unfair to customers and that the monopoly in question is anti-competitive. The exclusive rights in the drawings of toner cartridges were seen as pro-competitive in fact and there was indeed evidence of a strong market in refilling used toner cartridges in Hong Kong. The court therefore found that copier manufacturers can compete not only on quality and price but also on the allocation of the lifetime cost of their products between initial outlay and consumables. The outcome of this case was opposite that in *British Leyland*, where the exercise of the copyright in the design drawings of the exhaust pipes prevented repair of a car at a reasonable cost, which the House of Lords saw as unfair and anti-competitive.

Again, in *Mars UK Ltd v. Teknowledge Ltd*,[30] Jacob J (as he then was) held that the *British Leyland* defence could not apply in copyright infringement claims relating to computer software or to database rights. Mars was a leading designer and manufacturer of coin-receiving and -changing machines. The latter included 'discriminators' used to determine the authenticity and denomination of coins fed into the machines. Discriminators use sensors consisting of coils which take a series of electrical measurements of a coin as it passes through the discriminator. Signals from the coils are compared with pre-determined sets of data for valid coins. The data are recorded in an electronic memory on a chip. In 1990 Mars designed a new discriminator known as 'the Cashflow', which could be reprogrammed for new coins' data. Teknowledge was a small company that had succeeded in reverse engineering the Cashflow, and Mars claimed infringement of copyright and database right.

Mr Justice Jacob held that the two relevant authorities were *British Leyland*, which recognized a 'spare parts' defence to copyright infringement, and *Canon*,

29. [1997] FSR 817.
30. [2000] FSR 138.

where it was held that any such defence should not be extended and in particular should not be extended to 'consumables' such as copier cartridges. He then concluded that 'there is no overwhelming public policy reason entitling those who purchase machines with discriminators to use Mars copyright and database rights to convert those machines for new coins'.

Clarifications on the scope of the 'must match' and 'must fit' exclusions have been provided in both the High Court and Court of Appeal in *Dyson Ltd v. Qualtex (UK) Ltd*,[31] the first case to deal with UDRs in spares under the regime of the CDPA.

Dyson is the well-known household products company that manufactures 'bag-less' vacuum cleaners. Qualtex is a very successful European manufacturer of spares for vacuum cleaners, which marketed both identical and non-identical parts for Dyson vacuum cleaners including, for example, handles and brushes. The case involved roughly eighty designs.

Dyson brought proceedings against Qualtex alleging infringement of its UDRs in various spare parts. Expressly admitting copying, Qualtex claimed that it was entitled to do that and that this allowed consumers to preserve the look of their vacuum cleaners. The defendant mainly relied on the following six arguments: (1) that most of Dyson's designs were merely copies of earlier designs and therefore lacked originality; (2) the 'must fit' exception; (3) the 'must match' exception; (4) that parts of the design were commonplace; (5) that some were surface decoration; and (6) acquiescence and estoppel.

As regards originality, the court at first instance found that Dyson had design rights in the products, notwithstanding Qualtex's claim that they were not original because derived from spare parts that had been designed and manufactured by Dyson in previous years. In fact, Dyson had only claimed UDRs in respect of alterations recently made to, for instance, some handles of its vacuum cleaners (and not to the vacuum cleaners as a whole).

With respect to the 'must fit' exception, Mr Justice Mann held that the fact that there is more than one way to achieve the necessary interface between articles does not prevent the exclusion applying. Interestingly, the judge also held that the 'must fit' exception would also cover a situation where the parts had to fit part of the human body as, for example, in the case of the handle of a vacuum cleaner which must fit the hand.

Importantly, the judge recognized in relation to the 'must match' exception that its interpretation would have the widest potential consequences for the spare parts trade as a whole. Mann J held that the exclusion must be interpreted narrowly and that if Parliament had intended to confer far-reaching rights to repair and replace by virtue of section 213(3)(b)(ii) of the CDPA, it 'would have achieved that end far more naturally than the wording of the . . . must match [sic] provisions'. He considered that an independent manufacturer of spare parts must consider whether there is dependency of the kind or to the extent that would make the overall product in question radically different in appearance if the spare part

---

31. [2005] RPC 19 and [2006] RPC 769.

was not the shape it was. In other words, if the design of a spare part could be different from the original without radically altering the overall appearance of the whole article, then it was not necessary for the manufacturer to copy the design and the 'must-match' exclusion will not apply. Mann J relied on *Ford Motor Company Ltd's Design Applications*[32] in which the Registered Designs Appeal Tribunal held that the 'must-match' exclusion applied to car door panels because such panels required replacement by one that looked like the original. Given the narrow interpretation of the exclusion, the judge unsurprisingly concluded that the parts at issue, for example handles, stair tools, tool adaptors and brush tools, did not require replacement by a replica and were therefore protected by UDRs.

On Qualtex's argument that some of Dyson's designs were commonplace, Mann J held that whether the design is commonplace is not to be confused with whether it is novel. The fact that a design may exist elsewhere does not necessarily mean it is commonplace. It is interesting to note that Mann J limited his reasoning to whether a design was commonplace in the UK and ignored the extraterritorial prior art upon which Qualtex sought to rely.

The defence based on exclusion from protection of surface decoration also failed. The judge held that a design feature that also has a functional element (in the present case the ribbing of the wand handle that acted as a grip) can be enough to take it out of being mere surface decoration although the functional element must be more than subsidiary to the decorative element of the design feature. The judge agreed with Dyson that the ribbing detail was part of the shape or configuration of the article at issue and thus protected by UDR. On the contrary, colours including flecks of silver in the grey plastic were held to be surface decoration.

Finally, on acquiescence and estoppel, Mann J found that Qualtex was unable to demonstrate that Dyson had the requisite knowledge of the defendant's activities at the appropriate corporate level.

Qualtex appealed unsuccessfully.[33]

Lord Justice Jacob held that the 'must -fit' exception should not be applied to any of Qualtex's pattern spares. In general, however, a design feature that performs a 'fitting function' will not be protected by UDR, even if there are other ways of achieving that fit or interface. Also, he found that Mann J had not erred in his consideration of the 'must-match' exception. Jacob LJ considered the judgment in *Ford's Design Appn*[34] and concluded that, if a pattern spare is shaped so that it is different from the original, yet when employed did not result in the whole article becoming 'radically different in appearance', then there would be no need for copying to take place, no infringement would have occurred and the 'must match' exception would not apply. Therefore, if 'design freedom' is there, no dependency of the kind required by the 'must-match' exclusion exists.

The very narrow interpretation which was given to the exclusions in *Dyson v. Qualtex* appears to be at odds with the reasoning behind the Commission's

---

32. [1994] RPC 545.
33. [2006] RPC 769 (Tuckey, Jacob and Lloyd LJJ).
34. [1994] RPC 545.

Proposal and with Article 8 of the CDR, which exclude registered and unregistered design protection for designs dictated by a purely technical function. It is to be noted, however, that among the articles considered in the case, none had been created after March 2002 when the CDR entered into force.

IV. SPARE PARTS AND TRADEMARKS

Trademark rights have long been used to protect spares, as for example in the case of car front grilles or decorative elements, such as BMW's front grille, the Mercedes' star, or the Rolls-Royce Flying Lady.

Under EU (and UK) trademark law, the shape of a product can be registered as a trademark. According to the relevant provisions of the Trade Marks Directive[35] and the Trade Marks Act 1994 (TMA), a shape mark must satisfy the following requirements: (1) it must be distinctive of the relevant product; (2) must not consist exclusively of the nature of the goods covered; (3) must not be exclusively necessary to obtain a specific technical result; and (4) must not consist exclusively of a shape that gives substantial value to the goods.[36]

The Trade Marks Directive (and its equivalent provision in the TMA)[37] expressly provides that

> The trade mark [sic] shall not entitle the proprietor to prohibit a third party from using, in the course of trade, the trade mark [sic] where it is necessary to indicate the intended purpose of a product or service, in particular as accessories or spare parts provided that he uses them in accordance with honest practices in industrial or commercial matters.

In the UK, the issue of whether a mark can be registered to be used (by its owner) on goods that have been repaired after they have been sold was addressed as long ago as 1945, when the House of Lords decided the *Aristoc Ltd v. Rysta Ltd* case.[38]

The European Court of Justice (ECJ) has had on many occasions to comment on the use by a third party of a trademark of which it is not the owner in order to indicate the intended purpose of the product marketed and the case law is now settled on the issue. In *Parfums Christian Dior v. Evora* the Court held that when trademarked goods have been put on the Community market by the proprietor of the trademark or with his consent, a reseller, besides being free to resell those goods, is also free to make use of the trademark in order to bring to the public's attention the further commercialization of those goods.[39]

---

35. First Council Directive of 21 Dec. 1988 to approximate the laws of the Member States relating to trademarks, OJ L 159, 1989, 60.
36. See Arts 2 and 3(e) of the Trade Marks Directive and ss 1(1) and 3(2) of the TMA. See also Council Regulation 40/94 of 20 Dec. 1993 on the Community trademark, OJ L 11 1994, 1, Arts 4 and 7(1)(e).
37. Section 11(2)(c) of the TMA.
38. [1945] RPC 68.
39. Case C-337/95 *Parfums Christian Dior v. Evora* [1997] ECR I-6013, para. 38.

In *Volvo*[40] and *Renault*[41] the ECJ addressed the issue of whether the use of an intellectual property right could amount to an infringement of Article 82 of the EC Treaty, that is, to an abuse of a dominant position. The case concerned Volvo's refusal to grant third parties a license of its design rights on its car parts. The ECJ held that the refusal to grant a license does not in itself constitute an abuse of dominant position. The principle was then expanded in *Renault* where the Court clarified the circumstances in which a refusal to grant a license could amount to an abuse of dominant position. The case involved proceedings brought by a trade association (comprising a number of Italian undertakings which manufactured and marketed bodywork spare parts for motor vehicles) against the French OEM with respect to the latter's refusal to supply spare parts.

The ECJ held:

> Exercise of the exclusive [design] right may be prohibited . . . if it gives rise to certain abusive conduct on the part of an undertaking occupying a dominant position such as an arbitrary refusal to deliver spare parts to independent repairers, the fixing of prices for spare parts at an unfair level[,] or a decision no longer to produce spare parts for a particular model even though many cars of that model remain in circulation, provided that such conduct is liable to affect trade between Member States.[42]

In *BMW v. Deenik* (advertisement relating to car repair and maintenance in the context of sales of second-hand BMW cars) the Court held that the use of a trademark to advertise to the public the repair and maintenance of products constitutes use indicating the intended purpose of the service that is legitimate, provided the use is necessary to indicate that purpose and is in accordance with honest practices in industrial or commercial matters. As stated by the Court:

> In that regard, the requirement that use of the trademark be made in accordance with honest practices in industrial or commercial matters constitutes in substance the expression of a duty to act fairly in relation to the legitimate interests of the trademark owner, similar to that imposed on the reseller where he uses another's trademark to advertise the resale of products covered by that mark.[43]

With specific reference to a case of allegedly misleading advertisements concerning spare parts, the ECJ held:

> [T]he indication, in the catalogue of a supplier of spare parts and consumable items suitable for the products of an equipment manufacturer, of product

40. Case 238/87 *AB Volvo v. Erik Veng* [1988] ECR 6211.
41. Case 53/87 *Consorzio Italiano della Componentistica di Ricambio per Autoveicoli (CICRA) CICCRA and Maxicar v. Renault* [1988] ECR 6039.
42. *Renault ibid.* para. 16. The issues of refusal to grant a license of an intellectual property right – and in particular copyright – and compulsory licenses has been addressed in case C-418/01, *IMS Health GmbH & Co. OHG v. NDC Health GmbH & Co. KG* [2004] ECR I-5039.
43. C-63/97 *Bayerische Motorenwerke AG (BMW) and BMW Nederland BV v. Ronald Karel Deenik* [1999] ECR I-905, paras 55-61.

numbers (OEM numbers) by which the equipment manufacturer designates the spare parts and consumable items [that] he himself sells[,] may constitute comparative advertising [that] objectively compares one or more material, relevant, verifiable and representative features of goods.[44]

Finally, the issue of 'necessary use' and 'honest practices' with particular reference to spare parts was addressed by the ECJ in the *Gillette* case.[45] The case was referred to the ECJ by the Finnish Supreme Court in proceedings between Gillette Group Finland, the claimant, and LA Laboratories. The latter was a manufacturer of various razors (both razors composed of a handle and replaceable blade, as well as replaceable blades sold separately) marketed in Finland under the trademark Parason FLEXOR. Its blades were marketed with red stickers attached to the packaging that stated: 'All Parason FLEXOR® and all Gillette SENSOR® HANDLES are COMPATIBLE with this razor blade'. The Gillette Group Finland, which has the exclusive right to use the trademarks GILLETTE and SENSOR in Finland, claimed infringement of its trademarks before the court of first instance of Helsinki, which found in favour of Gillette. The judgment was reversed by the Court of Appeal of Helsinki, and Gillette appealed to the Supreme Court.

The ECJ reasserted that a trademark owner may not prohibit a third party from using the trademark where it was necessary to indicate the intended purpose of a product or service, in particular as accessories or spare parts. In line with its case law, the Court held that such use, however, must be in accordance with honest practices in industrial and commercial matters. Use of the trademark by a third party would be 'necessary', according to the Court, where it is the only means of providing the public with comprehensible and complete information as to the intended purpose of the third party's product. This meant that the third party must act fairly in relation to the legitimate interests of the trademark owner. The ECJ also provided guidance on the concept of 'honest use', albeit in the form of 'negative' exclusions. Accordingly, such use would not be honest where: (1) it gives the impression that there is a commercial connection between the third party and the trademark owner; (2) it affects the value of the mark by taking unfair advantage of its distinctive character or repute; (3) it entails discrediting or denigration of the mark; or (4) it is such that the product is presented as an imitation of the original product bearing the mark.

Although the ECJ has clarified in *Gillette* what may or may not be fair commercial use, national courts may interpret the concept in different ways. For the time being, however, the Finnish Supreme Court,[46] where the case went after the ECJ's ruling, ruled in favour of the defendant's use of the Gillette mark which was the only way to inform consumers on the characteristics of its products. The national court noted, however, that the message on the stickers could have been

---

44. Case C-112/99 *Toshiba Europe GmbH v. Katun Germany GmbH* [2001] ECR I-7145, para. 40.
45. Case C-228/03 *The Gillette Company and Gillette Group Finland Oy v. LA-Laboratories Ltd Oy* [2005] ECR I-2337.
46. Judgment of 22 Feb. 2006, Decision 2006/17.

more neutral, for example simply saying: 'This razor blade is compatible with Gillette Sensor handles.'

V.   PATENTS

Spare parts that have a technical effect capable of industrial application can be patented as can any other kind of article which satisfies the requirements of patentability. As inventions are protected for twenty years from the date of application for a patent (assuming the patent is granted), in Europe a patented spare part would be afforded a long period of monopoly protection. Further, it is to be remembered that when a product is patented as a whole, the manufacture or sale of unauthorized spare parts for such a product would constitute an infringement.

One important question involving patented products is whether, and if so to what extent, third parties are entitled to repair or modify such products. Under UK law the right to repair has traditionally been based on the idea of implied license.[47] In *United Wire Ltd v. Screen Repair Services Ltd and Others*[48] the House of Lords held that 'making' and 'repair' vis-à-vis a patented product are two exclusive rights. The repair right is not an independent right conferred upon the owner by license, express or implied, but is a residual right forming part of the right to do whatever does not amount to making the product. The case concerned the infringement of two UK patents for improvements to sifting screens used to recycle drilling fluid in the offshore oil-drilling industry. The defendants had attempted to enter this market by selling reconditioned screens made from the plaintiffs' own frames. The defendants argued that although the product they sold was a screen made in accordance with the invention, they did not infringe the plaintiff's rights because they only repaired screens that had been marketed with the consent of the plaintiff. Therefore, in marketing the screens, the plaintiff impliedly licensed anyone who acquired a screen to prolong its life by repair. It was also argued that the marketing of the screens constituted an exhaustion of any rights that a repair might infringe. Furthermore, it was said that a person who repairs a screen does not 'make' that screen in the sense required to infringe the patent.

At trial the judge (Robert Walker J) followed *Solar Thomson Engineering Co. Ltd v. Barton* and held that there was an implied license to repair. He was 'narrowly persuaded' that the defendants' activities should be considered to be repairs as the frame in question was an essential component and that when the defendants attached a new double mesh 'the screen's useful life [was] in that way prolonged'. The Court of Appeal, however, disagreed on the concept of implied license and Lord Justices Evans, Aldous and Ward focused on whether the defendant had 'made' the product. It was thus held that if a repair was not an infringement, it was because it did not infringe the patentee's right to prevent others from making the product. In this case, the defendants had made the product as they had repaired

---

47. See *Solar Thompson Engineering Co. Ltd v. Barton* [1977] RPC 537.
48. [2001] RPC 439.

or reconditioned the frame and then used that frame to make a screen in exactly the same way as if they had bought the frames as components from a third party.

The question of how much of a patented product a third party is able to repair or modify before infringing the owner's right to make the product remains open and the answer to it would depend on the particular circumstances of the relevant case. The factors that most likely will be taken into consideration are the relevance of the repair service, that is the amount of the patented product repaired, and the importance of the parts repaired in the patented product in relation to the latter.[49]

As a matter of principle, entitlement to repair a patented product means that purchasers of such products 'must be entitled to carry out what is a genuine repair whether it is economical to do so or not and whether the part repaired or replaced in the course of what is truly a repair is crucial to the function of the patented product or not'.[50] It is also worth noting that the fact that the repaired article may not work as well or as safely as the original product will not be relevant to the decision as to whether the repair is legitimate.[51]

---

49. See *Sirdar Rubber v. Wallington Weston* (1905) 22 RPC 257 and *United Wire v. Screen Repairs Service* [2001] RPC 439.
50. See *Solar Thompson Engineering Co. Ltd v. Barton*, see fn. 47.
51. Cf. *Dellareed v. Delking Developments* [1988] FSR 329.

Chapter 2

Repair and Recycle between IP Rights, End User License Agreements and Encryption

Estelle Derclaye

I.   INTRODUCTION

A wide range of everyday products that can be protected by various intellectual property rights (IPR) can be repaired or recycled. This includes mainly technical products such as vehicles (cars, planes, trucks, ships), electrical appliances (printers, photocopiers, phones, radios, CD, DVD and MP3 players, irons, ovens, mixers, etc.), buildings, as well as hardware and software. It also sometimes involves 'purely artistic' works such as literary, musical, dramatic, audiovisual and artistic works, films and sound recordings, if they have been damaged and need to be restored.

This article deals with the question whether it is lawful to block repair and recycle of intellectual property-protected products by way of end user license agreements (EULAs) or technological protection measures other than software (TPMs). Before this question can be answered, it is necessary to ascertain what repair and recycle mean and what their legal effects are. It must then be determined whether under the copyright, design, patent and trademark laws, there is a user's right to repair and to recycle the protected products they purchased. This is what the first section will attempt to discover. Thereafter, the central question can be tackled, that is: if those rights exist, are they imperative? In other words, are those

Christopher Heath, Anselm Kamperman Sanders (eds.), *Spares, Repairs and Intellectual Property Rights*, pp. 21-56.
© 2009 Kluwer Law International BV, The Netherlands.

copyright, patent, design and trademark law limits public policy rules from which no one can derogate, or on the contrary are they default rules? May the limits of these laws allowing repair and recycle, if and when they exist, be overridden by contract and/or TPMs? Sections III and IV will attempt to answer this question. The final section seeks to determine whether, as a matter of policy, those limits should be overridden. To do so, it uses several arguments and legal theories. The article will review European and American laws and only addresses the issue of whether contracts overriding limits allowing repair and recycle are valid under intellectual property rather than under contract law. Some answers to this latter aspect may be found in L. Guibault's thesis.[1]

II. PRELIMINARY QUESTIONS

A. Notions of 'Repair' and 'Recycle' and Their Legal Effects

Before answering whether intellectual property laws allow the blocking of repair or recycle, the determination of the meaning of those terms is in order. Recycling is defined neither in the intellectual property statutes nor in case law. Its ordinary meaning is therefore found in dictionaries. To recycle is defined as 'to collect waste, to valorize or reutilize it as such or to reintroduce it in the production cycle from which it originates'[2] or 'to pass again through a series of changes or treatments, to process (as liquid body waste, glass, or cans) in order to regain material for human use; to adapt to a new use; to make ready for reuse'.[3] Although recycling may sometimes involve a change in the product, for the purposes of this article the concept of recycling will not involve such changes, to contrast it with repair.

The notion of repair is rarely defined in intellectual property statutes, but has been interpreted in the case law. In the United Kingdom, the definition of repair for the purposes of copyright law is 'to restore to good condition by renewal and replacement of decayed and damaged parts'.[4] Therefore, repair includes the replacement of a defective component but not the replacement of the whole article.[5] The same applies in British patent law.[6] A similar rule applies to architectural works. Section 65 of the British Copyright Act (CDPA) provides that

---

1. L. Guibault, *Copyright Limitations and Contracts: An Analysis of the Contractual Overridability of Limitations on Copyright* (The Hague: Kluwer Law International, 2002).
2. Le Petit Larousse Illustré 1999.
3. Merriam-Webster Online Dictionary <www.m-w.com/cgi-bin/dictionary> (last visited 9 Apr. 2006).
4. See Foster J. in *Gardner & Sons Ltd v. Paul Sykes Organisation Ltd* [1981] F.S.R. 281, 284 quoted in *British Leyland Motor Corporation and Others v. Armstrong Patents Company Limited* [1986] RPC 279, at 348.
5. *British Leyland* (above, fn. 4), at 343, 348.
6. *Solar Thomson Engineering Co. Ltd v. Barton* [1977] RPC 537; *United Wire v. Screen Repair Services (Scotland) Ltd* [2001] RPC 439.

copyright in a building or in plans of a building is not infringed by reconstructing that building. However, extending a building without the permission of the copyright holder so that a substantial part of the building or plans is reproduced is likely to infringe.[7] In the United States, repair is defined in section 117 of the Copyright Act, which relates to computer programs. It states that 'the "repair" of a machine is the restoring of the machine to the state of working in accordance with its original specifications and any changes to those specifications authorized for that machine'. This means fixing a broken machine, that is, when there are worn or defective components.[8] In patent law, one court defined repair as the 'restoration to a sound, good or complete state after decay, injury, dilapidation, or partial destruction'.[9] This conception of repair in the United Kingdom and the United States more or less coincides with the dictionary definition of repair: 'to put back to its original state something that is damaged or deteriorated'[10] or 'to restore by replacing a part or putting together what is torn or broken'.[11] The slight difference is that the dictionary definitions could include replacing the whole product.

On the basis of these definitions of repair and recycle, it is then necessary to discover what those actions entail as far as intellectual property rights (IPRs) are concerned.

Repair generally involves using, making, reproducing, selling, offering to sell or adapting the product protected by an IPR, generally in the course of trade (i.e. if not done privately).[12] Therefore, it involves a restricted act under copyright, patent, design and trademark laws. The principle of exhaustion is not involved here since we are dealing with the making of a part of the product, not a further transfer of the unadulterated – albeit used – original article. Repair may also involve simply gluing the original parts of an article together or pasting the pages of a book back together, and thus involve no act restricted by intellectual property laws. In this case, therefore, no authorization is needed from the IPR holder. However, these cases are not the most important ones. Usual cases of repair involve the making of spare parts for example for cars, printers, and the like.

On the other hand, recycling a product involves a re-use or transfer of the original product. This does not involve any of the exclusive rights in copyright, patent, design, and trademark laws as the principle of exhaustion or the first sale

7. J. Phillips & A. Firth, *Introduction to Intellectual Property Law*, 4th edn (London: Butterworths, 2001), 214, citing *Meikle v. Maufe* [1941] 3 All ER 144.
8. *StorageTek v. Custom Hardware Engineering and Consulting* (Fed. Cir. 2005), at 7, available at <www.fedcir.gov/opinions/04-1462.pdf> (last visited on 1 Jun. 2006).
9. *Goodyear Shoe Mach. v. Jackson*, 112 F. 146, 150 (1st Cir. 1901).
10. Le Petit Larousse Illustré 1999.
11. Merriam-Webster Online Dictionary (above, fn. 3).
12. Section 271 US of the Patent Act; s. 60 of the UK of the Patent Act; Art. 27 of the Belgian Patent Act; Art. L. 613-3 of the French Patent Act; s. 1114 of the US Trade Mark Act; Art. 5 of the Trade Mark Directive (Directive 89/104/EEC of 21 Dec. 1988 to approximate the laws of the Member States relating to trademarks, OJ L 040 ,11 Feb. 1989, 1-7); s. 106 of the US Copyright Act; s. 16 of the CDPA; Art. 1 of the Belgian Copyright Act; Art. 122-1 and 122-2 of the French Copyright Act; Art. 12 of the Designs Directive (Directive 98/71 of 13 Oct. 1998 on the legal protection of designs, OJ L 289, 28 Oct. 1998, 28-35) and s. 271 of the US Patent Act.

doctrine applies. As a reminder, this principle, which applies to all IPR, provides that the right of distribution of the IPR holder is exhausted once he first puts his product on the market.[13] Nevertheless, sometimes the law allows IPR holders to limit the exhaustion principle.

Repair and recycle therefore involve some of the exclusive rights of IPR holders on their protected products.

B.   INTELLECTUAL PROPERTY LAWS' LIMITS IN RELATION
                WITH REPAIR AND RECYCLE

While repair and recycle may involve acts restricted by intellectual property laws, they also sometimes involve limits provided in those laws and therefore are not infringements. In all intellectual property laws, there are two important limits to the rights: the principle of exhaustion and the principle that IPR only last for a set term.[14] Therefore, it is not an infringement to recycle or repair a product if the term of protection of the IPR on the product expired or the product has been put on the market by the IPR holder or with his consent. In addition, each intellectual property law has other specific limits: the exceptions to the rights. This section examines whether European and American intellectual property laws include an exception for repair. As stated above, recycling is in principle allowed under the doctrine of exhaustion.

1.   Copyright Law

a.   Europe

The Copyright Directive provides for an exception for repair in Article 5.3(l): 'Member States may provide for exceptions or limitations to the rights provided

---

13. For the United States, see case law below, Section IV.B.; Art. 4 of the Copyright Directive (Directive 2001/29 of 22 May 2001 on the harmonization of certain aspects of copyright and related rights in the information society, OJ L 167, 22 Jun. 2001, 10-19), Art. 7 of the Trade Mark Directive; Art. 15 of the Designs Directive; Art. L. 613-6 (patents) and L. 713-4 (trademarks) of the French Intellectual Property Code and Art. 28.2 of the Belgian Patent Act and Art. 13.8 of the Benelux Trade Mark Law. The UK patent act does not provide for the principle but *Centrafarm v. Sterling Drug*, case 15/74 [1974] ECR 1147 which established the principle of exhaustion in the European Union applies. The right of destination, which exists in France, Belgium and the Netherlands (see A. Strowel & E. Derclaye, *Droit d'auteur et numérique: logiciels, bases de données et multimédia, droit belge, européen et comparé* (Bruxelles: Bruylant, 2001), 55; F. De Visscher & B. Michaux, *Précis du droit d'auteur et des droits voisins* (Bruxelles: Bruylant, 2000), 85; A. Lucas & H.-J. Lucas, *Traité de la propriété littéraire et artistique*, 2nd edn (Paris: Litec, 2001), n. 246-255; Hoge Raad, 19 Jan. 1979, N.J. 1979, n. 142, note L.W.H. (*Poortvliet*)) and allows the author to prevent a change of destination in the use of the material copies of his work by the acquirers of these copies, will not be involved as recycling is assumed in this article to put the product back to the same original use.
14. This does not apply to trademarks, which, if continually renewed in the register and/or used, can last forever.

for in Articles 2 and 3 in the following cases: ... (l) use in connection with the demonstration or repair of equipment'. In the same vein, Member States can provide for an exception to the rights of reproduction and communication to the public for the use of an artistic work in the form of a building or a drawing or plan of a building for the purposes of reconstructing the building (Article 5.3(m)). These exceptions however were optional. Therefore, very few Member States have implemented them. The Netherlands, Germany, Italy, France and Belgium, for instance, have not implemented them. In the United Kingdom, the exception for reconstructing a building (section 65), which already existed before the implementation of the Directive, has been kept.

In British copyright law, a right of repair may subsist although an exception for repair purposes is not explicitly provided in the CDPA. This results from the *British Leyland* case[15] and its progeny, the *Canon*[16] and *Mars*[17] cases. It seems that the sale of an article carries with it a license to repair it.[18] In the *Canon* case, the court said that the defence of repair only applies when it is plain and obvious that there is unfairness to the consumer and the monopoly is anticompetitive.[19] However, it seems that the *Mars* case in effect abolished the right of repair.[20] The reading of the case suggests this although it is not absolutely certain. Therefore, in cases where it is obvious that consumers are unfairly treated and the monopoly of the IPR owner is anticompetitive, the defence could still apply. The practical impact of the repair exception is nevertheless limited. While industrial articles are not protected by copyright anymore, this is different for works of artistic craftsmanship, that is, works that are not only original but aesthetic and are generally made by hand. In any case, even if the defence is abolished, it leaves Article 82 EC Treaty intact. So is Article 171(3) of the CDPA, which provides that 'nothing in this Part affects any rule of law preventing or restricting the enforcement of copyright, on grounds of public interest or otherwise'.

b.   *The United States*

In the United States, repair may qualify as fair use. Section 107 of the US Copyright Act provides:

> Notwithstanding the provisions of sections 106 and 106A, the fair use of a copyrighted work, including such use by reproduction in copies or phonorecords or by any other means specified by that section, for purposes such as

---

15. Above, fn. 4.
16. [1997] FSR 817.
17. [2000] FSR 138.
18. L. Bently & B. Sherman, *Intellectual Property Law*, 2nd edn (Oxford: Oxford University Press), 257.
19. *Canon* (above, fn. 16), 826.
20. Bently & Sherman (above, fn. 18), 229, quoting G. Llewelyn, Does Copyright Law Recognise a Right to Repair [1999] EIPR 599.

criticism, comment, news reporting, teaching (including multiple copies for classroom use), scholarship, or research, is not an infringement of copyright. In determining whether the use made of a work in any particular case is a fair use the factors to be considered shall include:

(1) the purpose and character of the use, including whether such use is of a commercial nature or is for non-profit educational purposes;
(2) the nature of the copyrighted work;
(3) the amount and substantiality of the portion used in relation to the copyrighted work as a whole; and
(4) the effect of the use upon the potential market for or value of the copyrighted work.

The fact that a work is unpublished shall not itself bar a finding of fair use if such finding is made upon consideration of all the above factors.

There is no case law under section 107 that states that repairing a copyrighted product is fair use. However, on the basis of the third fair use factor, repair could be fair use because the part repaired and thus reproduced is only a small part of the copyrighted work. To determine whether the use is fair, the criterion of quantitative and qualitative substantiality is used. Thus, if the work is reproduced in its entirety, it is not fair use (it would not be repair but replacement as in patent law). Under the first factor, the fact that a use is commercial does not necessarily mean that the defence is not available; however, generally the use will be presumptively unfair. Courts will look at whether the use was primarily for public benefit or private commercial gain.[21] The defence is more readily recognized when the use is for educational, scientific, or historical purposes.[22] Thus, if a Picasso painting is repaired, the public benefits, as a great work of art is again available for public viewing. This type of repair would be fair use. However, if a part of a jewel is repaired by a repairer for profit, this would most probably not be fair use. Still in respect of the first factor, the Supreme Court held in *Sony* that there must normally be a productive use for the defence to apply although the defence is not 'rigidly circumscribed' by the productive use requirement. In other words, the distinction between 'productive' and 'unproductive' uses is not wholly determinative.[23] Most repairs are generally not productive: for instance, repairing a car spare part is simply slavishly copying the original, while repairing a Picasso painting could be said to be productive (as Picasso cannot do it himself anymore). Under the fourth factor, the effect upon the plaintiff's potential market, if the defendant's work affects the value of a right in the copyright work (e.g. the adaptation right), the use is unfair. Whether there is fair use will depend on the circumstances. If repair of a work whose author is deceased is involved, it would probably be fair, but if the author is still alive, it would not be. In any case, 'fair use resists any

---

21. See *MCA, Inc. v. Wilson*, 677 F. 2d 180 (2nd Cir. 1980). Nimmer on Copyright, n. 13.05[A] updated to 1988.
22. *Ibid.*, i.e. Nimmer (above, fn. 21), n. 13.05[A] updated to 1988.
23. *Sony Corp. v. Universal City Studios, Inc.*, 104 S. Ct 774 (1984).

theoretically integrated methodology'.[24] Courts give the fourth factor more weight in some cases. However, as cases become more complex, courts weigh the factors differently in each case.[25] In conclusion, repair may be fair use in some cases; it all depends as the factors are weighed differently depending on the circumstances and on the courts.

Section 117(c) provides for an exception to enable the repair of machines:

Machine Maintenance or Repair. – Notwithstanding the provisions of section 106, it is not an infringement for the owner or lessee of a machine to make or authorize the making of a copy of a computer program if such copy is made solely by virtue of the activation of a machine that lawfully contains an authorized copy of the computer program, for purposes only of maintenance or repair of that machine, if –

(1) such new copy is used in no other manner and is destroyed immediately after the maintenance or repair is completed; and
(2) with respect to any computer program or part thereof that is not necessary for that machine to be activated, such program or part thereof is not accessed or used other than to make such new copy by virtue of the activation of the machine.

(d) Definitions. – For purposes of this section –

(1) the 'maintenance' of a machine is the servicing of the machine in order to make it work in accordance with its original specifications and any changes to those specifications authorized for that machine; and
(2) the 'repair' of a machine is the restoring of the machine to the state of working in accordance with its original specifications and any changes to those specifications authorized for that machine.

This exception allows the loading of software only 'for the purposes of repairing the machine into which it is loaded, not the software itself'.[26]

In contrast to the defence of fair use (where there is no case law on repair), there is – recent – case law on the application of section 117(c). In *Storage Technology Corp. v. Custom Hardware Engineering & Consulting, Inc.*,[27] Storage Technology ('StorageTek') sought to prevent Custom Hardware Engineering & Consulting ('CHE') from reproducing its computer programs when repairing its automated tape cartridge libraries. It also claimed that CHE violated the Digital Millennium Copyright Act (DMCA), section 1201(a) of the Copyright Act, when CHE circumvented StorageTek's protection system in order to force the Control Unit of the machine to transmit error codes so that the machine could be repaired. As a defence, CHE invoked section 117(c) and the fair use doctrine. The court's

---

24. M. Nimmer & P. Geller, *International Copyright Law and Practice* (New York: Matthew Bender, c1988-updated 2005), para. 8.2[a][i].
25. *Ibid.*
26. *Ibid.*, para. 8[2][c][iv].
27. 24 Aug. 2005 (Fed. Cir.).

interpretation of the meaning of section 117(c) was a matter of first impression. As the computer program was deleted after the repair was completed because when the machine was turned off it was erased automatically from the RAM, CHE's acts fell within section 117(c). CHE made a copy of the copyrighted code for purposes only of maintenance or repair. Because CHE's acts fell within section 117(c), the court did not have to address whether it fell within fair use.

Finally, section 120(b) of the Copyright Act provides for an exception for alterations done to buildings. It provides:

> Alterations to and Destruction of Buildings. – Notwithstanding the provisions of section 106(2), the owners of a building embodying an architectural work may, without the consent of the author or copyright owner of the architectural work, make or authorize the making of alterations to such building, and destroy or authorize the destruction of such building.

Section 120(b) therefore allows repairs of buildings because repairs can be said to be alterations (they are at least reproductions).

2.   Patent Law

a.   Europe

In some countries, courts have allowed an exception for the purposes of repairing a patented article. In the United Kingdom, the House of Lords, in *United Wire Ltd v. Screen Repair Services (Scotland) Ltd*,[28] confirmed that the notions of repair and making are mutually exclusive. This means that repairing an article is not making and therefore is not an infringement. Repair is consequently not an independent right conferred by express or implied license. However, if the repair of a patented product is so extensive as to amount to making it anew, it will infringe.[29] How much of a product can be repaired is judged on a case-by-case basis. Both quantitative and qualitative considerations such as the relative importance of the part of the patented product are taken into account.[30] As a result, normally, it will not be an infringement if an immaterial part of the patented product is repaired. However, in *Solar Thomson*,[31] the court held that purchasers must be able to carry out the repair even if the part repaired or replaced is crucial to the function of the patented article. The court also held that it does not matter if the repaired article does not work as well or as safely as the original one. This will not affect the decision of whether the repair is legitimate or not.

---

28. [2001] RPC 439; [2001] FSR 24. See also P. Torremans, Holyoak & Torremans, *Intellectual Property Law*, 4th edn (Torremans Holyoak: Oxford University Press, 2005), 137; Bently & Sherman (above, fn. 18), 520-521.
29. *Solar Thomson* (above, fn. 6); [2001] FSR 365.
30. *Sirdar Rubber v. Wallington Weston* [1905] 22 RPC 257.
31. Above, fn. 29.

In Germany, a recent Supreme Court decision lays down the rules for admissible repair.[32] One is allowed to replace parts 'which are usually expected to have to be replaced during the life of the device.' However, it is not allowed to reproduce a part 'if the technical effects of the invention are reflected exactly in the replaced parts.'[33] The Court concluded that 'the replacement of a wearing part which usually will have to be replaced – perhaps several times – during the excepted life of a machine, as a rule, does not represent a reproduction'.[34] This means that the 'more often the part must be replaced and the less its overall share in the combination and its closeness to the "actual" invention, the more likely exhaustion can be assumed even if the patent proprietor only sells the device'.[35] And 'the more the technical or economic advantage of the invention is realized by the very replacement, the more likely the replacement represents an inadmissible reproduction that is not covered by the intended use'.[36]

In Belgium and France, unless the repair is done privately,[37] it will be an infringement as there is no specific exception for repairs.

Further details are provided in the following Sections IV and V, where the issue of repair is discussed in the light of direct and indirect patent infringement.

b.   *The United States*

There is no explicit exception for repair in the Patent Act. However, the purchaser of a patented product may use the product free of control by the patent owner. 'Th[is] right to use includes a right to make repairs on the product necessary for continued use.'[38] In this respect, US law is similar to UK law. The right of repair includes the replacement of parts but does not include a complete reconstruction of a completely spent or worn-out product as this will infringe the patent holder's right to make the patented invention.[39] The first case that held there was a right of repair is *Wilson v. Simpson*.[40] It held that if the use of a patented product depends upon the replacement of parts of it, even if they are 'an essential and distinct constituent of the principle . . . of the invention, frequently replacing them . . . is not a reconstruction of the invention, but the use only of so much of it as is absolutely necessary to identify the machine with what it was in the beginning of its use, or before that part of it had been worn out'.[41] Thereafter, a series of cases

---

32. BGH, case n. X ZR 48/03, 2004 GRUR 758 (*Flügelradzähler*), commented by N. Hölder, Contributory patent infringement and exhaustion in case of replacement parts – Comment on a recent Supreme Court decision in Germany 36 IIC 889 et seq. [2005].
33. Hölder (above, fn. 32), 894.
34. BGH, case n. X ZR 48/03, 2004 GRUR, 758, at 762.
35. Hölder (above, fn. 32), 897.
36. *Ibid.*, 899.
37. Article L. 613-5 of the French Intellectual Property Code and Art. 28 of the Belgian Patent Act.
38. D. Chisum, *Chisum on patents* (New York: Matthew Bender, updated 1997), para. 16.03[3].
39. *Ibid.*
40. 50 U.S. (9 How.) at 123-26 (1850).
41. Chisum (above, fn. 38), para. 16.03[3][a].

confirmed this ruling and the current leading case is *Aro Mfg Co. v. Convertible Top Replacement Co.*:

> [R]reconstruction of a patented entity, comprised of unpatented elements is limited to such a true reconstruction of the entity as to 'in fact make a new article',... after the entity, viewed as a whole, has become spent... mere replacement of individual unpatented parts, one a time, whether of the same part repeatedly or different parts successfully, is no more than the lawful right of the owner to repair his property.[42]

It goes as far as including the sequential replacement of all the parts of a patented invention unless it is done in a single instance of reconstruction.[43] Therefore, *a contrario*, completely and contemporaneously reassembling the invention with new parts is an infringement.[44] As a result, if a patent exists on an ink cartridge rather than a whole printer, making the cartridge is clearly an infringement.[45] Thus, one way to prevent repair is to obtain a patent on each single part of a complex device.

Lower courts have affirmed and further elaborated the concept of repair.[46] Repair includes the replacement of soft or temporary, but also more durable parts which are broken, worn-out or destroyed.[47] Some decisions further extended the right of repair to changes designed to improve or alter performance rather then rectify wear or breakage.[48] However, the right of repair does not encompass the

---

42. 365 U.S. 336, 346 (1961), *reh'g denied*, 365 U.S. 890 (1961). For a similar ruling, see *Porters v. Farmers Supply Service, Inc.*, 790 F. 2d 882, at 886 (Fed. Cir. 1983). In *Cues Inc. v. Polymer Industries Inc.*, 680 F. Supp. 380, 385 (N.D. Ga. 1988), the court held that 'replacement of even a majority of the parts of a patented device does not constitute infringement of the patent.' The right of repair seems to also derive from the exhaustion doctrine. As was held in *ACRA v. Lexmark*, 290 F. Supp. 2d 1034 (N.D. Cal. 2003), at 1043, '[P]ut another way, when a consumer purchases a patented product, the consumer "has an implied license under any patents of the seller that dominate the product or any uses of the product to which the parties might reasonably contemplate the product will be put. *Hewlett-Packard Company v. Repeat-O-Type Stencil Manufacturing Corporation, Inc.*, 123 F. 3d 1445, 1451 (Fed. Cir. 1997). This includes the authority to repair a patented device (e.g. refill an empty printer cartridge)." *ACRA*. citing *Aro Mfg. Co. v. Convertible Top Replacement Co.*, 365 U.S. 336, 346 (1961)'.
43. *FMC Corp. v. Up-Right, Inc.*, 21 F.3d 1073, esp. 1077 (Fed. Cir. 1994). See Chisum (above, fn. 38), para. 16.03[3][d][ii].
44. *Hydril Co. v. Crossman Engineering, Inc.*, 152 USPQ 171 (E.D. Tex. 1966).
45. Some printer manufacturers successfully exerted their rights to suppress third-party competition in the replacement ink and cartridge market in this way. See e.g. *Canon Computer Sys., Inc. v. Nu-Kote Int'l, Inc.*, 134 F. 3d 1085 (Fed. Cir. 1998) (upholding a preliminary injunction against a third-party manufacturer because its replacement ink cartridges for Canon's Bubble Jet printers infringed Canon's patent). But contra: see *Hewlett-Packard Co. v. Repeat-O-Type Stencil Mfg. Corp.*, 123 F. 3d 1445, at 1452 (Fed. Cir. 1997) (competitors' acts were more akin to permissible repair than impermissible reconstruction. Therefore, there was no patent infringement).
46. Chisum (above, fn. 38), para. 16.03[3][b].
47. See e.g. *Gillette Safety Razor Co. v. Standard Razor Co.*, 64 F. 2d 6 (2nd Cir. 1933), *cert. denied*, 290 U.S. 649 (1933) (blades for razor-blade combination).
48. Chisum (above, fn. 38), para. 16.03[3][b].

right to replace a lost component.[49] A critical analysis of US case law is provided by Mineko Mori in Chapter 3 of this book.

3.   Design Law

a.   Europe

In European design law, there are exceptions to exclusive rights, yet the relevant provisions in relation to repair are those that exclude some subject matter from protection. Article 7 Design Directive provides that design rights shall not subsist in features of appearance of a product that are solely dictated by their technical function, or in those that must necessarily be reproduced in their exact form and dimensions in order to permit the product in which the design is incorporated or to which it is applied to be mechanically connected to or placed in, around, or against another product so that either product may perform its function (also called 'must-fit' designs or designs of interconnections). Whereas the first exclusion will not exclude many designs,[50] the second has been expressly provided to exclude the protection of functional spare parts, so that independent repairers may freely exercise their trade.

In addition, Recital 19 and Article 14 of the Directive left open the possibility for Member States to exclude from protection the design of component parts of complex products upon whose appearance the protected design is dependent (also called 'must-match' designs). Hence, in some countries, such as the Benelux countries[51] and the United Kingdom,[52] it is not an infringement of the registered design to make a new component part to repair the product so as to restore its original appearance. The Commission has recently proposed a Directive to include a repairs clause within Directive 98/71.[53] According to the proposal, the design of must-match parts would remain protectable, but it would not be an infringement to make and distribute such parts for repair purposes by others as long as consumers are duly informed about the origin of the part.[54] If the proposal sees the light of day, repair will be fully allowed, as the protection of spare parts will become inexistent.

Finally, Articles 3(3) and (4) of the Directive also leave certain designs unprotectable to the extent that they are component parts of complex products not visible during normal use. Thus, a component part that is only visible when repairing the product is not protectable by design right. This potentially excludes many designs.

---

49. *Universal Electronics Inc. v. Zenith Electronics Corp.*, 846 F. Supp. 641, at 650 (N.D. Ill. 1994). See Chisum (above, fn. 38), para. 16.03[3][d][e].
50. This is because only part of the design of a product will generally be excluded.
51. Article 14*ter* of the Uniform Benelux law on designs and models, 1973 as amended
52. Section 7A(5) of the Registered Designs Act.
53. Proposal for a Directive of the European Parliament and the Council amending Directive 98/71/EC on the legal protection of designs SEC(2004) 1097/* COM/2004/0582 final – COD 2004/0203.
54. J. Drexl, R. Hilty & A. Kur, Design Protection for Spare Parts and the Commission's Proposal for a Repairs Clause [2005] 36 IIC 448. See proposed new Art. 14(2).

b.   *The United States*

In the United States, designs are protected under the Patent Act (sections 171-173) and are called design patents. The law applicable to patents applies unless otherwise provided (section 171).[55] Designs that are solely dictated by functional considerations are unpatentable.[56] Therefore, the design of an article is more likely to be patentable when there are several ways to achieve the function of this article. If other designs could produce the same or similar functional capabilities, the design is likely ornamental, not functional.[57] As in European law, an exception for repair is not necessary, as the law excludes the protection of functional spare parts altogether. However, unlike in Europe, must-match designs are protectable and there is no exception for repair.

4.   Trademark Law

a.   *Europe*

Article 6 Trade Mark Directive concerns the limitation of the effects of a trademark and provides in paragraph 1 that:

> [T]he trade mark shall not entitle the proprietor to prohibit a third party from using, in the course of trade, ... (c) the trade mark where it is necessary to indicate the intended purpose of a product or service, in particular as accessories or spare parts; provided he uses them in accordance with honest practices in industrial or commercial matters.[58]

This provision has been interpreted by the European Court of Justice (ECJ) in the *BMW v. Deenik* case.[59]

Deenik ran a garage and specialized in the sale of second-hand BMW cars and BMW repairs. He was not a BMW dealer, but used the BMW trademark in advertisements for the sale of second-hand BMW cars and repairs and maintenance of BMW cars. BMW sought an order to restrain this. The question was whether use of the BMW mark in advertisements such as 'Repairs and maintenance of BMWs', 'BMW specialist' or 'specialized in BMWs' without the authorization of the trademark owner constituted infringement of that mark. Such use was held to be use of the mark within the meaning of Article 5(1)(a) of the Directive.

---

55. The law is the same except that the right of priority is six months and the term fourteen years (35 U.S.C. ss 172 and 173).
56. *Power Controls Corp. v. Hybernetics Inc.*, 806 F. 2d 234 (Fed. Cir. 1986); *Chrysler Motor Corp. v. Auto Body Panels of Ohio Inc.*, 908 F. 2d 951 (Fed. Cir. 1990); *L.A. Gear, Inc. v. Thom McAn Shoe Co.*, 988 F. 2d 1117, at 1123 (Fed. Cir. 1993); *Rosco Inc. v. Mirror Lite Co.*, 304 F. 3d 1373 (Fed. Cir. 2002). Chisum (above, fn. 38), para. 1.04[2][d].
57. Chisum (above, fn. 38), para. 1.04[2][d] citing *Rosco, Inc. v. Mirror Lite Co.*, at 1378.
58. See also Art. 12(c) of the Community Trade Mark Regulation n. 40/94, OJ L 208, 11 Aug. 1994, 15-26.
59. *BMW v. Deenik*, case C-63/97 [1999] ECR I-905 (ECJ).

The Court held that the exhaustion principle did not apply to adverts because advertisements relating to car repair and maintenance did not affect the further commercialization of the cars.[60] However, if an independent trader carries out the maintenance and repair of BMW cars or is in fact a specialist in that field, he cannot in practice communicate this fact to his customers without using the BMW mark. Therefore, it is not a trademark infringement to use the BMW trademark in order to inform the public of the repair and maintenance of BMW cars. This rule applies as well if the mark is used to inform the public of the resale of goods covered by that mark.[61] It seems that the Court's ruling goes as far as covering the affixing of the mark on the product repaired or informing the public that the spare part fits particular products, as long perhaps as there is an indication that the part is not new but repaired (because the Court uses the word 'use' which is very broad). Also because the Court adds that the repairer can do so unless 'the mark is used in a way that may create the impression that there is a commercial connection between the other undertaking and the trademark proprietor, and in particular that the reseller's business is affiliated to the trademark proprietor's distribution network or that there is a special relationship between the two undertakings'.[62] The implications of the judgment are that a trademark can be used in advertisements and even on the repaired product so long as it is clearly stated in the advertisements and on the products repaired that it has been done by an independent repairer (i.e. who has no connection with the trademark owner). If the trademark owner could prevent this use it would unfairly restrict trade.[63] Article 6(1)(c) therefore insures that trademark law does not inhibit the free movement of goods and services.

The *Gillette* case has further detailed the condition of 'honest use' under Article 6(1)(c).[64] According to paragraph 49 of the decision:

> [u]se of the trade mark will not be in accordance with honest practices in industrial and commercial matters if, for example:
>
> – it is done in such a manner as to give the impression that there is a commercial connection between the third party and the trade mark owner;
> – it affects the value of the trade mark by taking unfair advantage of its distinctive character or repute;
> – it entails the discrediting or denigration of that mark;
> – or where the third party presents its product as an imitation or replica of the product bearing the trade mark of which it is not the owner.

A similar rule already existed in French law.[65] A third party cannot create a risk of confusion between the products or services of the trademark owner and his own

---

60. *Ibid.*, para. 56 and 57.
61. *Ibid.*, para. 63.
62. *Ibid.*, para. 64.
63. Bently & Sherman (above, fn. 18), 926-927.
64. *Gillette Group Finland Oy v. LA-Laboratories Ltd Oy*, case C-228/03 [2005] 2 CMLR 62, [2005] ECR I-2337, [2005] ETMR 67.
65. F. Pollaud-Dulian, *Droit de la Propriété Industrielle* (Montchrestien, 1999), 612.

products or services, that is clients must not attribute the products to the owner of the trademark.[66] This means that the producer of spare parts cannot reproduce the trademark without indicating that the products do not originate from the trademark owner.[67] In other words, the repairer cannot pass himself off as a licensee.[68] He must indicate that the products have been repaired by him.[69] As the activity of repairing products put legally on the market is lawful, everyone has the right to present himself as the repairer of products X, Y or Z.[70] In addition, the maker of spare parts cannot imitate the conditioning and presentation of parts in question to 'parasite' or palm-off the success of his competitor, as this would amount to unfair competition.[71] Furthermore, under French law, if a trademarked product is repaired or a part is replaced which does not affect the product essentially, the repairer can and must maintain the original trademark, while if the product has been rebuilt, transformed or there has been an essential modification, the original identity does not exist anymore and the trademark owner cannot be responsible for the product so transformed.[72] In this case, the repairer cannot use the trademark. If he does, he infringes.

The same rule also existed in Belgium. In a recent Belgian case,[73] the Court of Appeal of Ghent followed and further detailed the *Deenik* ruling. A garage owner, AD Motors, who was no longer a licensee of Mitsubishi, used the Mitsubishi mark in big characters and in graphic style on the façade of his repair shop. Mitsubishi claimed that AD Motors' use of the trademark confused consumers. The court followed the *Deenik* case. While it was not allowed to give the impression that there existed a link between the company (here a garage owner) and the trademark owner, it was permissible for the garage owner to indicate that he deals with certain types of cars. But he must do so in a discrete way without using a protected logo or emblem so as not to create a risk of confusion in the mind of the public. The court also cited Belgian rulings that held that a garage owner may exceptionally use the trademark even if he is not a licensee, yet in a discrete manner in order to avoid

---

66. TGI Paris, 10.04.1978, PIBD, 1979 n. 217.III.16. See also Art. 713-6, b of the IP code and J. Schmidt-Szalewski & J.L. Pierre, *Droit de la propriété industrielle*, 3rd edn (Paris: Litec, 2003), 245.

67. Cass. Com. 06.05.1991, Bull. Civ. IV, n. 156 D., 1993, somm. Com. 116; Paris, 28 Feb. 1991, PIBD, 1991, n. III.454 (*Xerox*); Paris, 30 Nov. 1998, PIBD, 1999, n. 668.III.32 (*Gillette v. Monoprix*).

68. Cass. Com. 13 Jan. 1998, PIBD, 1998, n. 653.III.249 (*Spécialiste Porsche*); Paris 15 May 1998, D. 1998, Inf. Rap. 196, RTD Com. 1998, 846, obs. J. Azema. See also A. Bertrand, *Le droit des marques et des signes distinctifs*, Cedat (2000), 361.

69. *Ibid.*, 361.

70. *Ibid.*, citing TGI Grasse, 05 May 1981 (unreferenced); Cass. Com., 02 May 1984, Ann. 1984, 50; Cass., 09.12.1981, D., 1984, somm. 65, note J.J. Burst (*Benoit v. BMW*).

71. See *Gillette v. Monoprix* (above, fn. 67).

72. Cass. Req. 04.04.1940, *Annals*, 1949.48, 167; Paris, 07 Feb. 1908 and Caen, 10 May 1909, *Annals*, 1911, 105. F. Pollaud-Dulian (above, fn. 65), 756.

73. Gent, 13 Dec. 2004 [2005] IRDI 331 (*NV AD Motors v. NV Mitsubishi Motors Belgium*).

confusion.[74] Use of the Mitsubishi mark in big characters and in graphic style on the façade of a repair shop can lead the average consumer to believe that the garage owner belongs to the regular network of the Mitsubishi dealers or that a commercial link exists between defendant and Mitsubishi. The defendant's way of using the trademark was not strictly necessary.

A similar ruling was handed down in a case before the English courts. In *Volvo v. Heritage*,[75] after the end of his authorized dealership with Volvo, the defendant used the word 'Volvo' with the words 'independent' and 'specialist', but in smaller characters. The court held that this use of the trademark was meant to cause confusion and thus could not fall within the defence of section 11(2)(c) 1994 Trade Mark Act. In a similar vein, one may not answer the phone by saying 'Volvo' because that falsely suggests that one is the trademark owner.[76] On the other hand, the *Deenik* case has been applied restrictively by the British courts. In *Pag Ltd v. Hawke-Woods Ltd*,[77] the defendant refurbished batteries containing the claimant's mark. Pumfrey J. held that:

> [T]he offering for sale of refurbished batteries which were originally sold under the mark 'PAG' without removing the mark 'PAG' constituted an act of infringement and that this provision could not be relied upon as there was no evidence to show that use of the claimant's mark was necessary to indicate the intended purpose of the product. In this case, there was no evidence to suggest that the battery had to be sold under the 'PAG' mark as to fit into, e.g. a PAG car.[78]

In conclusion, trademark law may only prevent the commercialization of a spare part that does not infringe copyright, patent or design laws when the independent repairer does not make clear there is no link between him and the trademark owner. In addition, trademark law may prevent the commercialization of a spare part if the use of the trademark affects the value of the trademark by taking unfair advantage of its distinctive character or repute, the use of the trademark entails the discrediting or denigration of the mark, or where the repairer presents its product as an imitation or replica of the product bearing the trademark, of which he is not the owner.

b.   *The United States*

US trademark law regarding repair is not very different from EU trademark law. The landmark case on the use of a trademark for the repairing and reconditioning of

---

74. Liège, 27 Nov. 1992 [1993] Ing.-Cons. 47 (*VW et Audi*); Liège, 30 Oct. 1990 [1991] JLMB 350 (*Daimler-Benz v. Petrizot*); Anvers, 22 Jun.1998 [1999] IRDI 49 (*Mercedes*).
75. [2000] FSR 253.
76. *Volvo Ltd v. DS Larm Ltd and Dick Edvinsson* [2000] ETMR 299 (Sweden) cited by J. Phillips, *Trade Mark law: A Practical Anatomy* (Oxford: Oxford University Press, 2003), 226.
77. [2002] FSR 46.
78. G. Tritton et al., *Intellectual Property Law in Europe*, 2nd edn (London: Sweet & Maxwell, 2002), 247.

products is the 1947 *Champion* case.[79] The outcome of this case is that one can use the trademark on used goods if they are clearly labelled 'used' and the address and name of the repairer is indicated. The used status must be indicated clearly, distinctly, and permanently on the product as well as on the packaging.[80] However, if the repair is too basic or there is total reconstruction, it is unlawful to use the trademark on the product even if the term 'used' or 'repaired' is indicated.[81] A dealer can state he is a specialist in the repair of a type of trademarked product as long as its advertising does not mislead the public into thinking he is an authorized dealer.[82] For instance, an independent car repairer's mark and sign 'Independent Volkswagen-Porsche Service' was not an infringement of the VW trademark.[83] But a dealer who wants to trade as an authorized dealer or repair outlet needs a license from the trademark owner to do so.[84] Therefore, if the parts' manufacturer uses the mark so as to give the impression that the parts are made or sponsored by the trademark owner, he infringes.[85]

Recently, the *Beanies* case[86] confirmed this case law rather clearly: 'We do not think that by virtue of trademark law producers own their aftermarkets and can impede sellers in the aftermarket from marketing the trademarked product.'

In addition, the theory of dilution cannot be used to control independent parties in the aftermarket who repair or rebuild used trademarked goods.[87]

III. BLOCKING REPAIR THROUGH END USER LICENSE AGREEMENTS AND TECHNOLOGICAL PROTECTION MEASURES

It now appears that repair is not always allowed in all intellectual property laws and in all countries. If the intellectual property laws do not provide for it, it is therefore lawful, on the basis of intellectual property law (to the exclusion of competition

---

79. *Champion Spark Plug Co. v. Sanders*, 331 U.S. 125 (1947). The defendant collected used Champion spark plugs, repaired and reconditioned them and sold them under the Champion mark.

80. *Ibid.*, See also McCarthy on *Trademarks and Unfair Competition*, 4th edn, sec. 18:41, updated March 2006, citing *Clairol, Inc. v. Boston Discount Center, Inc.*, 608 F.2d 1114 (6th Cir. 1979); *Osawa & Co. v. B&H Photo*, 589 F. Supp. 1163, 1173 (S.D.N.Y. 1984).

81. *Champion Spark Plug Co. v. Sanders*, 331 U.S. 125 (1947). See also *Bulova Watch Co. v. Allerton Co.*, 328 F.2d 20 (7th Cir. 1964).

82. *Union Tank Car Co. v. Lindsay Soft Water Corp.*, 257 F. Supp. 510 (D. Neb. 1966), *aff'd*, 387 F.2d 477 (8th Cir. 1967); *Trail Chevrolet, Inc. v. General Motors Corp.*, 381 F.2d 353 (5th Cir. 1967).

83. *Volkswagenwerk Aktiengesellschaft v. Church*, 411 F.2d 350 (9th Cir. 1969), supplemental op., 413 F.2d 1126 (9th Cir. 1969).

84. McCarthy (above, fn. 80), § 18:41.

85. *Myles Standish Mfg. Co. v. Champion Spark Plug Co.*, 282 F. 961 (8th Cir. 1922).

86. *Ty Inc. v. Perryman*, 306 F.3d 509 (7th Cir. 2002), *cert. denied*, 123 S. Ct. 1750 (U.S. 2003).

87. McCarthy (above, fn. 80), para. 24-106.

and possibly other laws such as the theory of misuse or abuse of rights), to use EULAs and TPMs. In sum, this means that EULAs and TPMs can lawfully be used to prevent the repair of:

- patented articles in Belgium and France and in some cases in Germany;
- copyrighted works in most EU Member States and in some cases in the United States.

This section will therefore determine whether it is lawful to use EULAs or TPMs to block repair in the other cases.

A.   COPYRIGHT LAW

1.   Europe

If the exception for repair does not exist in the copyright act of the country in question, then it is lawful, under copyright law, to block repair by a TPM or a contract. If on the other hand, the exception does exist, one needs to ask whether it is imperative.

In order to ascertain whether the exception is imperative, it is necessary to determine the rationale behind it. The following reasoning applies to both contracts and TPMs. However, as will be seen below, the Copyright Directive makes specific provisions for TPMs.

Some commentators have argued that the exception in connection with the demonstration or repair of equipment has a default character, as it is based on market failure (i.e. a practical impossibility that copyright be respected).[88] In other words, such an exception can be said to disappear as authors can now prevent digital copying of their works and enforce their copyright. However, several reasons speak in favour of the imperative nature of the exception for repair.

One reason is the intellectual property rationale itself. Under this rationale, the IPR holder is adequately rewarded for its efforts when he first sells its protected product. Therefore, there should be free competition in the market for spares, as free competition is the principle and intellectual property is the exception. Consequently, preventing repair does not respect the intellectual property rationale. Indeed, contrary to the intellectual property rationale, if the spare parts market is IPR-protected, rent-seeking is promoted. Another reason could be that if it was lawful to block repair, it would not respect the principle of free movement of goods (Articles 28-30 ECT). Indeed, the further sale of the good is prevented if it cannot be independently repaired (i.e. no one will be able to sell the product if broken). In addition, the Civil Code in some countries (namely France and Belgium) is clearly

---

88.   M. Buydens & S. Dusollier, *Les exceptions au droit d'auteur: évolutions dangereuses* [2001] Communication Commerce Electronique, 13, at 14. In their view, this exception does not involve a fundamental freedom or public interest.

in favour of the free circulation of goods and does not allow inalienability.[89] But this rationale only works if the IPR holder refuses to repair the good. If the IPR holder provides for the repair of his own products, the free movement of goods is not impaired. Yet another reason is that the user must keep the benefit of a normal and minimal use of the thing; if not, the sales contract could be cancelled for lack of object.[90] The strongest reason seems to be the intellectual property rationale itself. Even if there is no specific exception in the law, the principle of freedom to compete at the basis of commercial transactions – and the fact that intellectual property is an exception to this principle – implies that anyone should be able to repair an article protected by an IPR. This exception should therefore be, if not a public policy rule, an imperative one.

As far as computer programs are concerned, the law is clearer. Although there is no exception for repairing a computer program, there is an exception for correcting errors (Article 5.1 of the Software Directive).[91] Correcting errors can be said to amount to repairing a computer program, since a computer program does not function properly if there are errors in it. However, the article makes clear that it is lawful to override this exception by contract. But Recital 18 nuances this.[92] It seems to say that even if the exception is not imperative, the acts of loading and running cannot be prevented by contract while the other acts can.[93] The exception can in any case not be overridden in its entirety by contract, in case the use conforms to the objective destination of the programme.[94]

On the other hand, using TPMs to block repair (in general and of buildings) is lawful because the Copyright Directive allows it. This is because the exception for repair is not listed in Article 6.4 of the Directive, which encourages rights holders to take measures so that users can make use of the exceptions listed despite TPMs, and force states to do so if rights holders do not act voluntarily. Technical works protected by copyright that can be subject to such TPMs include any type of electronic appliance whose shape is original and whose functioning

---

89. J. Hansenne, *Les biens – Précis*, Collection Scientifique de la Faculté de Droit de Liège: Liège, 584, n. 631, cited by S. Dusollier, *Droit d'auteur et protection des oeuvres dans l'univers numérique, Droits et exceptions à la lumière des dispositifs de verrouillage des oeuvres* (Brussels: Larcier, 2005), 405, n. 517.
90. *Ibid.*, 406, n. 518.
91. Council Directive 91/250/EEC of 14 May 1991 on the legal protection of computer programs, OJ L 122, 17 May 1991, 42-46. Article 5.1 provides: 'In the absence of specific contractual provisions, the acts referred to in Art. 4 (a) and (b) shall not require authorization by the rightholder where they are necessary for the use of the computer program by the lawful acquirer in accordance with its intended purpose, including for error correction'.
92. 'Whereas this means that the acts of loading and running necessary for the use of a copy of a program which has been lawfully acquired, and the act of correction of its errors, may not be prohibited by contract; whereas, in the absence of specific contractual provisions, including when a copy of the program has been sold, any other act necessary for the use of the copy of a program may be performed in accordance with its intended purpose by a lawful acquirer of that copy.'
93. S. Dusollier (above, fn. 89), 498, n. 643-644.
94. *Ibid.*

can be restricted by a TPM. Thus if a copyright-protected printer, photocopier, kettle, or iron is broken and repairing it requires to circumvent a TPM, an independent repairer may not repair the machine without infringing Article 6 of the Copyright Directive. The copyright owner can therefore extend its monopoly to the aftermarket.

Other technical works that can be protected by copyright and subject to TPMs are computer programs. The copyright holder on a computer program can therefore use a TPM to prevent its repair. In this case, the Software Directive, not the Copyright Directive, applies.[95] Article 7(c) of the Software Directive prohibits 'any act of putting into circulation, or the possession for commercial purposes of, any means the sole intended purpose of which is to facilitate the unauthorized removal or circumvention of any technical device which may have been applied to protect a computer program'. To escape this provision, it is sufficient for the maker of the device to add another purpose to it. As it does not have the *sole* purpose of circumventing the protection attached to the computer program, it is legal to circumvent the TPM in order to repair the program. However, if the copyright owner has used a contract to restrict the repair or correction of errors in addition to this device, then it will normally be illegal to repair the program without authorization.

In conclusion, it is in principle lawful to block repair through EULAs and TPMs. Whether courts would uphold such EULAs is uncertain. They would surely uphold them in countries where the exception of repair does not exist. But this would be subject to the application of competition law and the theory of abuse of rights. In countries where an exception for repair exists, it would depend whether they consider this exception to be imperative or public policy. If they do, for instance because they think that it unfairly restricts the free movement of goods or competition in the EU, then such contracts are void and they are not an effective means to prevent repair. As far as the use of TPMs is concerned, it seems that the law allows their use to prevent repair, since Article 6.4 of the Copyright Directive does not include the exception in its list and it is therefore impossible for a user to force a rights holder or the state to give him the means to disable a TPM to allow him to repair an article that is TPM-protected. As far as software is concerned, it is generally unlawful to use contract to prevent the correction of errors. In conclusion, the copyright holders' combination of contracts and TPMs to protect copyright works ensures that repair is strictly prohibited.

2.   The United States

As far as contracts are concerned, the issue is similar to that in Europe. If repair can fall within fair use, the question is whether the exception of fair use is imperative or a public policy rule. The same reasons as in Europe are valid. Therefore, a contract that prevents repair would be void if the repair falls within

---

95. Recital 50 of the Copyright Directive (above, fn. 13).

fair use. If it does not fall within fair use (e.g. the repair is too extensive), contracts can be used to prevent repair. As to the exceptions of sections 117(c) and 120(b), they could be said to be based on the same rationale of free competition and therefore be imperative.

Can copyright holders lawfully use TPMs to block the repair of copyrighted works? The short answer is yes, but they may not indirectly block the repair of machines not protected by copyright, as the *Chamberlain* case illustrates.[96] A distinction must therefore be made. The use of a TPM is lawful only if it is used to protect a copyright work from unauthorized copying or communicating to the public, as the DMCA was intended to protect copyright holders against infringement of their copyright works.[97]

Section 1201(a)(1)(A) of the Copyright Act (or DMCA) states that 'No person shall circumvent a technological measure that effectively controls access to a work protected under this title.' Although there is no explicit exception for circumvention for purposes of fair use in the DMCA,[98] section 1201(c)(1) states that 'Nothing in this section shall affect rights, remedies, limitations, or defenses to copyright infringement, including fair use, under this title.' Therefore, TPMs can lawfully be used to block the repair of a copyrighted work, unless the specific repair can be said to be fair use or fall within sections 117(c) or 120(b).

The DMCA provisions have however been stretched further and have been used by claimants to prevent the repair of articles not protected by copyright, such as cartridges and garage door openers ('GDOs').[99] In other words, section 1201(a)(1)(A) has been used to prohibit aftermarket competition although it seems that Congress never intended that the DMCA affects the aftermarket.[100] Competitors circumvented TPMs in order to make replacement parts and were sued by copyright holders. In *Chamberlain*,[101] the defendant, Skylink, was making universal GDOs transmitters. In order for its transmitters to work, it had to allow users to circumvent Chamberlain's TPM that controls access to Chamberlain's computer programs.

The Federal Circuit held that the DMCA anti-circumvention provisions establish a cause of action for liability not a new property right. Circumvention is not per se an infringement. According to the court, there are 'significant differences between defendants whose accused products enable copying and those, like

96. See below.
97. D. Higgs, 'Lexmark International, Inc. v. Static Control Components, Inc. & Chamberlain Group, Inc. v. Skylink Technologies, Inc.: The DMCA and Durable Goods Aftermarkets', *Berkeley Tech. L.J.* 19 (2004): at 80.
98. X, 'Control of the Aftermarket Through Copyright, *Lexmark v. Static Control Components*', [2003] *Harvard Journal of Law and Technology*, at 315.
99. See *Lexmark Int'l v. SCC*, 387 F.3d 522 (6th Cir. 2004); *The Chamberlain Group, Inc. v. Skylink Technologies, Inc.*, 381 F. 3d 1178 (Fed. Cir. 2004).
100. M. Howell, 'The Misapplication of the DMCA to the Aftermarket', *B.U. J. Sci. & Tech. L.* 11 (2005): 128, at 152.
101. Above, fn. 99.

Skylink, whose accused products enable only legitimate uses of copyrighted software'.[102] No protected uses were in question because Skylink's universal remote control did not copy Chamberlain's software, it only circumvented Chamberlain's TPM to access the software. For the Federal Circuit, section 1201(a) cannot allow copyright owners to use TPMs to block all access to their copyrighted works. This would create two copyright regimes. The first one would be the traditional one, where fair use and other exceptions apply. Under the second, which Chamberlain proposes, the copyright holders of a work protected by copyright and a TPM would have 'unlimited rights to hold circumventors liable under s. 1201(a) merely for accessing that work, even if that access enabled only rights that the Copyright Act grants to the public'.[103] This regime frontally contradicts section 1201(c)(1). The court also held that if Chamberlain's construction of section 1201 was upheld, it would allow any company to leverage its sales into aftermarket monopolies, something that antitrust law and the doctrine of copyright misuse prohibit.[104] Intellectual property laws are not immune from copyright misuse and antitrust liability. Therefore, if Chamberlain's construction was upheld and such circumvention was prohibited under copyright law, it would violate those two branches of the law.

Recently, the Federal Circuit confirmed its *Chamberlain* precedent, where it had for the first time to interpret the relationship between the exception for repair (section 117(c) of the Copyright Act) and the protection of technological measures by the DMCA.[105] The defendant, CHE, reproduced StorageTek's computer programs when repairing its automated tape cartridge libraries. StorageTek also claimed that CHE violated section 1201(a) of the Copyright Act when CHE circumvented StorageTek's protection system in order to force the Control Unit of the machine to transmit errors codes so that the machine could be repaired. The court applied its ruling in *Chamberlain*[106] and held that as the defendant's acts were not infringing the claimant's copyright, the circumvention of the technological measure was not a violation of the DMCA. These two cases show that TPMs cannot be used to prevent fair use and other exceptions. Therefore, if a specific repair is fair use or otherwise exempted by sections 117(c) or 120(b), users can circumvent the TPM without impunity in order to repair the underlying copyright work and *a fortiori* any non-copyrighted article protected by the TPM.[107] The downside is that sections 1201(a)(2) and 1201(b) strictly prohibit the manufacture, distribution etc. of devices whose main purpose is to allow the circumvention of TPMs.

---

102. *Chamberlain* (above, fn. 99), at 1198.
103. *Ibid.*, at 1199-1200.
104. *Ibid.*, at 1201, citing *Eastman Kodak Co. v. Image Tech. Servs.*, 504 U.S. 451, 455 (1992) and *Assessment Techs. of WI, LLC v. WIREdata, Inc.*, 350 F. 3d 640, 647 (7th Cir. 2003).
105. See *StorageTek* (above, fn. 8).
106. A copyright owner alleging a violation of s. 1201(a) must prove that the circumvention of the technological measure 'either infringes or facilitates infringing a right protected by the copyright act'. *Chamberlain* (above, fn. 99), at 1202-1203.
107. See also D. Higgs (above, fn. 97), 79.

Therefore, in practice, only savvy users are able to benefit from their fair use repair exception.

B.   PATENT LAW

1.   Europe

In Belgium and France, TPMs and EULAs can lawfully be used to block the repair of patented articles because there is no exception for repair in the Belgian and French patent laws. In Germany, TPMs and EULAs can be used to block repair only when a part that embodies the technical effects of the invention is reproduced. In the United Kingdom, where there is an exception for repair, the question is again whether this exception is a public policy rule or is imperative. In this respect, the same arguments as under copyright law are valid for the same reasons (see section III.A.1.). Therefore, where an exception allows the repair of a patented article, patent holders may not use EULAs or TPMs to prevent repair.

2.   The United States

This question will be examined under Section IV.B.1, as the law is the same for repair and recycle.

C.   DESIGN LAW

1.   Europe

On the face of it, it is lawful to block repair through TPMs and EULAs because there is nothing in the design law that prevents it unless one considers that the provisions excluding some subject-matter (functional, must-fit and must-match designs) are imperative. This subject-matter is clearly outside the scope of intellectual property protection and into the realm of free competition. Hence the arguments developed in Section III.A.1 for copyright law apply with even more strength as we are not dealing with exceptions to rights but outright non-protected subject-matter. In conclusion, it should not be allowed to prevent repair through TPMs and EULAs.

2.   The United States

The answer to this question is the same as for patent law and will be examined under Section IV.B.1 as the law is the same for repair and recycle.

D.   TRADEMARK LAW

1.   Europe

Nothing in the trademark law prevents a trademark owner from prohibiting by contract or a TPM to repair a trademarked good, or rather to prevent the affixing of the trademark on a repaired good or on spare parts. However, some of the arguments developed above for copyright (Section III.A.1) are applicable. Such contracts or TPMs are against Articles 28-30 ECT providing for the free movement of goods. In addition, the sales contract could be cancelled for lack of object if users cannot keep the benefit of a normal and minimal use of the thing.

The use of TPMs to prevent the affixing of the trademark on the good certainly will be less common than the use of contracts. One such possibility is the sale of services only available online (e.g. an online software company). In this case, the trademark is only available online and the trademark owner could protect the trademark (icon, logo) with a TPM so that the trademark cannot be reproduced (at least in its usual form, style, and colour). In this way, the repairer could not use it (at least in that form, style, colour) to sell repair services. However, as the trademark can be printed and scanned, the TPM is thereby easily circumvented. And there is not yet any legal protection of TPMs that protect trademark goods. This is so unless the trademark is affixed on a good protected by copyright. On this issue, see below Section III.E.

2.   The United States

The answer must be the same as for Europe for the same reasons. The *Beanies* case[108] reinforces this finding.

E.   USE OF EULAs OR TPMs TO PREVENT REPAIR WHEN A PRODUCT
          IS PROTECTED BY SEVERAL IPRs AT THE SAME TIME

The simultaneous protection of goods by several IPRs may happen quite often. For instance, in Belgium, products such as shoes, bags, clothes, tables, baffles, and an aquatic game have been held to be protected by copyright law.[109] Jewels and lighters as well as kitchen utensils[110] are other examples of utilitarian products that can be copyright protected. They generally bear a trademark and may sometimes be protected by design and/or patent law. The question is whether, if a product is protected simultaneously by several IPRs, the law which prevents repair by independent parties (i.e. copyright law in both Europe and the United

---

108.   Above, fn. 86.
109.   See A. Strowel & E. Derclaye (above, fn. 13), 30 and 34 and decisions cited in fn. 85 and 106.
110.   In France, a salad receptacle (Cass. Crim., 02.05.1961, JCP G, 1961, II, 12242) and a bottle opener (Cass. Crim. 09 Oct. 1974, JCP G, 1976, II, 18311) were held to be protected.

States and patent law in Belgium and France) prevails over the other laws that allow it. If the answer is that that law prevails, repair of the product by independent repairers is impossible, although it may be allowed under other intellectual property laws such as design or trademark law. It seems that if copyright can be claimed on a utilitarian object that is also protected either by patent, design, or trademark law (which will happen more often in Europe than in the United States because of the US copyright's separability rule[111]), it may prevent repair of the product. Similarly, a trademarked good that is patented in France or Belgium may not be repaired even if trademark law allows it. Indeed, the *Dior v. Evora*[112] case does not directly apply to this situation. In that case, the ECJ held that the advertising of trademarked goods by resellers was lawful according to the principle of exhaustion. It also held that the protection conferred by copyright as regards the reproduction of protected works in a reseller's advertising may not, in any event, be broader than that which is conferred on a trademark owner in the same circumstances. This meant that such reproduction was not a copyright infringement. The case does not require that the same conclusions should be drawn in other cases. Reproducing for the purposes of repair is not the same as reproducing for the purposes of advertising to sell the initial good. In the case of repair, because part of the product is made anew, the exhaustion principle does not come into play. However, the Court may have signalled that the cumulative use of IPRs on the same product may be subject to reinforced scrutiny by the Community courts. As some have argued, the idea behind European intellectual property law is that the IPR holder has to be rewarded, but that it must be rewarded only once.[113] A single price is charged for the product and it stands for all the producer's IPRs.[114] Extrapolating this reasoning, the rights holder on a product protected by both trademark/design and copyright or trademark/design and patent should not be able to enforce its right of reproduction/making if trademark/design law allows repair. Therefore, using a contract or TPM to block repair should not be allowed for the same reasons as explained above (Section III.A.1). Harmonization of European intellectual property laws on repair would in this respect render the state of play clearer.

On the other hand, the problem of the prevention of repair by one IPR whilst it is allowed by another is less pertinent in the United Kingdom. Works of applied art need to be aesthetic in addition to being original to be protected by copyright law;[115] therefore, many such objects – and most of those that are not made by hand – may only be protected by design law. In addition, section 51 of the CDPA

---

111. Copyright can only subsist in features capable of existing separately from the utilitarian aspects of the article. See s. 101 Copyright Act and *Mazer v. Stein*, 347 U.S. 201 (1954), *Kieselstein-Cord v. Accessories by Pearl*, 632 F. 2d 989 (2nd Cir. 1980).
112. Case C-337/95 [1998] ETMR 26; [1998] 1 CMLR 737.
113. I. Stamatoudi, 'From Drugs to Spirits and From Boxes to Publicity (Decided and Undecided Issues in Relation to Trade Marks and Copyright Exhaustion)', *IPQ* 1(1999): 95, at 106-107.
114. *Ibid.* On this issue, see also A. Kur, The 'presentation right – Time to create a new limitation in copyright law?', 31 IIC 203-218 [2000].
115. Section 4 of the CDPA. See e.g. *George Hensher Ltd v. Restawile Upholstery (Lancs) Ltd* [1975] RPC 31 (HL); *Merlet v. Mothercare* [1986] RPC 115 (CA).

makes sure that it is not an infringement of the copyright in a design document (e.g. drawings, photographs) or model recording or embodying a design for anything other than an artistic work to make an article to the design or to copy an article made to the design.[116] Therefore, copyright in the drawing of an exhaust pipe will not be infringed if a spare exhaust pipe is made. This applies regardless of whether the exhaust pipe is protected by patent, design, or trademark law. Since British patent, design, and trademark laws allow repair, and copyright by implication does as well, the problem of one IPR preventing repair although the other IPRs allow it does not occur.

IV.   IS IT LAWFUL TO BLOCK RECYCLE THROUGH
             EULAs and TPMs?

A.   EUROPE

As was said earlier (Section II.A.1), recycling a product involves a re-use or transfer of the original product. This does not involve any of the exclusive rights in copyright, patent, design, and trademark laws, since the principle of exhaustion applies. The principle of exhaustion is the same in all European intellectual property laws. It was first established by the ECJ in the 1970s[117] and is now codified in the several Directives and Regulations relating to intellectual property (see above, Section II.B). A contract or a TPM preventing the recycling of products protected by an IPR would clearly contradict the principle of the free movement of goods (Articles 28-30 ECT). This applies only if the recycling (as has been defined in Section II.A above) does not entail a change in the product. If it does, the above analysis on repair applies. Therefore, it seems rather clear that Articles 28-30 ECT cannot lawfully be set aside by a EULA or a TPM.[118] Furthermore, in Belgium and arguably also in France, inalienability clauses have been held void because they are against the very definition of property, and against the Civil Code, which favours the free circulation of goods.[119]

In addition, this type of contract (and by analogy one could say TPMs as well) may also conflict with EU environmental rules. A number of directives in the

---

116. This section codified the famous British Leyland case (above, fn. 4) in which this very problem arose. This non enforcement of copyright in case an article is also protected by patent law, which carries with it the right of repair, also arose in *Solar Thomson* (above, fn. 6).

117. *Centrafarm v. Sterling Drug* (above, fn. 13); *Deutsche Grammophon GmbH v. Metro-SB-Grossmarkte GmbH & Co KG*, case 78/70, [1971] ECR 487; *Centrafram v. Winthrop*, case C-16/74, [1974] ECR 1183.

118. In French patent law, it is for instance clear that the application of the principle of exhaustion cannot be set aside by a clause of the license contract, which would forbid the licensee from exporting the goods he makes. See J. Schmidt-Szalewski & J.L. Pierre (above, fn. 66), 82. This could be said to apply by analogy to a clause of a contract that would prevent recycling.

119. J. Hansenne, *Les biens – Précis*, Collection Scientifique de la Faculté de Droit de Liège: Liège, 584, n. 631, cited by S. Dusollier (above, fn. 89), 405, n. 517.

field of environmental law require Member States to promote recycling in the packaging,[120] vehicle,[121] batteries,[122] electronic equipment[123] and oils[124] sectors. For instance, under the end-of-life vehicles Directive,[125] Member States must ensure that economic operators increase the rate of re-use and recycling to around 85% of each vehicle (Article 7(2)) and that collection systems are set up by economic operators to collect end-of-life vehicles (Article 5). Similarly, under the waste electrical and electronic equipment (WEEE) Directive,[126] producers must set up systems to provide for the treatment and recovery of such waste. Directive 75/439 requires the Member States to take the necessary measures to ensure that, as far as possible, the disposal of waste oils is carried out by recycling (Article 3) and Directive 91/157 requires the same for batteries (Article 4). Finally, as far as packaging waste is concerned, Member States must meet increasing recycling targets at set periods (Article 6 of Directive 94/62). Therefore, it is illegal to prevent the recycling of such products even if they are IP protected. This includes at least all end-of-life vehicles, oils, packaging, batteries, refrigerators, microwaves, lamps, and other electrical and electronic equipment such as printers, phones, and computers (see Annex IA of the WEEE Directive).

If a product is copyright protected, these rationales are subject to the right of integrity. In some countries (mainly France), it is a violation of the right of integrity to change the context of a work (e.g. presenting the work in misleading or disparaging circumstances) even if no modification was made to it.[127] Hence, if a copyrighted product is recycled, the recycler must take care not to change the work's context.

B.   THE UNITED STATES

1.   **Patent and Design Law**

In US patent law, although the principle of exhaustion, more commonly known there as the first sale doctrine, is a well-recognized principle of law,[128] it does not apply if the sale is conditioned. In other words, a restriction or condition may

---

120. Directive 94/62 of 20 Dec. 1994, on packaging and packaging waste, OJ L 365, 31 Dec. 1994, 10.
121. Directive 2000/53/EC of 18 Sep. 2000 on end-of life vehicles, OJ L 269, 21 Oct. 2000, 34.
122. Directive 91/157 of 18 Mar. 1991, on batteries and accumulators containing certain dangerous substances, OJ L 78, 26 Mar. 1991, 38.
123. Directive 2002/96/EC of 27 Jan. 2003 on waste electrical and electronic equipment (WEEE), OJ L 37/24 as amended by Directive 2003/108/EC of 8 Dec. 2003, OJ L 345, 31 Dec.2003, 106-107.
124. Directive 75/439/EEC of 16 Jun. 1975 on the disposal of waste oils, OJ L 194, 25 Jul. 1975, 23-25.
125. Above, fn. 121.
126. Above, fn. 123.
127. See e.g. Paris, 4th Ch., 12 Dec. 1995 [1996] 169 RIDA 372.
128. D. Chisum (above, fn. 38), para. 16.03[2][a].

lawfully, under intellectual property and contract laws, be placed on the sale of a patented product.[129] In *General Talking Pictures Co. v. Western Elec. Co.*, the Supreme Court held that a restrictive license is legal. 'The patentee may grant a license "upon any condition the performance of which is reasonably within the reward which the patentee by the grant of the patent is entitled to secure".'[130] However, if a patent owner tries to restrain the use of a patented product after the first authorized sale, this exceeds the scope of the patent monopoly. Such attempts may constitute patent misuse.[131] In fact, *General Talking Pictures* only allows a patent owner to restrict his manufacturing licensee's use of the invention and to enforce the restriction under patent law. But *General Talking Pictures* does not mean that express restrictions are per se valid, bind purchasers, and can be enforced in actions for infringement. In *Mallinckrodt*, the court held:

> The case is distinguishable . . . from any situation where the purchaser buys directly from the patent owner, rather than through a manufacturing licensee . . . and also from the situation where licensees manufacture and sell, thinking the devices they are selling are destined for an authorised use, but the purchaser nevertheless uses the device in an unauthorised manner. Thus the holding in *General Talking Pictures* does not disturb the holdings in earlier cases, from *Adams v. Burke* forward, that restrictions on future use, even express ones, are not enforceable against purchasers because patent owners exhaust their rights when they sell.[132]

Later, the Federal Circuit reiterated that 'unless the condition violates some other law or policy (in the patent field, notably the doctrine of misuse or antitrust law), private parties retain the freedom to contract concerning conditions of sale'.[133] The court held that a 'single use only' restriction 'does not per se violate the doctrine of patent misuse or antitrust law'.[134] 'In other words, if a patented device is licensed for single use only, any re-use is unlicensed and is a patent infringement, and there is no reason to choose between repair and reconstruction; the contract determines what is impermissible reconstruction not the public law.'[135] The *Mallinckrodt* ruling has been endorsed in other cases.[136] Consequently, express conditions accompanying the sale of a patented product are generally upheld.[137]

---

129. *Ibid.*, para. 16.03[2][a][iii].
130. 304 U.S. 127 (1938), quoting *United States v. General Elec. Co.*
131. D. Chisum (above, fn. 38), para 19.04[3]. See also below, section V.
132. *Mallinckrodt, Inc. v. Medipart, Inc.*, 976 F. 2d 700, at 708 (Fed. Cir. 1992).
133. *Ibid.*, cited by Chisum (above, fn. 38), para. 16.03[2][a][iii].
134. *Mallinckrodt* (above, fn. 132), at 701.
135. A. Gajarsa, 'How Much Fuel to Add to the Fire of Genius? Some Questions About the Repair/ Reconstruction Distinction in Patent Law', *Am. U. L. Rev.* 48 (1999): 1205, at 1225, summarizing *Mallinckrodt* at 709.
136. *The Kendall Co. v. Progressive Medical Technology, Inc.*, 85 F.3d 1570 (Fed. Cir. 1996); *Hewlett-Packard Co. v. Repeat-O-Type Stencil Mfg. Co., Inc.*, 123 F.3d 1445, 1453-55 (Fed. Cir. 1997).
137. A. Gajarsa (above, fn. 135), 1225.

Recently, the scope of the first sale doctrine has been revisited in a case concerning the recycling of used printer cartridges. In *Arizona Cartridge Remanufacturers Association v. Lexmark Int'l*,[138] Lexmark gave a discount to purchasers of Lexmark printer cartridges. In return, consumers agreed to send the emptied cartridges back to Lexmark. Consumers thus had a choice to buy the cartridge at discounted price with the restriction or at regular price without restriction. If the consumer bought a regularly priced cartridge, he could choose to trash it or give it to anyone for recycling. Lexmark's contract therefore did not prevent competitors from recycling, that is, take used cartridges sold at the regular price, fill them with ink and sell them back to consumers. Among other claims, Arizona Cartridge Remanufacturers Association (ACRA) contended that Lexmark could not impose such an obligation on buyers of discounted cartridges because it had exhausted its patent rights. On the other hand, Lexmark invoked its patent rights to impose the single-use condition on discounted cartridges. In the first instance, the court held that a patent owner exhausts its rights under the patent when it sells its goods[139] but reminded that the exhaustion principle only applies where the sale of the patented product is unconditional.[140] This means that the buyer of a product sold unconditionally has the right to repair (or recycle) the product but the buyer of a product sold conditionally does not.[141] The court held that Lexmark had not exhausted its patent right because the sale was validly conditioned. The circumstances of the sale indicated that '(1) purchasers, including end-users, [we]re on notice of the single-use condition; (2) purchasers ha[d] an opportunity to reject the condition; and (3) the Prebate [wa]s offered at a special price that reflect[ed] an exchange for a single-use condition'.[142] In this case, end-users may be subject to conditions even if the product is sold through an intermediary. The upshot of this case is that thanks to its patent, Lexmark had the right to impose conditions on the sale of its patented product, such as the restriction of a purchaser's ability to repair or recycle it.[143]

In conclusion, if the patent owner does not specify any condition when he puts patented goods on the market, repair and recycle are allowed on the basis of the exhaustion doctrine; but if he puts patented products on the market under the condition that repair or recycle cannot be performed, then this contractual condition prevails over the exhaustion principle. Therefore, a patent owner can use contract to restrict repair and recycle. It is allowed under US patent and contract law. Arguably, the same applies for TPMs as it works as a condition on the resale of the patented product.

---

138. 290 F. Supp. 2d 1034 (N.D. Cal. 2003), *aff'd*, 421 F.3d 981 (9th Cir. 2005).
139. *Ibid.*, at 1043.
140. *Ibid.*, citing *Monsanto Co. v. Scruggs*, 249 F.Supp.2d 746, 753 (N.D. Miss. 2001).
141. *Ibid.*, citing *Mallinckrodt, Inc. v. Medipart, Inc.*, 976 F.2d 700, 709 (Fed. Cir. 1992).
142. *Ibid.*, at 1045.
143. *Ibid.*

2.   Trademark and Copyright Law

In trademark law, the first sale doctrine derives from the *Champion* case.[144] It allows anyone who has acquired branded goods to resell them in an unchanged state without authorization of the trademark owner. But if the goods are materially different, the exhaustion principle does not apply.[145] The trademark first-sale doctrine is the same as that in copyright law.[146] It means that the first sale or other transfer of the copyrighted or trademarked goods exhausts the right of distribution of the copyright or trademark holder. Anyone is subsequently free to dispose of the copyrighted copy of the work or trademarked good without the copyright holder's or trademark holder's authorization. It is therefore the same principle as in Europe. However, it seems that in trademark law, whilst a trademark owner can impose conditions as to the terms and scope of the resale to the first buyer of goods, these conditions do not 'run with the goods'.[147] The same seems to apply in copyright law. In *Independent News Co. v. Williams*,[148] it was held that a restriction on the use of a copyrighted work did not bind subsequent purchasers of the work, whether or not they had notice of the restriction. Therefore, downstream users who wish to recycle are not prevented from doing so because of the condition imposed on the first buyer.

V.   SHOULD LIMITATIONS TO REPAIR AND RECYCLE BE ALLOWED?

A.   BLOCKING REPAIR

The above analysis has shown that both American and European intellectual property laws generally do not allow blocking the repair of copyright, trademarked,

---

144. Above, fn. 78.
145. *Davidoff & CIE, S.A. v. PLD Intern. Corp.*, 263 F.3d 1297 (11th Cir. 2001). See also *Original Appalachian Artworks, Inc. v. Granada Electronics, Inc.*, 816 F.2d 68, 2 U.S.P.Q.2d 1343, 1349 (2d Cir. 1987), *cert. denied*, 484 U.S. 847 (1987); *Denbicare U.S.A. v. Toys 'R' Us, Inc.*, 21 U.S.P.Q.2d 1711 (N.D. Cal. 1991), *subsequent appeal*, 84 F.3d 1143 (9th Cir. 1996) ('The "first sale" or "exhaustion" doctrine is well recognized in trademark law.'). See also Restatement (Third) of Unfair Competition § 24, comment b (1995).
146. For copyright see, 17 U.S.C.A. §§ 109(a), 109(d). See also *Sebastian Int'l v. Longs Drug Stores Corp.*, 53 F.3d 1073 (9th Cir. 1995); *Denbicare U.S.A. v. Toys 'R' Us*, 84 F.3d 1143 (9th Cir. 1996) ('Since the trustee's sale qualified as a first sale for copyright purposes, it is a trademark first sale as well'). See Nimmer (above, fn. 21), para. 8.12[B][3]; M. Nimmer & P. Geller (above, fn. 24), USA, para. 8[1][b][ii].
147. At least one court has held so. See *Denbicare U.S.A. v. Toys 'R' Us*, 84 F.3d 1143, 38 U.S.P.Q.2d 1865 (9th Cir. 1996) ('bankruptcy court injunction, limiting resale to nations other than the U.S. and Canada, does not bind downstream buyers with no notice of the injunction') cited by McCarthy (above, fn. 80), para. 25:41.
148. 293 F.2d 510, 516-17 (3d Cir. 1961).

patented and design-protected products. Nonetheless, the intellectual property laws are silent as to the imperative or public policy nature of these prohibitions. In some cases, however, intellectual property laws clearly allow the blocking of repair, namely in respect of French and Belgian and in some cases German patents, copyrighted works protected by TPMs, and software protected by contracts in Europe. However, in these cases, blocking repair is nevertheless subject to the intellectual property rationale and the principle of the free movement of goods.[149] This means that repair is allowed as a matter of public policy. In addition, in the United States, contract law, which is state law, may not conflict with intellectual property laws, which are federal laws. The principle of pre-emption prevents states, and *a fortiori* private parties, from departing from federal law.[150] As a result, contracts cannot depart from intellectual property laws. Therefore, EULAs and TPMs blocking repair should in principle not be enforceable. This is particularly clear in respect of American copyright law for the use of both EULAs and TPMs. Furthermore, in US law it may be difficult for right holders to enforce restrictions on repair against subsequent purchasers and users because of the privity principle.[151]

B.   Blocking Recycle

Blocking recycle is clearly not allowed in Europe because of the prevalence of the principle of exhaustion and Articles 28-30 ECT. In addition, in some sectors it is against European environmental rules. In US trademark and copyright law, blocking recycle is similarly prohibited under the first-sale doctrine and the principle of the free movement of goods. On the other hand, contracts or TPMs forbidding the recycling of US patented products would not fall foul of US environmental rules.

---

149.   In the United States, the free movement of goods derives form the Commerce Clause of the United States Constitution and case law applying it. See e.g. *Douglas v. Seacoast Products*, 431 U.S. 265, 286 (1977); *Philadelphia v. New Jersey*, 437 U.S. 617, 623 (1978); *Hood & Sons v. DuMond*, 336 U.S. 525, 533 (1949). States cannot prevent the free movement of goods for their economic advantage, except when there is a threat to health or safety, or fraud. *Healy v. Beer Institute*, 491 U.S. 324, 335-336 (1989) (purpose of the Commerce Clause was to maintain a national economic union unencumbered by limitations on interstate commerce imposed by states); *Boston Stock Exchange v. State Tax Commn.*, 429 U.S. 318, 328 (1977) (Commerce Clause sets up a free trade among the states); *Hunt v. Washington State Apple Advertising Commn.*, 432 U.S. 333 (1977) (a national common market). As the rule prevents states from putting barriers to interstate commerce, *a fortiori* private parties cannot contractually enact the same, albeit private restriction.
150.   Under the Supremacy Clause, 'a particular cause of action may be pre-empted if its enforcement would stand as an obstacle to the accomplishment of the full purposes and objectives of Congress.' See L. Guibault, 'Copyright Limitations and Contracts: Are Click-Wrap Licences Valid?', *Journal of Digital Property Law* 2, no. 1 (2002): 148, at 161, citing G. Founds, 'Shrink-Wrap and Click-Wrap Agreements: 2B Or Not 2B', *Federal Communications Law Journal* 52 (2000): 99, at 114.
151.   A. Gajarsa (above, fn. 135), 1231.

First, there are no federal rules making recycling mandatory.[152] Second, the few state laws that may make recycling mandatory would be pre-empted by the federal intellectual property laws because there would be a conflict between the state law requiring recycling and the contract or TPM derived from the exclusive rights granted by federal law to the patent owner, which would forbid it.[153] However, although the practice of conditioning sales clearly is allowed, it is subject to the misuse doctrine and antitrust law. This leads us to examine the laws that, in addition to the principle of the free movement of goods and the intellectual property rationale, safeguard repair and recycle.

C.   ADDITIONAL SAFEGUARDS

In both Europe and the United States, the competition rules and the abuse of rights theory (called misuse doctrine in the United States), always play the role of safeguard when an IPR holder abuses its power. Thus, were the rationales above not sufficient to secure the possibility to repair or recycle IPR-protected products, these two branches of the law can come to the rescue.

1.   **Europe**

The theory of abuse of rights differs in every European country, as it has not been harmonized. It is beyond the scope of this article to develop its characteristics in several European countries. Suffice it to say that it may apply when IPR holders override the scope of the IPR grant by contract or TPM.

   European competition law is so far unclear as to whether it is anticompetitive to secure a complete monopoly in the aftermarket. In *Hugin*,[154] the ECJ held that the market of spare parts for Hugin's cash registers was a market on its own, as there were no spare-parts substitutes for these machines. It then held that Hugin had a dominant position in that market. However, as there was no effect on trade between Member States, the court did not address whether Hugin's behaviour was an abuse of dominant position. In the *Maxicar* and *Volvo* cases, the ECJ held that in any case the holding of a dominant position by an IPR holder cannot per se entail abuse of it. In the *Maxicar* and *Volvo* cases, it was held anticompetitive for the owner of the IPR to refuse to supply spare parts, fix prices at an unfair level,

---

152. M. Short, 'Taking Back the Trash: Comparing European Extended Producer Responsibility and Take-Back Liability to U.S. Environmental Policy and Attitudes', *Vand. J. Transnational Law* 27 (2004): 1217, at 1220, 1226.

153. This is known as conflict pre-emption. There is conflict pre-emption when state law conflicts with or frustrates the purpose of federal law or the Constitution. The Supreme Court found such pre-emption 'where compliance with both federal and state regulations is a physical impossibility'. See e.g. *Florida Lime & Avocado Growers, Inc. v. Paul*, 373 U.S. 132, 142-143 (1963).

154. *Hugin Kassaregister AB & Hugin Cash Registers Ltd v. Commission*, case C-22/78 [1979] ECR 1869.

or discontinue production.[155] The *Maxicar* and *Volvo* cases dealt with designs but apply to all IPRs. Thus, on the basis of these EU competition rulings, the scope of the exclusive rights contains the right to make spares (except for designs as the law now provides it does not). In other words, EU competition law ratifies the absence of a right of repair if the intellectual property law is unclear. But if the statutory law clearly provides for a right of repair, and the IPR holder tries to suppress it through a EULA or TPM, it seems that on the basis of these cases, it would be anticompetitive.

The subsequent EU case law, culminating in the *IMS Health* case, implicitly confirms this state of play. It held that a refusal to license is only abusive on several cumulative conditions, namely when it (1) concerns a product the supply of which is indispensable for carrying the business in question in that the person wishing to make the product would find it impossible to do so; (2) prevents the emergence of a new product for which there is a potential consumer demand; (3) is not justified by objective considerations and (4) is likely to exclude all competition in the secondary market.[156] Arguably, a spare part is an exact copy of the original IPR-protected subject matter and a refusal to license a repairer would not be anticompetitive (if the law does not provide a right of repair). Thus, competition law is not very useful to render EULAs and TPMs that restrict repair unenforceable. Nevertheless, the British *Canon* case held that the defence of repair applies when it is plain and obvious that there is unfairness to the consumer and the monopoly is anticompetitive.[157] This case could be usefully extrapolated to all IPR at EU level. This would mean a change in EU competition case law, which would be welcome, especially in cases where a right of repair does not exist, for example in French and Belgian patent law and in some copyright laws. The national theories of abuse of right may also be helpful in going further than current European competition law.

2.   The United States

As mentioned above, in the United States competition law and the doctrine of misuse apply to instances where contracts or TPMs block repair or recycle. Under US antitrust law there are two sources of antitrust liability that can apply when an IPR holder restricts repair or recycle: refusals to deal under section 2 of the Sherman Act, and the essential facilities doctrine. The essential facilities doctrine

---

155. *Consorzio italiano della componentistica di ricambio per autoveicoli & Maxicar v. Régie nationale des usines Renault*, case C-53/87 [1988] ECR 6039; *AB Volvo v. Erik Veng (UK) Ltd*, case C-238/87 [1988] ECR 6211. Maxicar and Veng wanted to obtain a license to produce spare parts for cars protected by design right, but Renault and Volvo refused. The ECJ rejected Maxicar and Veng's argument that this was an abuse of dominant position. Subsequently, however, the law was changed to exclude spare parts from design protection. Here it was the refusal to enter into a contract to allow repair rather than a contract itself that was at stake. However, it amounts to the same as having a contract stating it is forbidden to repair.
156. *IMS Health GmbH & Co OHG v. NDC Health GmbH & Co KG*, case C-418/01 [2004] 4 CMLR 28 (ECJ), para. 38.
157. Above, fn. 16, 826.

has never been endorsed by the Supreme Court and has attracted numerous negative comments.[158] It has now been so reduced that it hardly exists.[159] The focus is therefore on section 2 of the Sherman Act and its application to refusals to license IPRs. Refusals to license are on point as preventing repair or recycle by contract or TPM are akin to refusals to license the IPR to perform such acts.

The general rule is that a firm with market power may not refuse to deal with a competitor if it does not have a valid business reason and the mere lure of additional profit is not a valid business justification.[160] However, as the case law shows, different rules apply for IPRs. In *Data General v. Grumann*,[161] the First Circuit held that 'while exclusionary conduct can include a monopolist's unilateral refusal to license a copyright, an author's desire to exclude others from use of its copyrighted work is a presumptively valid business justification for any immediate harm to consumers'.[162] According to this case, it seems that claimants seeking to establish an IPR holder's unlawful refusal to supply its protected product 'may be required to show that the defendant's control over the downstream market in which the plaintiff competes extends above and beyond the control that naturally flows from the exercise of the IP rights themselves'.[163] This is illustrated in the *CSU* litigation,[164] in which Xerox implemented a policy of not selling parts of its copiers to independent repairers unless they were also end-users of the copiers. The court held that Xerox could refuse to sell its IPR-protected replacement parts to independent repairers. The court refused to look at Xerox's motivation for relying on intellectual property laws to refuse to sell its protected products. It held that it will not enquire into the IPR holder's 'subjective motivation for exercising intellectual property rights even though his refusal to sell or license his patented invention may have an anticompetitive effect, so long as it is not illegally extended beyond the statutory patent grant.'[165] According to commentators, *CSU* means that so long as the patent owner does nothing more than exclude another from making, using or selling his patented invention, the patentee does not violate the antitrust laws even if the exclusion leads to a monopoly in a market for a non-patented product.[166] This is in sharp contrast with the position taken in the

---

158. See mainly P. Areeda, 'Essential facilities: an epithet in need of limiting principles', *Antitrust L. J.* 58 (1989):_ 841.
159. *Verizon Communications IC v. Trinko LLP*, 540 U.S. 398 (2004). See also V. Korah, 'Refusals to deal in IP, The after-sales market and consumer welfare', paper given at the Seventh IEEM Intellectual Property Seminar, Jun. 2006, 4-5.
160. *Aspen Skiing Co. v. Aspen Highlands Skiing Corp.*, 472 U.S. 585 (1985).
161. *Data General Corp. v. Grumman Systems Support Corp.*, 761 F. Supp. 185 (D. Mass. 1991), *aff'd*, 36 F. 3d 1147 (1st Cir. 1994).
162. *Ibid.*, 36 F.3d at 1181, at 1187.
163. G. McCurdy, 'Intellectual Property and Competition: Does the Essential Facilities Doctrine Shed Any New Light', *EIPR* October (2003): 472, at 476.
164. *CSU, L.L.C. v. Xerox Corp.* 203 F. 3d 1322 (Fed. Cir. 2000), *cert. denied*, 531 U.S. 1143 (2001).
165. *Ibid.*
166. P. Boyle, P. Lister & J. Everett, Jr, 'Antitrust Law at the Federal Circuit: Red Light or Green Light at the IP-Antitrust Intersection?', *Antitrust L. J.* 69 (2002): 739, at 754.

Kodak[167] case that the Federal Circuit in *CSU* expressly denied following. Kodak decided to discontinue the supply of spare parts to independent repairers because they were cheaper than Kodak's. The Supreme Court held that the sale of Kodak replacement parts only to customers who use Kodak's repair service could be a violation of section 2 of the Sherman Act unless there was a valid business justification. On remand, the district court held that the business justification that Kodak advanced (its desire to protect its copyright and patent rights on parts) was pretextual.[168] This was because there were thousands of parts and only sixty-five of them were patented. The result is that it is unclear whether IPR holders are sheltered from antitrust liability. It seems nonetheless that if they do not go beyond the bounds of the intellectual property laws, they are. However, if they use their IPR to monopolize the market of non-protected items, their power, according to some case law, is subject to antitrust scrutiny. It would also seem, *a contrario*, that if they bypass intellectual property laws' limits (e.g. if repair is allowed by law without limitation) and have no valid business reason for it, they violate antitrust law.

Misuse, which is well established in patent, copyright, and trademark laws, is an equitable doctrine that acts as a defence in an IPR infringement action, and under which a court refuses to enforce the rights of a claimant who has violated the rights of others.[169] It applies where the ends to which an IPR is put exceed the reasonable grant of that right.[170] There is a difference between copyright and patent misuse. Since the 1988 Patent Misuse Reform Act, to assert the patent misuse defence, the claimant must have committed an antitrust violation under the Sherman Act.[171] It seems also that the patent misuse doctrine has been abolished in *Mallinckrodt* as the court subsumed it into antitrust law.[172] This is normally not the case for copyright misuse (the copyright misuse doctrine's conditions vary from court to court; some courts require the presence of an antitrust violation to find

---

167. 504 U.S. 451 (1992).
168. *Image Technical Services Inc. v. Eastman Kodak*, 125 F. 3d 1195 (9th Cir. 1997), *cert. denied*, 523 U.S. 1094 (1998).
169. For patents, see e.g. *Morton Salt Co. v. G. S. Suppiger Co.*, 314 U.S. 488 (1942). For copyright, see e.g. *Lasercomb Am., Inc. v. Reynolds*, 911 F.2d 970, 978 (4th Cir. 1990). For trademarks, see 15 U.S.C. s. 1115(7).
170. D. Higgs (above, fn. 97), 82. For instance, there was copyright misuse in *Alcatel USA, Inc. v. DGI Technologies, Inc.*, 'in which the Fifth Circuit held that a manufacturer of telephone switching equipment was using the enforcement of the copyright on software inside of microprocessor cards to prevent competitors from developing compatible microprocessor cards. Because the plaintiff was using its copyright in the software to obtain a monopoly in the uncopyrighted hardware, the court held that the copyright misuse defense was applicable.' 'Control of the Aftermarket Through Copyright, *Lexmark v. Static Control Components*', *Harv. J. L. & Tech.* 17(2003): 307, at 318.
171. G. Davis, 'The Rapidly Growing Defense of Copyright Misuse and Efforts to Establish Trademark Misuse: Legitimate Restraints on Copyright Owners or Escape Routes for Copyright Infringers? Ways of Protecting Domain Names?', [1999] III 566 PLI/P at 639, 646.
172. X, 'Is the Patent Misuse Doctrine Obsolete?', *Harv. L. Rev.* 1922, 1928 110 (1997). ('Mallinckrodt confirms that . . . the Federal Circuit will decide allegations of patent misuse by looking solely to antitrust principles.')

misuse, some don't[173]), but if there is antitrust violation there is probably also copyright misuse. This is the same for trademark law: if the IPR owner violates the antitrust laws, it will be denied relief in an infringement action.[174] In *Lasercomb*, the landmark case on copyright misuse, the Fourth Circuit held that 'the question is not whether the copyright is being used in a manner violative of antitrust law . . . but whether the copyright is being used in a manner violative of the public policy embodied in the grant of a copyright'.[175] In short, a copyright may not be used to secure rights beyond the strict boundaries of the conferring statute.[176] The main question the courts ask themselves is whether the claimant's practices fall within the grant of the intellectual property monopoly or, on the contrary, whether the claimant used its copyright in a manner that violates the public policy embodied in the grant of the IPR. Most courts find copyright misuse 'when a copyright owner (1) illegally attempts to use his copyright to gain market power or to extend the monopoly beyond the scope of the copyright; or (2) violates the public policies underlying the copyright laws'.[177] In practice, copyright misuse will be found when anticompetitive clauses are used in contracts and licensing agreements and when IPR owners refuse to license competitors, for instance to dominate a separate market.[178] Arguably, this defence should also apply to 'paracopyright', that is liability created by the DMCA. Although the *Chamberlain* case seems to have clearly put a stop to the use of TPMs to block the repair of both copyrighted works and non-copyrighted products, the doctrine of misuse can achieve the same.[179]

In conclusion, the yardstick used in both antitrust and misuse cases seems to be that if the contract or TPM grants more rights than the law grants to the IPR holder it can amount to private legislation, upset the balance established in the intellectual property laws, and therefore be unlawful. In other words, if the contract or TPM is within the scope of the rights granted to the IPR holder, it should normally be

---

173. A. Fellmeth, 'Copyright Misuse and the Limits of the Intellectual Property Monopoly', *J. Intell. Prop. L.* 6 (1998): 1, at 11 et seq.; G. Davis (above, fn. 171), 649 et seq.
174. Nimmer (above, fn. 21), n. 13.09[A], and cases cited.
175. Above, fn. 165.
176. W. Thomson Jr & M. Chu, 'Overstepping the Bounds: Copyright Misuse', *Computer Law.* 15 no. 11 (1998)1. See *Lasercomb* (above, fn. 165); but also *F.E.L. Publications, Ltd. v. Catholic Bishop of Chicago*, 214 U.S.P.Q. 409 (1982) (citing *Mercoid Corp. v. Mid-Continent Investment Co.*, 320 U.S. 661 (1944)); *Broadcast Music, Inc. v. Columbia Broadcast Sys., Inc.*, 441 U.S. 1 (1979); *Mazer v. Stein*, above, fn. 111.
177. A. Fellmeth (above, fn. 173), 24-25; W. Thomson & M. Chu (above, fn. 176), 4.
178. A. Fellmeth (above, fn. 173), 24 et seq.
179. D. Higgs (above, fn. 97), 82-83 states:

Based on the preceding evaluation of the legislative intent behind the DMCA, it is apparent that the anti-circumvention measures were intended to protect independently-marketable copyrighted works. Extending the anti-circumvention measures into the realm of durable goods, where copyrighted software is only ancillary to a product's desirability, can therefore be classified as a misuse since this constitutes extending the paracopyright beyond its intended scope. Thus, under the misuse doctrine, courts may refuse to enforce the paracopyright of a plaintiff who has restricted the types of toner cartridges, GDO transmitters, or other aftermarket products its consumers may use. (footnotes omitted).

enforceable and vice versa. For instance, the Lexmark Prebate programme left a choice to the consumer between the purchase of discounted and regularly priced cartridges. It also promoted recycling by enticing users to buy discounted cartridges and left it possible for other companies to recycle regularly priced cartridges. Because of these two possibilities, the contract was not against the law. On the other hand, the Supreme Court held that 'a patentee's attempt to secure royalties beyond the grant of its patent was void as the patentee was trying to achieve through contract what the patentee could not obtain under the patent law'.[180]

VI.   CONCLUSION

The result of our enquiry is that intellectual property laws are far from uniform in their treatment of acts of repair and recycle. Sometimes, the law clearly allows IPR holders to prevent the repair and recycle of their goods. This is the case for the repair of copyrighted software in Europe, of copyrighted works protected by TPMs, and of patented articles in Belgium and France and in some cases in Germany. It is also the case for the recycling of American patented goods. However, the prevention of repair or recycle in these cases is not sheltered from competition law and abuse-of-rights doctrines. In other cases, while the law provides exceptions for repair and the exhaustion principle, it does not provide whether those limits are overridable. Based on the rationale of intellectual property laws (which are exceptions to the free competition principle) and on the free movement of goods principle, these practices should not be allowed. In case these two principles should not be strong enough to preserve repair and recycle, competition law and the abuse-of-rights doctrine are final safeguards. In Europe, competition law does not allow repair if it is not provided in the intellectual property laws but it prevents anticompetitive conduct by the IPR holders who keep their monopoly on repairs; that is, they cannot fix prices at an unfair level nor discontinue production. National abuse-of-rights doctrines may apply to fix the lacuna of current EU competition law. In the United States, it seems that under antitrust law, IPR holders who possess market power cannot bypass the limits of intellectual property laws unless they have a valid business reason to do so. But the misuse doctrine is generally more severe than antitrust law as all IPR holders (except patent owners), not only those with market power, may not override the limits of the grant of the IPR in question, even if they have a valid business reason. In conclusion, repair and recycle are reasonably well safeguarded in both legal systems. Nevertheless, the fact that competition law and the misuse doctrine allow IPR holders to prevent repair and recycle if the intellectual property laws do not provide for such exceptions may in some cases call for the need to reform intellectual property laws where such exceptions do not exist and where they perhaps should.

---

180.   A. Gajarsa (above, fn. 135), 1228-1229, citing *Brulotte v. Thys Co.*, 379 U.S. 29, 33-34 (1964) (holding that an attempt to 'project [the expiration of patents] into another term by continuation of the licensing agreement is unenforceable').

Part 2

Issues under Patent Law

Chapter 3

Repair and Recycle as Direct Patent Infringement?

Mineko Mohri

I. INTRODUCTION: PATENT EXHAUSTION ON REPAIR AND RECYCLING

Patent law grants an inventor a 'right to exclude' others from using, selling, or importing the invention for a limited period in the country where the patent is granted.[1] Under the domestic exhaustion doctrine, the patentee's monopoly effectively ends at the first lawful, unconditional sale[2] of the patented products. Thus, purchasers of patented products may use or resell them without interference from patentees. Such a phenomenon is referred to as that the patent was 'consumed' or 'exhausted'.[3] A purchaser's right to 'use' includes a right to make 'repairs' on a

---

1. Such powers of the patent right are provided in the US under 35 USC. s. 154(a)(1) (provides grant of the patent right), and s. 271(a) (defines patent infringement) (1952), in Japan by the Japanese Patent Act s. 2(3)(i), and s. 68 (Law No. 121 of 1959, as amended), and under the German Patent Act s. 9(2)(i) (1981 as amended).
2. The patent exhaustion doctrine may not apply to an expressly conditioned sale or license. See below, Section IV.
3. G. Benkard, *Patentgesetz*, 10th edn (Munich: C.H. Beck, 2006), at 372; R. Kraßer, *Patentrecht*, 5th edn (Munich: C.H. Beck, 2004), at 819.

Christopher Heath, Anselm Kamperman Sanders (eds.), *Spares, Repairs and Intellectual Property Rights*, pp. 59-83.
© 2009 Kluwer Law International BV, The Netherlands.

patented product necessary for continued use.[4] Yet, the term 'repair' does not include a complete reconstruction of a completely spent or worn-out product.[5] The basic rule of domestic exhaustion seems simple; however, distinguishing between permissible repair and impermissible reconstruction is difficult.

The varieties of commercial activities in the after-sales market ('aftermarket'), adds complexities to this issue. Maintenance services, sales of replaceable parts for consumed parts, recycling used products: these activities could be offered not only by patentees, but also by third parties. Patentees might seek an injunction against third parties' activities in the aftermarket, claiming 'impermissible construction' as direct infringement, or asserting the sales of replaceables as 'indirect infringement' (see the following chapter). To what extent patentees can control these activities in the aftermarket has a direct influence upon a patentee's business strategy. Patentees might sell whole patented products at a relatively low profit margin in order to profit by selling spare parts to the product. Therefore, whether or not the producers of patented products can maximize the turnover of spare parts sales by invoking patent law is an economically important issue.[6] Or patentees could simply prohibit recycling so that they can promote the sale of new-patented products. For the purpose of clarification, patentees sometimes set special agreements upon the sale of a patented product, such as maintenance agreements or single-use agreements, in order to prohibit repair or recycling services of third parties. The ruling of courts directly affects the interests of patentees, repair, and recycling manufacturers, and it is also a concern to society, namely consumers.

The rationale of patent law, which gives the patentee a monopoly and regards the latter's exhaustion as a limit, might give a clue to the solution. Currently, case law and mainstream theory concerning repair or recycling, or the replacement of spare parts somewhat differs in each jurisdiction.[7] Each theory is worth a closer look. This article will highlight the key similarities and differences in various jurisdictions and the interests behind the issues involved. Section II reviews some important cases on 'repair and recycling' in different jurisdictions: the US, Japan, and Germany. Section III compares the legal theories of each jurisdiction using the 'single-use-camera' case as an example. In Section IV, the paper analyses the enforceability of common 'single-use' agreements from the perspective of patent law. Finally, Section V provides a synthesis and thoughts on the road ahead.

---

4. D.S. Chisum, '5 Chisum on Patents', 16.03 [3] (1998), at 16-158; K. Yoshifuji & K. Kumagai, [Tokkyohô Gaisetsu] (*Outline of Patent Law*), 13th edn (Tokyo: Yuhikaku, 1998), at 434; *ibid.*, see above, fn. 3, Benkhard, at 387.
5. *See* Chisum, *id.*
6. *See* Chisum, *id.* According to Chisum, 'The issues of repair versus reconstruction frequently arise in suits against the manufacturer or seller of replacement parts for contributory infringement.' Corresponding provisions are 35 U.S.C. 271(1)(c) (as of 1994), Japanese Patent Act s. 101(1) (Law No. 121 of 1959, as amended). German Patent Act s. 10(1) (as of 1998). The angle of 'Repair and Recycle as Indirect Patent Infringement' is analysed by Heath in Chapter 4 of this book.
7. See Sections II and III.

II.   REPAIR AND RECYCLING IN DIFFERENT
             JURISDICTIONS: THE US, JAPAN, THE UK AND
             GERMANY

A.   THE US[8]

1.   The Origins of Patent Exhaustion in the
             US Supreme Court

On 9 June 2008, the US Supreme Court issued a decision in *Quanta Computer, Inc. v. LG Electronics, Inc.*[9] This eagerly awaited decision confirmed the longstanding doctrine of patent exhaustion, which was established around the middle of the nineteenth century.[10] The origin of the principle of repair/reconstruction can be traced back to *Wilson v. Rousseau.*[11] In *Wilson v. Rousseau* the court established the principle that '[T]he right of property of the inventor to his invention or discovery passed from him as soon as it went into pubic use with his consent'.[12] The established rule was succeeded and elaborated in later cases.[13] In *Adams v. Burke,*[14] the court held:

> [W]here a person had purchased a patented machine of the patentee or his assignee, this purchase carried with it the *right to the use of that machine so long as it was capable of use* ...[15] 'But ... when the patentee ... sells a machine or instrument whose sole value is in its use, *he received the consideration* for its use and the parts with the right to restrict that use'.[16] ... once

---

8. The following texts review the repair and reconstruction theory in the US: M.J. Adelman, 'Patent Law Perspectives', s. 3.8; Matthew Bender (file 2nd edn 2007); Donald S. Chisum, '5 Chisum on Patents', 16.03[2](a) (1998). Case analysis and proposals for an adequate legal framework by legal practitioners are provided by J.W. Osborne, 'A Coherent View of Patent Exhaustion: A Standard Based on Patentable Distinctiveness', *Santa Clara Computer & High Tech. L. J.* 20 (2004): 643, A.H. Rovner, 'Practical Guide to Application of (or Defense against) Product-Based Infringement Immunities under the Doctrines of Patent Exhaustion and Implied License', *Tex. Intell. Prop. L. J.* 12 (2004): 227.
9. *Quanta Computer, Inc. v. LG Electronics, Inc.*, 533 U.S. _____ (2008). *See* Section IV. Unfortunately, the court did not rule on another important issue, namely, the validity of the concept of conditional sales to avoid exhaustion.
10. The starting points of the exhaustion principle concerned William Woodworth's patent. He had a patent on a planning machine, which was cutting edge technology and his products dominated the marketplace.
11. *Wilson v. Rousseau*, 45 U.S. 646 (1846).
12. *Ibid.*, at 674.
13. *Bloomer v. McQuewan*, 55 U.S. 539 (1852):'And when the machine passes to the hands of the purchaser, it is no longer within the limits of the monopoly. It passes outside of it, and is no longer under the protection of the act of Congress. . . .' *Id.*, at 549-550 (*Bloomer v. McQuewan* was cited later in *Mitchell v. Hawley*, 83 U.S. 544 (1872)). The 'right to use' was confirmed by the U.S. Supreme Court long before the *Aro I* case.
14. *Adams v. Burke*, 84 U.S. 453 (1873).
15. *Ibid.*, at 455 (emphasis added).
16. *Ibid.*, at 456 (emphasis added).

lawfully made and sold, there is no restriction on their use to be implied for the benefit of the patentee.[17]

The Court confirmed that a patentee loses its right to control patented product upon lawful sales, because it receives the consideration to the use of product. On the other hand, a purchaser obtained 'right to use' a patented product until the product was incapable of use.

The Supreme Court in *Quanta* confirmed further two rules. First, the sale of an uncompleted article of combination product results in exhaustion of the patent covering the whole combined patented product, if such uncompleted article *embodies essential features of its patented invention*.[18] The Court in *Quanta* held '[I]f the device practices patent A while *substantially embodying* patent B, its relationship to patent A does not prevent exhaustion of patent B.'[19] Second, the exhaustion does apply to method claims,[20] so method patents can also be exhausted upon the first sale.[21]

2.   Replacement of Unpatented Parts of Combination Products

In *Wilson v. Simpson*,[22] the court held that the replacement of worn-out cutting knives from a patented wood planing machine, after several months of use, constituted permissible repair. In the court's view, reconstruction could only be assumed when 'one of the elements of the combination has become so much worn as to be inoperative, or has been broken, so that the machine no longer exists'. But 'when wearing or injury is partial, then repair is restoration, not reconstruction'.[23] It confirmed that a purchaser has a right to use until the useful lifespan of the patented product comes to an end. This ruling of *Wilson v. Simpson* has been continuously supported by the Supreme Court.[24]

The intention of the Supreme Court to limit the extension of a patentee's monopolies over unpatented spare parts became even clearer in the *Aro I* case.[25] The Supreme Court ruled on 'whether the replacement of an unpatented part, in a patented combination, that has worn out, been broken or otherwise spent,

---

17. *Ibid.*, at 457 (emphasis added).
18. *United States. v. Univis Lens Co.*, 316 U.S. 241, 250-251 (1942). The case concerns the Sherman Anti-Trust Act.
19. *Quanta Computer, Inc. v. LG Electronics, Inc.*, 533 U.S. _____, 15 (2008).
20. *Ethyl Gasoline Corp. v. United States*, 309 U.S. 436, 457 (1940). This was also a Sherman Anti-Trust Act case. The court held that the sale of a motor fuel produced under one patent also exhausted the patent for a method of using the fuel in combustion motors.
21. The court in *Quanta* found it is unfair if patentees could avoid patent exhaustion by simply drafting their patent claims to describe a method rather than an apparatus.
22. *Wilson v. Simpson*, 50 U.S. 109 (1850).
23. *Ibid.*, at 123-124.
24. *Morgan Envelope Co. v. Albany Perforated Wrapping Paper Co.*, 152 U.S. 425 (1894), *Heyer v. Duplicator Mfg. Co.*, 263 U.S. 100 (1923).
25. *Aro Mfg. Co. v. Convertible Top Replacement Co.*, 365 U.S. 336 (1961).

is permissible "repair" or infringing "reconstruction".[26] This case involved a convertible sports car of which the folding top was patented.[27] The defendant supplied a replaceable top fabric, and the car manufacturer alleged patent infringement. The Court held:

> [R]econstruction of a patented entity, comprised of unpatented elements, is limited to such a true reconstruction of the entity as to 'in fact make a new article', after the entity, viewed as a whole, has become spent...It must, indeed, be a second creation of the patented entity...*Mere replacement of individual unpatented parts, one at a time, whether of the same parts repeatedly or different parts successively, is no more than the lawful right of the owner to repair his property.*[28]

Thus, under this precedent, subsequent lower courts had to consider whether a patented entity was, as a whole, 'spent' and 'the sold machine no longer exists'. Otherwise, the lifespan of a patented product has not come to an end, and its modification can be a permissible repair. The *Aro I* case followed the line of *Wilson and Simpson*, and interpreted the scope of unlawful reconstruction narrowly.[29]

3.   Multiple Factors and Extrinsic Conditions

In *Aro I*, in deciding the lawfulness of repair, the majority refused to consider whether the 'essential' element or 'heart' of the invention was replaced, by holding that 'the combination patent covers only the totality of the elements in the claim and that no element, separately viewed, is within the grant'.[30] One of the concurring opinions by Judge Brennan, who thought the majority view was too narrow a standard of what constitutes impermissible reconstruction,[31] is also noteworthy. He stated 'repair' and 'reconstruction' should be considered based on numerous factors, including:

> the life of the part replaced in relation to the useful life of the whole combination, the importance of the replaced element to the inventive concept,[32]

---

26. *Ibid.*, at 342.
27. The Court noted that:

    The folding top as such was new. Yet, the patent covered the combination of several unpatented individual parts, such as top fabric, supporting structures, and a mechanism for sealing the fabric against the car. After some years, the top fabric becomes worn out and needs replacement (*Ibid.*, at 337).

28. *Ibid.*, at 346 (emphasis added).
29. According to D.S. Chisum, 'the impact of the *Aro* cases on the lower court decisions seems to have been one of broadening the scope of permissible repair' (see above, fn. 4 'Chisum on Patent', para. 16.03[3](d)).
30. *Aro Mfg. Co.*, at 344.
31. *Ibid.*, at 362.
32. Judge Gajarsa of the Court of Appeals of the Federal Circuit (CAFC) points out in his article that the heart of the invention could be (1) the part that is non-obvious over the prior art; (2) the

the cost of the component relative to the cost of the combination, the common-sense understanding and intention of the patent owner and the buyer of the combination as to its perishable components, whether the purchased component replaces a worn-out part or is bought for some other purpose, and other pertinent factors.[33,34]

In addition, it should be noted that extrinsic conditions may limit the patent exhaustion. The very first case where the Supreme Court found alleged repairs and 'illegal reconstruction' was the *American Cotton-Tie* case,[35] in which the patented products were sold with the words 'Licensed to use once only'.[36] Later in the *Aro I* case[37] the Supreme Court confirmed the importance of marking 'Licensed to use once only', when the Court found impermissible reconstruction in the *American Cotton-Tie* case. The Supreme Court in *Quanta* left open the issue whether relatively common single-use license agreements can avoid patent exhaustion. Under US case law, patent exhaustion may be restricted when the first lawful sale was conditional. In the US, the exhaustion doctrine, or whether purchasers of patented products can freely use, repair, or replace spare parts, is often explained as implied license theory.[38] See Section IV, below.

4.   Not 'Repair', but 'Akin to Repair'

The vague meaning of 'spent' becomes even more problematic when purchasers or third parties intend to replace the component with superior functions to improve the quality of patented products. In *Wilbur-Ellis Co. v. Kuther*,[39] the patentee owned a combination patent covering a fish-canning machine, including a combination of

---

most expensive component of the patented device; or (3) the largest element of the patented device, and says it is difficult to understand how one would apply the 'heart of invention' test. A.J. Gajarsa et al., 'How Much Fuel to Add to the Fire of Genius? Some Questions about the Repair/Reconstruction Distinction in Patent Law', *Am. U. L. Rev.* 48 (1999): 1205, 1210 at fn. 32.

33. *See* above, n. 25, *Aro Mfg. Co.*, at 363, 364.
34. In *Aktiebolag v. E. J. Co.*, 121 F. 3d 669 (Fed. Cir. 1997), and the instruction to the jury in *Lummus Industries, Inc. v. D. M. & E Corp.*, 862 F. 2d 267 (Fed. Cir. 1988), it seems that the court followed Judge Brennan's 'numerous factor' test (see above, n. 32, Gajarsa, at 1215 et seq. and 1220 et seq.).
35. *American Cotton-Tie Co. v. Simmons*, 106 U.S. 89 (1882). Founding of 'impermissible reconstruction' was followed by *Leeds & Catlin Co. v. Victor Talking Mach. Co.*, 213 U.S. 325 (1909).
36. *See American Cotton-Tie Co. v. Simmons*, at 91. To the contrary, the Court did not find infringement in *Morgan Envelope Co. v. Albany Perforated Wrapping Paper Co.*, 152 U.S. 425 (1894) and held: 'In this case, however, the purchaser of the new roll does precisely what the patentee intended he should do: he replaces that which is in its nature perishable, and without the replacement of which the remainder of the device is no value.' *Ibid.*, at 434.
37. See above, fn. 25, *Aro Mfg. Co.*, at 343.
38. *Lawther v. Hamilton*, 124 U.S. 1 (1888); *De Forest Radio Telephone & Telegraph Co. v. United States*, 273 U.S. 236 (1927); *United States. v. Univis Lens Co.*, 316 U.S. 241 (1942) (in relation to anti-trust law, Sherman Act), *Anton/Bauer, Inc. v. PAG, Ltd*, 329 F. 3d 1343 (2003).
39. *Wilbur-Ellis Co. v. Kuther*, 337 U.S. 422 (1964).

unpatented components. The purchaser, who retained a repair person, cleaned and resized six of the thirty-five elements, and made it suitable for use with a smaller can. The Supreme Court held that such acts 'were doing more than repair in the customary sense; but what they did was "akin to repair", for it bore on the useful capacity of the old combination, on which the royalty had been paid'.[40]

The United States Court of Appeals for the Federal Circuit (the 'Federal Circuit') followed *Wilbur-Ellis Co. v. Kuther* and used the magical formula '(a)kin to repair' in the *Hewlett-Packard*[41] and *Surfco Hawaii* cases.[42]

In *Hewlett-Packard*, the plaintiff manufactured and sold ink-jet printers and disposable ink cartridges, and held a variety of patents on 'ink-jet printing technology, including patents on ink-jet printers, cartridges, and ink formulations'. The ink-jet cartridges were intended for one-time use. The defendant bought two types of patented cartridges, and modified the new cartridges' plastic caps, which covered the ink reservoirs, making the caps removable and the cartridges refillable. The Federal Circuit focused on the defendant's lawful purchase of the cartridges and modification before the cartridges had been, as a product, 'spent'. Consequently, the court found the defendant's modification of an unspent cartridge '*more akin to* permissible "repair" than to impermissible "reconstruction"' (emphasis added).[43]

When the Federal Circuit expanded the scope of permissible repair granting 'akin to repair', the court focused on a number of elements, as Judge Brennan in the *Aro I* case had proposed. In the *Surfco* case, *Surfco* manufactured fins that were specifically fitted for use with the Fin Control Systems surfboard.[44] The *Surfco* fins differed from the patentee's fin only in that the *Surfco* fins incorporated rubber edges as a safety feature.[45] These rubber edges prevented the fins from cutting the user of the surfboard. The Federal Circuit reversed the judgment of the lower court, and interpreted that 'permissible 'repair' also included replacement of parts that were neither broken nor worn.[46] *Unless a device or substantial parts thereof are reconstructed, or the sale has been conditional*, the law does not prevent the purchaser of a patented device from prematurely replacing an unpatented part.[47,48]

---

40. *Ibid.*, at 425 (emphasis added).
41. *Hewlett-Packard Co. v. Repeat-O-Type Stencil Mfg. Corp.*, 123 F. 3d 1445 (Fed. Cir. 1997).
42. *Surfco Hawaii v. Fin Control Systems, Ltd*, 264 F. 3d 1063 (Fed. Cir. 2001).
43. See above, fn. 41, *Hewlett-Packard Co.*, at 1452. Stracker criticizes that 'the court decreased HP's incentives to invest the time in creating superior ink cartridges', and adds the decision was not supported in light of 'just rewards theory' because, 'upon setting a price based on a one-time use of the ink-jet cartridge, the selling price for the cartridge would not reflect multiple uses of the product . . .'. E. Stracker, 'I. Intellectual Property: B. Patent: 2, Infringement: a) Modification: *Hewlett-Packard Co. v. Repeat-O-Type Stencil Manufacturing Corp.*', *Berkeley Tech L. J.* 13 (1999): 175, 192 and 194.
44. See above, fn. 42, *Surfco* at 1064.
45. *Ibid.*
46. The Federal Circuit cited *Aro I* case.
47. See above, fn. 42, *Surfco* at 1065. See *Kendall Co. v. Progressive Medical Technology, Inc.*, 85 F. 3d 1570 (Fed. Cir. 1996).
48. *Husky Injection Molding Systems, Ltd v. R&D Tool Engineering Co.*, 291 F. 3d 780 (Fed. Cir. 2002). The court said, 'The critical question is: how much repair is fair before the device is deemed reconstructed.' *ibid.*, at 784.

5.   Overview: Permissible Repair in the US

There is some confusion between the decisions of the Supreme Court and the Federal Circuit in this respect.[49] First, although the Supreme Court denied the multifactor test, the Federal Circuit showed in some cases[50] that multiple factors should be taken into account, and that there might be a legally protected 'essential' element or 'heart' of the invention in a combination patent.[51] Second, conditional sales may avoid patent exhaustion under the case law of the Federal Circuit, although the Supreme Court has not given any answer to the validity of conditional sales. Comparing the approach of the two courts, it seems the Federal Circuit is more conservative in finding 'permissible repair'.

It seems the courts and scholars rest their decisions on 'the exercise of sound common sense and an intelligent judgment'.[52] However, thanks to the volume of cases, we can find some clear rules from the Supreme Court as follows. First, purchasers of patented products can use the defence of patent exhaustion as long as the lifespan of the entire product has not yet come to an end. Second, even when purchasers do not repair the broken (spent) parts of patented products, the acts of an alleged infringer might still be deemed 'permissible repair' as long as the acts are deemed 'akin' to repair.[53] Third, mere replacement of individual unpatented parts, one at a time, whether for the same or different parts successively, is within the 'right to use' of the owner of the patented product. The third point is often argued as an indirect infringement claim. However, the direct infringement is a prerequisite for indirect infringement in the US, therefore the 'spent' criterion is the most important in deciding repair or reconstruction.

B.   Japan[54]

1.   Japanese Cases and Patent Exhaustion

Compared to the US, Japanese courts seem to find for infringement rather than non-infringement in repair and recycling cases. The courts were trying to draw a

---

49. See above, fn. 32, Gajarsa et al., 1210.
50. In *Aktiebolag v. E. J. Co.*, 121 F. 3d 669 (Fed. Cir. 1997), and the instruction to the jury in *Lummus Industries, Inc. v. D. M. & E Corp.*, 862 F. 2d 267 (Fed. Cir. 1988), it seems that the court followed Judge Brennan's 'numerous factor' test (see above, fn. 32, Gajarsa et al., at 1215 et seq. and 1220 et seq.).
51. See above, fn. 42, *Surfco* 'When a device or substantial parts thereof are not reconstructed, or condition of sale is not violated'. How does this harmonize with *Univis Lens* case?
52. M.D. Janis, 'A Tale of the Apocryphal Axe: Repair, Reconstruction, and the Implied License in Intellectual Property Law', *Md. L. Rev.* 38 (1999): 423, 426.
53. See above, fn. 39, *Wilbur-Ellis Co. v. Kuther*.
54. Introduction and analysis of recent Japanese cases on repair/reconstruction issues are available in English by C. Heath & M. Môri, 'Ending Is Better than Mending: Recent Japanese Case Law on Repair, Refill and Recycling', *IIC* 37 (2006): 856; Zeitschrift für Japanisches Recht [*Journal of Japanese Law*] 23 (2007): 65.

line between infringement and non-infringement. The rulings are generally classified into two categories by Japanese scholars:[55] (1) rulings based on the repair/
reconstruction theory,[56] and (2) rulings based on the doctrine of patent exhaustion
and its exception.[57]

Japanese courts follow the theory of patent exhaustion.[58] There are old cases
of lower courts that ruled the principle that 'once a patented product is put on the
market by an authorized person such as a patentee, the patented product is no
longer subject to patent enforcement'.[59]

The Japanese Supreme Court expressed its view on Patent Exhaustion in the
BBS case in 1997.[60] A German company, *BBS*, brought a lawsuit claiming the
unlawfulness of parallel importation of their aluminium wheels for automobiles.
The court ruled on the international exhaustion as *ratio decidendi*, but it also
explained the rationale of national exhaustion doctrine as an *obiter dictum*.

---

55. H. Yokoyama, case review – *Acycrovir*, Jurist No. 170, 130 (2004); H. Yokoyama, [Tokkyo-
    seihin no recycle to shôjinriron] ('The Recycle of Patent Products and the Exhaustion Doctrine')
    Jurist 34 (2006): 1316.
56. *Hammer* case, *Acycrovir* (Tokyo High Court), *Step Tool* case, *Canon* case (Tokyo District
    Court).
57. *Konica* case, *Fuji I* case, *Fuji II* case, *Acycrovir* case (Tokyo District Court).
58. N. Nakayama, [Kōgyō shoyūken hō (Jō) Tokkyohō] (*Industrial Property Rights, Patent Rights*),
    361, second revised and enlarged edition (2000); see above, fn. 4; K. Yoshifuji & K. Kumagai,
    above fn. 4, at 431; K. Tamai, [Nihon kokunai ni okeru tokkyoken no shôjin] ('Patent Exhaus-
    tion in Japan'), in T. Makino & T. Iimura (eds), *Shin Saiban Jitsumu Taikei* (Tokyo: Yuhikaku,
    2001), 233; Y. Tamura, [Shûri ya buhin no torikae to tokkyokenshingai no seihi] ('Recycle or
    Replacement of Spare Parts and Possibility of Patent Infringement'), *Chiteki zaisan hô seisa-
    kugaku kenkyû* 6 (2005): 33.
59. Osaka District Court, 9 Jun. 1969, Mutaishū 1-160; Nara District Court, 26 May 1975, 329
    Hanrei Times 287.
60. Supreme Court of Japan, 1 Jul. 1997, 29 IIC 331, 333 (1998) – *BBS Car Wheels III*:

    If patented products are sold domestically, either by the patentee or with his consent, the patent
    is deemed exhausted because it has fulfilled its purpose. The patent does not give rights to
    subsequent use of the patented product by acts of transfer or lease. First, patent law has to be
    understood as balancing the interests of invention protection, and the public benefit of society at
    large. Next, if a tangible object is transferred, the corresponding rights are obtained by the
    transferee, and the transferee obtains those rights that were originally vested in the transferor.
    Also insofar as patented products are distributed on the market, the transferee obtains an object
    from the patentee whose exercise of the right suggests that the right in further acts of resale has
    been transferred as well. If with respect to any acts of marketing patented products, the paten-
    tee's consent were necessary each time a transfer occurs, the free movement of goods would be
    seriously impeded, the smooth distribution of patented products would be hampered and as a
    result, the interests of the patentee himself would suffer. This would run counter to the purpose
    of the Patent Act 'to encourage inventions by promoting their protection and utilization so as to
    contribute to the development of industry' (s. 1 Patent Act). Finally, by making the invention
    available to the public, the patentee will have the opportunity to obtain the reward from selling
    the product or granting a license for the use of the patent and thereby obtain a licensing fee. In
    order to protect the financial interests of the patentee who has made his invention public, it
    would not seem necessary to give the patentee or the licensee rights beyond the first act of
    marketing, as the patentee would then obtain an unnecessary double reward in the course of
    further distribution.

The Supreme Court based domestic exhaustion on: (1) the free movement of goods, and (2) the patentee's opportunity to obtain a reward (by making the invention available to the public, the patentee will have the opportunity to obtain the consideration). These interests have to be analysed closely, since these substantial grounds of domestic patent exhaustion have influenced later repair and recycle cases.

2. *Canon* as Decided by the Supreme Court

After the *BBS* case, although some lower courts rendered judgments, no case has been argued before the Supreme Court on the issue of how to consider the repair or replacement of consumables in relation to the principle of patent exhaustion until the *Canon* case in 2007.[61,62]

In this case, the plaintiff (appellant) had an apparatus patent and a method patent concerning the ink tank for an ink-jet printer. The affiliated company of the defendant collected the used ink tanks, patented products, sold by the plaintiff from North America, Europe, and Asia (including Japan). Then the defendant (appellee) initially made a hole on the topside of the ink tank in order to rinse the tank and refill it with ink. After the ink was refilled into the tank, the hole in the ink tank was plugged and sealed. There is no dispute about the fact that the defendant's act falls within the exercise of plaintiff's patent rights.

The Court first referred to the above *BBS* ruling and commented on the national exhaustion doctrine:

> However, the exercise of a patent right is restricted regarding only a patented product which was assigned by the patent holder et al. in this county. Therefore, when a third party refurbished or replaced the parts of such product and thus, created a new product which has a different identity from the original product, a patent holder can enforce its right and claim patent infringement against such products ... The issue whether or not a third party has created a new product should be determined from a comprehensive standpoint such as the *attribute of a patented product, contents of a patented invention, aspects of refurbishment and replacement of parts*, in addition to *actual conditions of distributions*, etc. (emphasis added).

The material facts and the conclusion of this case were as follows. The patented product was intended to be used only once and should be replaced by a new one after consumption of the ink, because the refilling of ink could cause a quality loss

---

61. Supreme Court of Japan, 8 Nov. 2007, 1990 Hanrei Jihō 3, 1258 *Hanrei Times* 62 – *Canon Ink Tank*; (In English) 39 IIC 39 (2008), the appeal court IP High Court., 31 Jan. 2006, 30 Hanrei Jiho 1922.
62. Reviews: T. Nakayoshi, 39 *L&T* 60 (2008); R. Shitara, Prof. Saito Festschrift 405 (2008); Y. Tamura, 887 NBL 12 (2008), 878 NBL 22 (2008); H. Yokoyama, 45 Tokkyo Kenkyû 52 (2008), H. Yokoyama, 72 Forum of the Institute of Intellectual Property 24 (2008). K. Hirano, 6-65 Chizai Prism 21 (2008); M.S. Hashiguchi, 'Recycling Efforts and Patent Rights Protection in the United States and Japan', *Colum. J. Envtl. L.* 33 (2008): 169 (focuses on legal doctrine and business practice involving recycling activities and patent infringement in the US and in Japan).

in printing, or a disorder of the printing machine. The plaintiff's products did not have any hole which made it possible to refill the ink, and the hole on the top part of the ink tank which was needed to fill the ink into the tank was sealed after the tanks were filled with ink. Therefore, the refurbishment that was going to create the defendant's products was not just the refill of the consumable ink, but the deformation of the ink tank.

Concerning the plaintiff's product, the ink itself played a technical role in preventing the movement of air at the boundary surface of the insulation part, and when such ink was consumed to a certain amount, part or all of the boundary surface of the insulation part could no longer retain the ink. Concerning the used ink that remained in the tank, it would dry in the tank after approximately seven-to-ten days, and the function to prevent the movement of air at the boundary surface of the tank could not be revived even though the new ink filled the whole ink chamber and the boundary surface of the insulation part. Here, the defendant washed the inside of the ink tank, rinsed off the dried ink, and thus the function to prevent the movement of air at the boundary surface of the insulation part was recovered. Also, the conditions to keep the ink despite the position of the ink tank were reproduced through refilling the ink in the same amount as the original. The Court held that the aspect of refurbishment in this case involved reusing the used ink tank, and reproducing the configuration of the essential element of the invention, which had lost its function. Based on these facts, the defendant's refurbishment was regarded by the court as a reproduction of the substantial value of the invention and realizing the effect of the invention, which was to prevent the leakage of ink.

Thus, the Court concluded:

> Along with the actual conditions of distribution, we must conclude that *new patented products which lack the identity from the original products were created*, and thus, the plaintiff can enforce its right in seeking injunction of distribution of the defendant's product (emphasis added).

When the Supreme Court ruled on the issue in 2007, the discussions seemed to have come to an end. However, what the Court meant by saying that patent exhaustion should be determined based on 'whether or not the new products lack the identity from the original products' is not yet clear. Is the 'comprehensive standpoint' clear enough to give the market the outcome of legality? Could the patentee's intention have influence on the timing of patent exhaustion? Here, an analysis of the lower courts' ruling might give us clues.

3.   *Canon* **before the IP High Court**

The Intellectual High Court in Tokyo ('IP High Court') in the *Canon* case[63] ruled on the issue of national exhaustion and its two exceptions and ruled that refilled ink

---

63. Intellectual Property High Court, 31 Jan. 2006, 1922 Hanrei Jihō 30 – *Canon* (the second instance). English translation in 37 IIC 867 (2006). An official English summary is available

cartridges infringed Canon's patent[64] contrary to the first instance that had found no infringement.[65] The ruling of the IP High Court was detailed. Japanese practitioners and scholars appreciated the IP High Court's effort to seek a clear criterion of what is impermissible as overstepping patent exhaustion in order to give certainty to the market. Later, the Supreme Court did not apply the same criteria, but applied its own standard. But a judge at the Supreme Court explains that the Supreme Court did not reject the criteria that the IP High Court applied, and these criteria are still valuable and useful.[66]

The IP High Court made it clear that the exceptions to patent exhaustion should be determined based on the analysis of either: (1) the lifespan of the patented products, or (2) the nature of the patented invention. According to the decision, the relevant patent rights for the patented products should be deemed exhausted once the patentee sold the patented products in Japan, because the patent rights for these patented products have fulfilled their purpose. Thus, the patentee may no longer exercise the patent right over the defendant's acts of use or resale. However, patentees can enforce their patent rights under one of the following conditions that would be considered reconstruction rather than repair:

(1) The patented product is used or recycled after it has finished its service along with the lapse of its ordinary life as a product;
(2) A third party has made modifications or replacements to the whole or part of the components that *constitute an essential portion* of the patented product.[67]

The court thus determines the lifespan not only from the physical composition of the product, but also from a social/economical point of view. And even if the lifespan has not come to an end, there is patent infringement when an essential portion of the patented invention is repaired. The exception one above focuses on the lifespan of the patented product, while the exception two focuses on the patented invention. In the case at issue, the court determined that the part that was repaired by the defendants was the essential portion of the patented invention and found the defendant liable for infringement.[68]

---

at (last visited 15 Dec. 2008), <www.ip.courts.go.jp/eng/documents/pdf/g_panel/decision_summary.pdf>.
64. The outcome of the *Canon* case is often compared with the *Hewlett-Packard* case, where the US court held that recycled ink cartridges did not infringe the patent. Considering the specification and claims of the *Canon* patent, the outcome of Japanese Supreme Court is not unreasonable.
65. Tokyo District Court, 8 Dec. 2004, 1889 Hanrei Jihô 110 – *Canon* (the first instance).
66. See above, fn. 62, Nakayoshi, at 69.
67. This second point 'essentialness' was reversed by the Supreme Court. The Supreme Court thought the sole fact that modification was made to the 'essential' part cannot always make repair impermissible. The Court wanted more flexibility for permissible repair.
68. Numerous articles on the *Canon* case are available in Japanese: H. Furusawa, [Shiyôzumi tokkyoseihin wo sairiyô shita inktank ni tsuki shôjin ga hitei sareta rei] ('A Case Where the Patent Exhaustion Was Not Found as to the Re-usage of the Consumed Ink Tanks') *Chizai Kanri* 56-59 (2006): 1425; M. Suzuki, [Tokkyo hatsumei no jisshihin de aru ink tank no iwayuru recycle hin ni tsuki tokkyoken ni motozuku sashitome seikyû tô wo kôshi suru koto ga

At the same time, the court held that exception one did not apply, as the patented products had not spent their life as a product even if the initial ink was used up, because: (1) no physical alteration had been added to the components of the products other than the refill ink; (2) ink is an interchangeable part; (3) the recycled cartridges and ink refills are available on the market of ink products for ink jet printers, and they are widely accepted by users due to their lower price; (4) recycling should be encouraged; and (5) no laws or regulations prohibit the recycling of used ink tanks. The elements that should be analysed for determining exception one are rather complicated. First, the lapse of the product's ordinary life should be determined by taking into account social and economic views. In addition, the lifespan of a product may end due to: (1) physical reasons; and (2) reasons determined by the applicable laws or 'common understanding of society'. The replacement of consumable parts is permissible, if this amounts to 'usual repair'. When alterations are added to dominant and/or substantial parts of the patented product, such alterations are not a 'usual repair', and therefore impermissible. Furthermore, the replacement of spare parts is permissible, even when a patented product has a structure making it difficult to replace the consumable component. But in Japan it can be illegal either when: (1) such structure is indispensable in light of the purpose of the invention; or (2) such structure is the one that products of the same kind generally have.

4.   Other Early Cases[69]

There are two cases concerning a utility model and indirect infringement: the *Hammer* case (a hammer for crushing stones), and the *Step Tool* case (a trap/ step tool for construction sites).

In the *Hammer* Case,[70] the plaintiff had sold hammers for crushing stones, which consisted of an arm, mount, and battering plate, and these hammers were

---

yurusareru to sareta jirei] ('Requesting Injunctive Relief against the Exchange of an Ink Tank as Part of an Invention'), *L&T* 32 (2006): 71; K. Kondo, 'Canon Case Review (IP High Court)', *CIPIC Journal* 172 (2006): 22; T. Takenaka, [Tokkyo seihin no kakô, buhin kôkan ni tomonau hôritsu mondai no hikakuhôteki kôan] ('Comparative Analysis: Legal Issues on Repair and Replacement of Patented Product'], in Monya Nobuo kyôju koki kinen (*Writings in Honour of the70th Birthday of Professor Dr. Nobuo Monya*), (Tokyo: Hatsumei Kyokai, 2006), 379; Y. Tamura, [Shôhi zumi inktank ni ink wo saijûten suru kôi to tokkyoken shingai no seihi] ('The Patent Infringement and the Refilling the Ink into the Consumed Inktank'), NBL 836 (2006): 18; NBL 837 (2006): 44; Y. Tamura, [Tokkyoken no shôjin riron to shûri to saisei mondai] ('The Issue Concerning to the Patent Exhaustion Doctrine, and Repair and Reconstruction – *Canon* Case Review') I.P. Annual Report, 116 Bessatsu NBL 180 (2006). For a comment in English, See above, fn. 54, Heath & Môri.

69.   Other cases: Osaka District Court, 23 Jul. 1992, 2399 Hanrei Kôgyô shoyûkenhô 282 – *Seaweed Machine*, Tokyo District Court., 6 Jun. 2000, 1712 Hanrei Jihō 175 – *Konica*; Tokyo District Court, 31 Aug. 2000, 170 Jurist Bessatsu 128 – *Fuji Photo I*; Tokyo High Court, 29 Nov. 2001, 1799 Hanrei Jihô 89 – *Acycrovir*.

70.   Osaka District Court, 24 Apr. 1989 – *Hammer*, 1315 Hanrei Jihō 120. Reviews: M. Kazuko, [Mutaizaisankenhô 2] ('Intangible Property Law 2'), *Jurist* 248 (1992): 1330 Hanrei Jihō 219, H. Kuroda, 40-6 Tokkyo Kanri 715, S. Tanaka, [Shūri to saido no seizō] (Repair and

covered by a utility model right. Although the hammers were made to last for one to three years,[71] the lifespan of the battering plates was three days to one week depending on the duration and amount of operation. The plaintiff claimed that the battering plate was the dominant part of the entire utility model; therefore, the replacement of this plate amounted to an infringement of the utility model. The Osaka District Court rejected the plaintiff's argument. The court took into account the plaintiff's sales method and held, '[W]e can not say that only the battery plate was the dominant part of the utility model, considering the fact that such plate was a spare part which is easily consumable...'. It nevertheless found infringement, because: (1) permissible 'repair' meant recovery of the condition of broken parts, and when plates were intended to be consumed and replaced in a short period, such plates were not broken, therefore the replacement of the plates was not permissible; and (2) when the plates were intended to be replaced in such a short period, purchasers were allowed to purchase plates only from the owner of the utility model but not from third parties, since later sales of plates were intended as the exercise of such utility model right. Concerning the substantial ground of patent exhaustion, the court stated that '[P]urchasers can use or resell products, because such acts are the recovery of the consideration which they paid to the utility model owner.'

To the contrary, in the *Step Tool* case,[72] the court found no infringement. Here the defendant sold connection metal fittings of traps. Although the trap itself is usable repeatedly, the connection metal fittings are to be destroyed every time after use. The court ruled that a utility model right to traps including connection metal fittings was exhausted by plaintiff's authorized sale to users. The connection metal fitting was not the essential part of the utility model device, and therefore the replacement of such is not an indirect infringement.

5.   Overview: Permissible Repair in Japan

In Japan, 'whether or not a new product which has a different *identity* from the original product has been created', (emphasis added) is the important criteria that a patentee has to prove in a lawsuit. The Supreme Court used the word 'identity', which the IP High Court intentionally avoided. Contrary to the IP High Court, which made an effort to draw a line between permissible repair and impermissible one, the Supreme Court focused on the modification, and took

---

Reconstruction), [chiteki zaisanken no gendaiteki kadai] (*Intellectual Property and Recent Problems*) (1995): 172, (in English) Y. Yamasaki, *AIPPI Journal* 151 (August 1989).

71. Arms were made to last one to two years and mounts were made to last two to three years (*see* Osaka District Court, (above, fn. 70), at 252).

72. Osaka District Court, 26 Nov. 2002 – *Step Tool*, available at <www.courts.go.jp/hanrei/pdf/0A6D1C7A7F008E4A49256CC60030DCB2.pdf> (last visited 15 Dec. 2008). Reviews: G. Kurauchi, [Tokkyoken no yōjinsonpi no handan kijun] (The Standard of the Exhaustion of Patent Right), [chiteki zaisan hō seisaku gaku kenkyū] (*Intellectual Property Law and Policy Journal*) 5 (2005): 153.

into account *the totality of circumstances* in order to determine 'identity'. The elements are taken into account such as the lifespan of the product, whether the replaced part embodies the essential feature of its patented invention, etc. Whether the replaced part was the 'essential part' is not a decisive criterion, contrary to the IP High Court and to the German Supreme Court.[73] Ruling that the replacements or refurbishments of the essential part always make it an impermissible reconstruction is too rigid a standard, unduly favouring the patentee.[74]

As a result, the standard of the Japanese Supreme Court is as vague as the US 'akin to repair' standard. The outcome will depend on how the case is litigated before the courts. Despite the burden of proof on rights holders, this will not be an obstacle in verdicts favourable to patentees.

One question remains. A judge of the Supreme Court explains that '[W]hether or not a patentee was supposed to obtain the consideration (*taika*) at the point of sale of the patented product in an objective view (public perception)' plays an important role as the rationale of the patent exhaustion. Yet, there are two issues that must be taken into account. When a patentee obtains such consideration, he has an opportunity to make a profit under the exclusive right, and the law protects such exclusive right. But what does 'consideration' mean regarding the second justification for the exhaustion doctrine, that is, legal certainty for trade (*torihiki no anzen*)? How should the question whether a patentee was supposed to obtain sufficient consideration be determined? Could public perception or the patentee's intention be an element of determination? And could such elements affect the limitation to the property right by way of exhaustion? These questions remain unsolved.

Concerning the replacement of easily consumable parts of patented inventions, there is no concrete ruling by the courts other than the *Hammer* or *Step Tool* cases.

C.   GERMANY

1.   'Intended Use' and the Exhaustion Doctrine

In Germany, the limitation of patent rights in the aftersales market was explained by the exhaustion doctrine.[75] The German cases concerning the repair or reconstruction of patented products mainly relate to cases of contributory

---

73. See below, Section II.3.c.
74. 1990 Hanrei Jihō 4. See above, fn. 62, Nakayoshi, at 68.
75. See above, fn. 3, G. Benkard, § 10 marginal note 15. German Federal Supreme Court, 21 Nov. 1958, 1959 GRUR 232 – *Förderinne*. German courts often base patent exhaustion on the patentee having recovered the just profit based on his right or the patentee gaining the rewards of his patent.

infringement.[76,77] Although just protection for the patentee's exclusive right must be given, such protection should not extend further than the consideration that a patentee received in exchange for his patent.[78]

Cases from the last century show the criteria for distinguishing infringement from repair or replacement of patented products.[79] Under the doctrine of national exhaustion, purchasers are always allowed to act in accordance with the 'intended use'.[80] Such 'intended use' must be determined from an objective point of view, and usual measures for starting operation or maintenance of patented products are included in the intended use.[81] However, there is an old case that showed that such conclusion could be questionable if the replacement of the consumable part required the 'job of craftsman'.[82] There is another criterion to distinguish permissible repair from impermissible remanufacturing. Maintenance or repair must take place during 'the normal lifespan of the patented product'.[83] Whether the lifespan of the patented product is expired is also assessed based on 'the concept of the interested circles involved',[84] namely how this is ordinarily perceived in the trade.

**2.   No Protection in Case of Replacement of Consumable
            Spare Parts**

In the *Gerbsäure* case,[85] the plaintiff distributed a patent protected device and a tannic acid spare part that was necessary for the patented device. The patent-protected invention was a device for the accessory of tannic acid to the kettle-water, which should serve the known purpose of preventing chlorination.

---

76. See above, fn. 3, Benkard, § 36.
77. A review of cases and determination of patent infringement are discussed in C. Ann, 'Identität und Lebensdauer' – 'Patentverletzung durch Instandsetzung patentierter Vorrichtungen', in *Materielles Patentrecht – Festschrift für Reimar König zum 70. Geburtstag*, eds C. Ann et al. (Köln: Heymann, 2003), 17; T. Kowal-Wolk & R. Schuster, Patentverletzung im Reparatur-, Ersatzteil- und Altteilgeschäft – Eine Bestandsaufnahme, in *Aktuelle Herausforderungen des Geistigen Eigentums – Festschrift für* F. K. Beier zum 70. Geburtstag, ed. J. Straus (Köln: Heymann, 1996), 87.
78. See above, fn. 3, Kraßer, 819.
79. German *Reich* Supreme Court, 25 Oct. 1924, GRUR 1926, 163 – *Schraubstöpselsicherung*; German *Reich* Supreme Court, 5 Nov. 1930, Mitt. 1930, 345 – *Heizkissen*; German *Reich* Supreme Court, 9 Jun. 1934, GRUR 1934, 534 – *Diskusscheleifrad II*; German *Reich* Supreme Court, 4 Oct. 1938, GRUR 1939, 184 – *Gerbsäure*; German Federal Supreme Court, 15 Jun. 1951, GRUR 1951, 452 – *Mülltonne II*; German Federal Supreme Court, 21 Nov. 1958, 1959 GRUR 232 – *Förderinne*;.12 Jun. 1951, 1951 GRUR 449; 8 Mar. 1973, 1973 GRUR 518 – *Spielautomat II*; etc.
80. *Ibid., Förderrinne* GRUR, 1959, 232, 234. In German 'bestimmungsgemäßer Gebrauch'.
81. *Ibid., Förderinne*.
82. German *Reich* Supreme Court, 4 Oct. 1938, GRUR 1939, 184 – *Gerbsäure*, at 187 'wenn die Erneuerung eine fachmännische Arbeit erforderte'.
83. See above, fn. 79 *Förderinne*.
84. See above, fn. 79 *Förderinne*. In German 'Verkehrsauffassung'.
85. German *Reich* Supreme Court, 4. Oct. 1938, GRUR 1939, 184 – *Gerbsäure*.

The defendant supplied tannic acid to refill the individual bin, which was part of entire patented product.

The court mentioned the purchasers' right to use the patented products. The purchaser's right included the supply of items for operation (*'Betriebsstoffe'*) like tannic acid, which was relevant to the case, and purchasers should be able to refill the supply items. The rule also applies to supply items for an operation that is particularly designed to match the patented device. Thus, renewing supply items will not be a patent infringement, even though it specially matches the invention at issue.

**3.   Alteration of the 'Identity' of Products:
         The *Flügelradzähler* Case**

In the recent *Flügelradzähler* decision,[86] the German Federal Supreme Court decided whether the defendant's selling of a removable measuring cup replacement as part of a patented product could be considered an indirect patent infringement.[87] The court applied the concept 'product identity'. When maintenance or repair of patented products have been made to keep the 'identity' of the specific patented product, such maintenance or repair is allowed within the scope of the purchaser's right to use.[88] The Court remanded the case back to the appeal court, which found that there was no indirect patent infringement. The Court held:

> The distinction between a (permissible) repair and a (prohibited) remaking depends on whether the measures taken maintain *the identity of the specific patented product* ..., or are the equivalent of the creation of a new product according to the invention[89] (emphasis added).

The German courts seem to find an impermissible reconstruction or new manufacturing particularly when replacing or renewing concerned the *essential part* of the patented invention. As the Court noted in *Flügelradzähler*:

> The replacement of a worn part that usually must be replaced – possibly several times – during the expected working life of the machine, as a rule does not constitute a new making of the product. The situation may be different, however, *if this part embodies essential elements of the invention.* For, if the replacement of this part implements the technical or commercial benefit of the invention a second time, it cannot be said that the patent holder

---

86.   German Federal Supreme Court, 4 May 2004. GRUR 2004, 758 = 36 IIC 963 (2005) – *Flügelradzähler*.
87.   Case review by N. Hölder, 'Contributory Patent Infringement and Exhaustion in Case of Replacement Parts: Comment on a Recent Supreme Court Decision in Germany', 37 IIC 889 (2006).
88.   See above, fn. 77, C. Ann at 23-24.
89.   See above, fn. 86, *Flügelradzähler*, 36 IIC 963, 969 (2005).

has already drawn the benefits from the invention as a result of the first putting into circulation of the device as a whole.[90]

4.   Overview: Permissible Repair in Germany

In Germany, when the issue of repair/reconstruction comes up, the court will examine if the act of the defendant is within the 'intended use' of the patented product, and if it has been done during 'the normal lifespan of patented products' judged by the concept of the interested circles involved. Some scholars support this view and find the 'concept of the interested circles' useful, while others take the view that patent infringement should be determined from an objective point of view.[91] The 'identity of the specific patented product' is a watershed for dividing permissible repair and impermissible reconstruction.[92]

Regarding consumable parts, the Federal Supreme Court has not construed a repair monopoly for patentees.[93] However, according to the *Flügelradzähler* decision, when the replacement is made to the essential element of the invention, the court will likely find an impermissible reconstruction. Then, the question should be asked whether the court abolished the rule that a patent monopoly does not cover consumable parts. What would be happen if consumable spare parts embody the essential character of invention?[94] Would the court find for reconstruction?

D.   THE UK: DENIAL OF IMPLIED LICENSE THEORY IN THE *UNITED WIRE* CASE

Interestingly enough, the German Supreme Court in *Flügelradzähler* cited not only its own precedents, but also the UK House of Lords' decision *United Wire Limited v. Screen Repair Service*.[95] It also cited the question posed by Lord Hoffmann: 'whether, having regard to the nature of the patented article, the defendant could be said to have made it'.

The UK lower courts[96] have traditionally applied the implied license theory, which is similar to the one applied by the US courts. In 2000, however, the House of Lords overruled one of these decisions and held that the act of impermissible

---

90. *Ibid.*, 36 IIC 963, 969-970 (emphasis added).
91. See above, fn. 77, T. Kowal-Wolk & R. Schuster, 87 at 105.
92. See above, fn. 86 'Flügelradzähler'.
93. See above, fn. 79 *Gerbsäure*; see above, fn. 77, T. Kowal-Wolk & R. Schuster, 87, 99.
94. German Federal Supreme Court, 27 Feb. 2007, GRUR 2007, 769 – *Pipettensystem* ruled on this point in relation to indirect infringement.
95. English House of Lords, *United Wire Ltd v. Screen Repair Services Ltd.* [2001] RPC 439 = [2001] FSR 24.
96. English Court of Appeal, *Solar Thomson Engineering Co. Ltd v. Barton* [1977] RPC 537.

refurbishment should be determined according to whether the act could be likened to one of manufacture.[97]

In *United Wire*, the plaintiff's UK patents aimed at improving the system of a sifting screen used to recycle drilling fluid in the oil industry. The defendant used the original frame of the patented product, refurbished the screen, and sold it. The defendant argued that such repair, which prolonged the lifespan of the product, should be covered by an implied license and not be considered a 'making' under the Patents Act 1977. The defendant further argued exhaustion of the patent right. The High Court decided for the defendant, but the House of Lords reversed. The court confirmed that the notion of repair and making are mutually exclusive, and held that where it was alleged that the defendant had infringed by *making* the patented product, the concept of an implied license or exhaustion of rights had no part to play. In the Court's view, what could be said to be *repair* can depend upon the perception of the person answering the question, so the court should focus on whether the act of the defendant amounted to the manufacture of a product rather than whether it could be called repair: 'The owner's right to repair is *not* an independent right conferred upon him by license. It is a residual right, forming part of the right to do whatever does not amount to "making" the product.' The court found infringement according to the nature of the invention as claimed and what was done by the defendant.

In both jurisdictions, Germany and the UK, the courts ask *whether or not the acts of the defendant amount to the creation of new products*. However, in the UK, how this should be determined is still unclear.

III.   INTERNATIONAL COMPARISON: SINGLE-USE
        CAMERA CASE AS THE TOUCHSTONE

For a comparison between different jurisdictions, the following case that was decided in Japan and the US is of particular interest. The core question was whether a patentee, a manufacturer of single-use cameras, could invoke its right in the aftermarket against a recycling business for such cameras? The facts are the same both in the US and Japan: The patentee, Fuji Film, manufactures paper-boxed, single-use cameras, and owns a patent on 'lens-fitted film packages'. The winding mechanism for the film was the core part of the invention. The defendant's affiliated companies collected the used, legally sold paper-boxed camera bodies from their original purchasers, and refurbished them for reuse. During refurbishing, the cardboard covers were removed, the bodies cut open, new films were inserted, the counters reset, the bodies resealed and newly covered. Fuji Photo claimed that the defendants infringed its patent.

How would the case be decided respectively under the current Supreme Courts' rulings in the US, Japan, and Germany?

In the US, there is a concrete rule that the mere replacement of unpatented parts is permissible repair (*Aro I*). The used cameras still had a useful function even

97.   Under the Patent Act 1977, s. 60(1)(a).

after being used one time, and the refurbishing steps merely helped to realize this capacity rather than create a new camera. Thus, in a series of *Jazz Photo* cases,[98] the US Federal Circuit found against *Fuji Photo* and held the patent exhausted.[99] For the US courts, also the structure of Fuji Photo's single-use camera, which must be broken in order to replace the spent film and film cartridges, did not justify a finding of impermissible reconstruction.[100] Whether or not the core part of the invention was altered does not matter in the US courts.

In contrast, the Tokyo District Court upheld the *Fuji Photo*'s arguments twice in the *Fuji Photo I*[101] and *II*[102] cases. However, the outcome could have been more unpredictable if the parties had to argue under the current *Canon* ruling. The repair/reconstruction must be determined from a comprehensive point of view, including the attributes of the patented article, the contents of the patented invention, the manner of the modification, and the parts replaced, as well as other conditions of trade. These are the elements to determine whether or not the refurbished product is still identical to the originally sold product.

What if Fuji brought a lawsuit in Germany? When courts recognize the replacement of consumable parts, there is no infringement. When courts do not find the replacement of consumable parts, the court must first examine if the defendant's act is according to the 'intended use', and if the refill was done 'during the lifespan of the patented product'. The recycling of single-use cameras is most likely outside the scope 'intended use'. The lifespan of the entire patented product must be determined according to the opinion of the interested circles. In the author's view, the German courts would likely reach the conclusion that the lifespan of the cameras had come to an end, because, according to the users or photo shops, which are the relevant circles to the single-use-camera, single-use-cameras become useless once used. However, should the courts focus on whether the replacement was made to the essential element of the invention, the court could find the replacement permissible. After all, the replaced part is a film, while it is the *winding mechanism* of the single-use camera that embodies the essential concept of the invention, and this mechanism was not replaced.

Judging from the above, each jurisdiction has its shortcomings:

(1) The *US* approach of 'spent' parts is a cul-de-sac, though, as was seen in the *Wilbur-Ellis Co. v. Kuther* case, which tried to expand the meaning and

---

98. *Jazz Photo Corp. v. Int'l Trade Commission*, 264 F.3d 1094, 59 USP.Q. 2d 1907 (Fed. Cir. 2001); *Fuji Photo Film Co. v. Int'l Trade Commission*, 386 F. 3d 1095 (Fed. Cir. 2004); *Fuji Photo Film Co. v. Jazz Photo Corp.*, 394 F. 3d 1368(Fed. Cir. 2005); *Jazz Photo Corp. v. United States*, 439 F. 3d 1344 (Fed. Cir. 2006); *Fuji Photo Film Co. v. Int'l Trade Commission*, 474 F. 3d 1281 (Fed. Cir. 2007).

99. There is a judgment that held to the contrary; *Fuji Photo Film Co. v. Jazz Photo Corp.*, 394 F. 3d 1368(Fed. Cir. 2005). The court affirmed the district court's finding that Jazz Photo was liable for direct infringement of Fuji Photo Film's patent.

100. *Fuji Photo Film Co. v. Int'l Trade Commission*, 474 F. 3d 1281 (Fed. Cir. 2007) at 1297.

101. Tokyo District Court, 31 Aug. 2000 – *Fuji Camera*, 170 Jurist 128.

102. Tokyo District Court, 24 Apr. 2007 – *Fuji Camera II*, Available at <www.courts.go.jp/hanrei/pdf/20070507105616.pdf> (last visited 15 Dec. 2008).

introduced the concept of '(a)kin to repair'. The scope of 'permissible repair' is continuously expanding, as patentees increasingly enforce their rights after the initial sales of their products. The aim of patent law is 'to promote the progress of science...by securing for limited times to...inventors the exclusive right to their respective...discoveries'.[103] Even when a spare part represents the inventive step of the invention over the prior art, would it still not be protected from replacement?

(2) In *Japan*, the 'common understanding of society' is one of the elements for finding the identity of the patented product. Should the identity of the patented product be determined by common sense, apart from the contents of the invention? Second, after the *Canon* case, the future plaintiffs have many possible rebuttals to prove an exception to patent exhaustion, perhaps too many. Both US and Japanese courts take the view that a business decision that anticipates that some parts of products will be broken in order to replace the spent spare parts does not justify a finding of impermissible reconstruction. Contrary to the US, however, Japanese courts take into account whether such structure is inevitable in light of the purpose of the patented invention, or such structure can be found commonly in the products in the same technical fields.[104] And when such requirements are met, replacements of such parts are an impermissible reconstruction. It is correct to find unlawfulness when replaced parts, which inevitably break, are part of an inventive concept, namely, the teaching of patent.

(3) *German* courts take the identity of the specific patented product and technical/essential elements of the invention into account in determining permissible repair and impermissible reconstruction. The Federal Supreme Court balances the interests of patentees, purchasers, and the nature of invention. However, the answer to 'the identity' of the specific patented product might not be predictable enough when the German courts cite and show sympathy for the UK *United Wire* case. The House of Lords has shown no consistent standard in this respect. Not only the concept 'repair', but also that of 'making' would depend upon the perception of the person answering the question. What Lord Hoffmann said sounds almost like 'we can tell infringement when we see it'. Furthermore, the concept of the 'essential element' is left open if this part implements the technical or commercial benefit of the invention. Would the term *'wesentliches Element der Erfindung'* ruled under mean the same under the national exhaustion doctrine and indirect infringement?[105]

The outcome in each jurisdiction is not easily predictable. Should the intent of patentees play a role here? Fuji Photo intended these cameras to be used only once

---

103. US Const. Art. I, 8, cl. 8.
104. See above, fn. 63.
105. See above, fn. 97. The Federal Supreme Court ruled on this issue in *Pipettensystem*. However further questions remain.

and discarded after use, but both courts in Japan and in the US did not recognize such intention as a condition of sale.

IV.   A POSSIBLE SOLUTION: SINGLE-USE RESTRICTIONS?

To avoid unforeseeable judgments after time-consuming legal processes, paten-tees might be more interested in making sales with conditions. Doing so, paten-tees could avoid the exhaustion of their patent right. In this respect, US cases on license agreements might offer the patentee an effective means for controlling the aftermarket.[106]

Under US law, a valid single-use restriction may be enforceable if it consti-tutes a genuine condition of an enforceable agreement (express or implied), as in the *Mallinckrodt* case.[107] Enforceability depends on whether the restriction was 'validly conditioned under the applicable law such as the law governing sales and licenses and [whether] the restriction on reuse was within the scope of the patent grant or otherwise justified'.[108] Just as in a sequence of recent *Monsanto* cases,[109] providing notice by placing the contract on the outside of the seed package and publicizing the restriction in relevant journals and meetings is a strong indication

---

106.   See E. I. Winston, 'Why Sell What You Can License? Contracting Around Statutory Protec-tion of Intellectual Property', *Geo. Mason L. Rev.* 14 (2006): 93; Symposium on 'The Scope of Downstream Licensing Restrictions', *Fordham Intell. Prop. Media & Ent. L. J.* 16 (2006): 1025. Analysis concerned with antitrust law: M. J. Meurer, 'Vertical Restraints and Intellec-tual Property Law: Beyond Antitrust', *Minn. L. Rev.* 87 (2003): 1871.
107.   *Mallinckrodt, Inc. v. Medipart, Inc*, 976 F.2d 700 (Fed. Cir. 1992). Mallinckrodt sold a pat-ented device for diagnosis and treatment to hospitals. Each device bore the statement 'For single patient use only', and the patentee instructed the hospital that the devices should be discarded after use. But some hospitals sent used units to cleaning and refurbishing services and used them again. Mallinckrodt sued the refurbishing party for patent infringement and inducement to infringe, based on the violation of the single-use 'restriction'. The Federal Circuit held that single-use restrictions were enforceable, and that the patentee must prevail on this issue as a matter of law. The court explained that a restriction on reuse would not be illegal if it (1) 'was within the scope of the patent grant', and (2) the sale was 'validly conditioned under the applicable law, such as the law governing sales and license'. It is clear that where the patented device is validly licensed for only a single use, it is unnecessary to choose between repair and reconstruction.
108.   *Ibid.*, at 709.
109.   *Monsanto Co., v. McFarling*, 302 F. 3d 1291 (Fed. Cir. 2002); *Monsanto Co., v. Swann*, 308 F.Supp.2d 937 (E.D. Mo.2003); *Monsanto Co., v. Good*, 2004 WL 1664013 (D.N.J. 2004); *Monsanto Co., v. Scruggs* 2004 WL 1598848 (N.D.Miss 2004). The Federal Circuit upheld an infringement injunction against a farmer who purchased patented seeds from the seed company Monsanto under an agreement that the seeds be used for 'planting a commercial crop only in a single season', and then replanted Monsanto's seeds that were genetically modified. The court did not find an anticompetitive tying agreement because the purchase of single-use seeds did not prevent farmers from choosing other seeds in the future, and seeds of different types are readily available in the market place. Thus, their use during subsequent seasons was patent infringement and could be enjoined.

of enforceability. Also in the *Lexmark* case,[110] the court found the printed, single-use restriction on the outside of the printer cartridges an adequate notice. In contrast thereto, courts have refused to enforce mere intents of single-use as in the *Hewlett-Packard*[111] and *Jazz Photo* cases.[112]

The long-awaited decision of the Supreme Court in *Quanta* did not decide whether such explicit intention can prevent patent exhaustion. It ruled only that there was no such explicit intention – license agreement – among the parties. Thus, we could still conclude that providing explicit contractual language on the packaging will likely assure an enforcement of the agreement, at least in the US. Moreover, it is desirable for purchasers to indicate that they accept such restrictions, for example, by way of a signature on the technology agreement in the *Monsanto* case, or tearing the package wrapping as in the *Lexmark* case.

In Japan, society might be more willing to accept single-use restrictions for medical devices than for cameras,[113] although in the US there are both cases where the courts recognized single-use restrictions[114] and those where they did

---

110. *Arizona Cartridge Remanufactures Association, Inc. v. Lexmark International, Inc.*, 03-16987 D.C. No. CV-01-04626- SBA/ JL OPINION (9th Cir. 2005). This is not a patent infringement case, but adds an interesting point to single-use agreements. Arizona Cartridge sued Lexmark for deceptive and unfair business practices under unfair competition law, alleging that Lexmark's 'prebate' programme and single-use restriction are not enforceable. Lexmark packaged some of its ink cartridges with a 'shrink-wrap'-type license. Upon opening the package or using the patented cartridge inside the packages, purchasers agreed to return the empty cartridge to Lexmark, which gave purchasers an upfront discount in exchange for their agreement to return the empty cartridges. The 9th Circuit determined that Lexmark imposed an enforceable condition on the sale of printer cartridges. The court said Lexmark's patent was not exhausted. And under contract law, the language on the outside of the cartridge specifies the terms under which a consumer may use the purchased item and the consumer can read the terms and conditions on the box before deciding whether to accept them or whether to opt for the non-rebate cartridges that are sold without any restrictions.

111. *Hewlett-Packard*, see above, fn. 41. The Federal Circuit found that the defendant's recycling did not infringe the patent, despite the fact that HP instructed consumers in its manual to 'discard old print cartridge immediately'. The court said that Hewlett-Packard's single-use-only restriction showed 'no contractual intention' and constituted a 'hope' or 'advice'. The court found that the instruction manual was a mere request and not sufficient to create an enforceable restriction, because consumers read and become aware of the plaintiff's instruction only after they purchased and opened the patented cartridges.

112. *Jazz Photo* and *Fuji Photo*, see above, fn. 98. The court gave no weight to the plaintiff's intention to restrict the use of cameras for only one time. The court applied contract law, and concluded that the statements were not enforceable as license agreements under contract law. Instead, the statements were 'instructions and warnings of risk, not mutual promises or a condition placed upon the sale'.

113. In *Canon*, see above, fn. 63, the IP High Court ruled that '[T]he lifespan of patented products should be determined based on a social and economic determination. And when patented medical products, such as single-use injection syringes or internal medicines, contain a limitation to their use due to hygiene, such products might be deemed to have come to an end of their lifespan after a single use under the common understanding of society.'

114. *Mallinckrodt*, see above, fn. 74; *B. Braun Med., Inc. v. Abbott Laboratories*, 124 F.3d 1419 (Fed Cir. 1997).

not.[115] A single-use restriction, or other limitations on the usage of patented product, etc., is enforceable as a contract unless it exceeds the expectation of the third parties and hurts the fair trade.[116]

In Germany, when a patentee agrees with a purchaser and puts a limitation on a patented product, such as limitation of use or resale, the limitation is valid only between the patentee and the purchaser (only in personam). And it is valid to the extent allowed by competition law. So when the purchaser breaches the agreement, he is responsible only under contract law but not under patent law. The agreement is ineffective against third parties. Thus, even when a patentee tries to limit activities of third parties in the aftermarket, the doctrine of exhaustion does not allow such control by the patentee.[117]

V.   SYNTHESIS AND THOUGHTS ON THE ROAD AHEAD

Patent law aims to protect inventions and promote industry. Inventors who take risks and invest money and time should be rewarded. On the other hand, protection of the patentee should be limited to ensure competition for new innovations, which include the repair and recycling industry in the aftermarket. The following questions should be asked: Would a competition between patentees and suppliers of spare parts bring more innovation, and meet the interest of consumers? Or is there no competition between patentees and suppliers at all, and suppliers are rather exploiting the invention of the patentee by selling spare parts for patented products, like a 'free rider'?

In the United States, 'permissible repair' or 'right to use' is covered by a broader exhaustion rule than in Germany or Japan, although patent exhaustion in the US might be avoided by specific license agreements. As a result, patent laws in Germany and Japan reward patentees more, and laws in the US do more to enhance business competition between patentees and emerging economies in the aftermarket. Rewarding patentees and promoting emerging innovation are both equally important in aftermarket. The real issue here is that the criteria for 'permissible' repair cases are not necessarily transparent for either patentee or repair services, especially for the latter, who have fewer resources to go through patent litigation. The spare-parts business requires less investment than the manufacturing of original products, and can expect constant demand as patented products wear and tear. There should be rigid criteria more than common sense or public conception.

---

115. *Sage Products, Inc. v. Devon Industries, Inc.*, 45 F.3d 1575 (Fed Cir. 1995), *Kendall Co. v. Progressive Med. Tech. Inc.*, 85 F. 3d 1570 (Fed Cir. 1996). In Kendall, the court held that '[U]nlike the facts in *Mallinckrodt*, the customers followed rather than disregarded the single use. They replaced the pressure sleeves after each use'. (*Ibid.*, at 1577).
116. T. Hashiba, [Tokkyo shômô riron no tokuyaku ni yoru seigen] (Contractual Restriction on the Application of Patent Exhaustion Doctrine), *Annual of Industrial Property Law, Japan Association of Industrial Property Law* (May 1989): 47, at 66-67.
117. See above, fn. 3, Benkard, at 378 and Kraßer, at 820.

'Consideration' is the word used when courts describe the principle of patent exhaustion. In the US, the court said 'consideration for its use' and in Japan, 'consideration for making the invention public'. But the limitation to the property right should have a clearer standard. In Germany, the rationale for the doctrine of exhaustion is explained that it is believed that a chance to exploit based on the exclusive right (patent right) must be given *just once* concerning one and the same product.[118] When the lawfulness of repair and recycling is decided by whether a patentee received the consideration, the meaning of 'consideration' must be clearly defined. It might be decided by social perception. There are many things left open for 'common sense' or social perception. Furthermore, can the art of receiving the 'consideration' be controlled by patentees by agreements based on their business strategy?[119] The single-use restriction increasingly plays a significant role in the current market. The introduction and analysis of these cases might be useful to balance the interests of repair services and patentees. However, enforceability of such restrictions should be carefully analysed in light of (1) the issue between freedom of contract and public intellectual property law,[120] (2) enforceability against subsequent purchasers and users,[121] and (3) enforceability under competition/antitrust law.

Comparative studies will help to outline the weaknesses of theories in each jurisdiction in order to overcome them. It provides a wide range of legal issues and facts that were argued before the courts. The sharp confrontation between patentees and repair services is increasing and will certainly be here to stay.

---

118. See above, fn. 3, Kraßer, at 820.
119. N. Hölder, Ersatzteile und Erschöpfung – Patentschutz für Geschäftsmodelle? – Die 'Kaffee-Filterpad' – Entscheidung des OLG Düsseldorf (2007) GRUR 96.
120. See above, fn. 32, Gajarsa, at 1226-1229.
121. *Ibid.*, at 1229-1231.

Chapter 4

Repair and Refill as Indirect Patent Infringement

Christopher Heath

I.   INTRODUCTION

A.   Direct and Indirect Infringement

The previous chapter dealt with the issue of spare parts replacement as a potential (direct) patent infringement. The main issue in this context is the interpretation and scope of the exhaustion doctrine and the way to distinguish permissible repair from impermissible reconstruction: Reconstruction can never be covered by exhaustion or a license to deal with the original product, while repair can. It is a common feature of all the repair cases that not the whole product is repaired or reconstructed, but only part thereof. If that very part is patented as such, the issue is straightforward and an exchange of the part leads to a finding for (patent) infringement at least for this part. If the part is not patented as such, or if an argument is made in favour of patent infringement for the composite product, the issue tends to be decided on whether the product is essential, or incorporates the inventive merit of the whole product or apparatus. Such a case of patent infringement, however, can only be made against the person putting the composite product back into its original state, but not those furnishing the essential product, although this person may assist in the (permissible or impermissible) repair/reconstruction. This is where indirect or contributory infringement comes into play. The indirect infringer

Christopher Heath, Anselm Kamperman Sanders (eds.), *Spares, Repairs and Intellectual Property Rights*, pp. 85-102.
© 2009 Kluwer Law International BV, The Netherlands.

regularly supplies the means for committing a direct infringement, yet does not commit the infringement himself. Going after the indirect infringer thereby broadens the scope of persons that may be sued for a certain patent infringement, may assist in drying up the supply of parts that can be used to commit a direct infringement, and may also be of use if the direct infringer cannot be sued for one reason or another. As the cases listed under Section II show, there is a broad range of different constellations, some of which are completely unrelated to the spare parts issue discussed here. Still, indirect infringement has also been used to go after the suppliers of spare parts, particularly in Europe. In order to make this clearer, the following case argued as indirect infringement in Germany and the Netherlands should serve as an example.

B.   SENSEO'S COFFEE MACHINE AS AN EXAMPLE

Sara Lee, the parent company of Douwe Egberts, owned European patent EP 0 904 717 for an 'Assembly for use in a coffee machine for preparing coffee, container and pouch of said assembly', claim 1 of which read as follows:

> An assembly for use in a coffee machine for preparing coffee, comprising a container having a bowl-shaped inner space bounded by a bottom having at least one outlet opening and a vertical sidewall and, included in the inner space of the container, a pill-shaped pouch manufactured from filtering paper and filled with ground coffee, which pouch rests on the bottom and extends over the bottom to a position adjacent the sidewall, while provided in the bottom are a number of channel-shaped grooves extending in radial direction of the bowl-shaped inner space to the at least one outlet opening and, in use, hot water is fed under pressure to a top side of the container by means of the coffee machine causing the hot water to be pressed from a top side of the pouch through the pouch for extracting the ground coffee included in the pouch, the coffee extract formed flowing from a bottom side of the pouch and from the container via at least one outlet opening, **characterized in that** each of said grooves extends from a position located at a distance from the side wall in a direction away from the side wall.

Claim 1 above does not claim the coffee machine, but an assembly, which is essentially an apparatus claim over the inner part of the machine bar the outer shell. Although millions of these machines were sold all over Europe due to their cheap price compared to other espresso machines, there was no question of anyone trying to copy the assembly as such. Due to the low price the machines were sold at, this may not have been commercially interesting. Far more lucrative, though, was the trade in the coffee pads. As can be seen from claim 1, the pads are part of the claim ('a pill-shaped pouch manufactured from filtering paper and filled with ground coffee'). If the patentee could prevent third parties from selling the pads

by way of the above patent, customers would essentially be required to purchase their supplies from the patentee. The monopoly, in other words, would extend to the refill market, not unlike a case where the sale of a car would tie the customer to fuel only supplied by the car maker. Neither the coffee as such, nor the filter paper, nor the specific shape and size of the pouch were any improvement over prior art. And yet, as the pads were mentioned as part of the claim, their manufacture and sale by third parties may qualify as a 'supply of means relating to an essential element of the invention', in the full knowledge that the pads would be used for the purpose of putting the assembly into effect. In other words, an act of indirect or contributory infringement, and the case was argued in this way in the Netherlands and Germany. It should be noted already here that different from the 'classical' concept of contributory infringement, European jurisdictions do not require a direct infringement to be committed in order to commit a contributory infringement. This is different from the law in the United States (see below), and was decisive for the coffee pad case: The 'direct' infringement here would be committed by private end users of the machines, and acts of private use are not infringing under patent law. In other words, there would have been no direct infringement to speak of, for which the action for indirect infringement did not open up an additional avenue of enforcement for the patentee, but actually the only one; if, of course, the supply of the patents could qualify as an act of indirect infringement, and the use of a new pad (when undertaken commercially) an act of direct infringement, an impermissible reconstruction rather than a permissible refill. Where an indirect infringement can be committed without an act of direct infringement, this may also extend to acts of 'incomplete' infringement, i.e., where only part of the patented product is manufactured or sold.

II.   THE CONCEPT OF 'INDIRECT' OR 'CONTRIBUTORY'
                 INFRINGEMENT IN DIFFERENT JURISDICTIONS

A.   EUROPE: GERMANY, THE NETHERLANDS AND THE UK

1.   The CPC

Although patent law has not yet been harmonized in Europe, the starting point for
many domestic patent laws on the issue of indirect infringement is Article 26
(Draft) Community Patent Convention 1989 (equals Article 30 Community Patent
Convention 1975):[1]

Art. 26 Community Patent Convention (not in force):

A Community patent shall also confer on its proprietor the right to prevent all
third parties not having his consent from supplying or offering to supply within
the territories of the Contracting States a person, other than a party entitled to
exploit the patented invention, with means, relating to an essential element of
that invention, for putting it into effect therein, when the third party knows, or
it is obvious in the circumstances, that these means are suitable and intended
for putting that invention into effect.

2.   The Netherlands

Section 73 of the Dutch Patents Act, inserted in 1987 in order to implement the
above CPC provision, reads as follows:

(1) The proprietor of the patent may institute the claims which are at his
disposal in enforcing his patent against any person who . . . in the Netherlands
offers or delivers, in or for his business, the means for working the patented
invention, in respect of an essential part of the invention in the Netherlands, to
others than those who . . . are empowered to work the patented invention,
provided that that person knows or that it is evident considering the circumstances that those means are suitable and intended for that application.

(2) Paragraph (1) shall not apply if the offer or delivery takes place with
the consent of the proprietor of the patent. Nor shall that paragraph apply if the
means delivered or offered are products which are generally available in
commerce, unless the person involved incites the third party to whom he
delivers to perform acts specified in Section 53 (1).

It was this provision that the patentee invoked in the above-mentioned coffee pad
case, perhaps the first case in the Netherlands where the provision on indirect

---

1. This provision has served as a blueprint for similar provisions in the UK, France, Germany, the
   Netherlands and about ten other European Countries: Keukenschrijver, *Flügelradzähler, Kaf-
   feetüte und Drehzahlermittlung – neue Entwicklungen bei der mittelbaren Patentverletzung*,
   Festschrift 50 Jahre VVP 2005, 331, 332.

infringement was used to prevent the supply of refills. Jan Brinkhof summarizes the case history as follows:[2]

> Sara Lee initiated *kort geding*[3] proceedings against a supplier of such coffee pods on the basis of indirect infringement. Sara Lee asked the court to prohibit the defendant from trading in the coffee pads. The procedure revolved around the question whether a coffee pod was 'an essential part of the invention'. The Presiding Judge of the District Court in the Hague answered this question in the affirmative.[4] He found that the defendant's pods fitted the container of the Senseo machine perfectly. In his opinion, it could remain moot whether the pods should be deemed new or inventive. There may also be indirect patent infringement if the means offered are not, in and of themselves, new or inventive. In this context the judge referred to Benyamini.[5] He found that the Dutch provision is based on Article 30 of the CPC 1975 (later changed into Article 26 CPC). The rationale of this provision is that third parties should not be allowed to benefit from the invention by providing means – the judge quotes Benyamini p. 182 – 'whose market flows from the invention and which are intended for utilizing it'. According to the judge, the defendant's advertisement shows that the pods are meant to be used in the Senseo machine. The judge added that to the extent the pods on offer were 'generally available in commerce', the defendant was inciting others to apply the invention. The injunction was granted.

The Court of Appeal arrived at a totally different opinion.[6] It ruled that the container is an essential part of the invention. Yet compared to the state of the art (US 3.620.155), only the container was changed. According to the Court of Appeal, not everything that is necessary to be able to use the patented assembly is an essential part of the invention. If that were the case, after all, the hot water and even the coffee machine in which the assembly is used, would also constitute an essential part of the invention. The Court felt that what Benyamini regards as the rationale did not change this, and added that pill-shaped pouches had been brought on the market by other parties for a long time. While those pads might perhaps not fit precisely in the container of Sara Lee's assembly, it would be possible to construct a container according to Sara Lee's patent that would be suitable for such existing pill-shaped pouches as well. The Court of Appeal did not consider the pad to be an

---

2. Jan Brinkhof, 'Pure Coffee? On Indirect Infringement', in *Festschrift für Jochen Pagenberg* (Cologne: Heymanns, 2006), 9, 13-14.
3. On *kort geding* proceedings see Wadlow, 'Enforcement of Intellectual Property in European and International Law, (London: Sweet & Maxwell, 1998): 14; Brinkhof, 'The Enforcement of Patent Rights in the Netherlands', in *Patent Enforcement Worldwide*, eds Christopher Heath & Laurence Petit, vol. 23 of *IIC Studies* (Weinheim: Richard Hart, 2005), 174.
4. 18 Jan. 2002, BIE 2004, 285.
5. Benyamini, 'Patent Infringement in the European Community', vol. 13 of *IIC Studies* (Weinheim: VCH Verlag, 1993): 199.
6. Court of Appeal The Hague 6 Jun. 2002, BIE 2004, 288.

essential part of the invention. The Court reversed the judgment of the court in first instance and declined the injunction.

Sara Lee disagreed with the decision of the Court of Appeal and submitted the case in cassation to the Dutch Supreme Court (Hoge Raad). It is up to the Supreme Court to examine whether the Court of Appeal applied the law correctly and gave clear reasons for its decision. The Supreme Court does not examine the accuracy of the facts. It is established case law that the interpretation of the patent is the reserve of the fact-finding court.

Even though this was the first time that the Supreme Court was asked to examine the application of the 'new' provision on indirect patent infringement, it devoted very little attention to the issue raised in this case.[7] Notably, the Supreme Court did not discuss the background and rationale of this provision at all, nor did it take into consideration opinions held abroad.[8] The Supreme Court confined itself to the following findings:

> The mere circumstance that a fitting coffee pod is necessary to apply the patented invention does not entail outright that this pod is a means that regards an essential part of the invention. Apparently, and in light of the interpretation of the patent by the Court of Appeal, understandably, the Court of Appeal concluded that the coffee pod that fit the container was not an element of what, according to the patent specification, distinguished the teaching of the patent from the state of the art. That conclusion does not reflect an inaccurate legal opinion.

Thus, the court interpreted the 'essential element' as one that must contribute to the inventive merit of the apparatus.[9]

3.   Germany

In Germany, indirect patent infringement seems to have led to a run of cases in the last five years,[10] apart from a good number of articles on the subject

---

7. Hoge Raad 31 Oct. 2003, BIE 2004, 285. The decision of the Advocate-General Verkade is reprinted there at 290-298 and contains further references.

8. In his opinion (advice to the Supreme Court), Advocate-General Verkade did pay attention to the background of s. 73 Patents Act and to foreign literature. He rightly notes that, given the conventional law underlying the provision, it should not be interpreted without paying due attention to the original provision in the CPC.

9. This was also held in the (parallel) proceedings in Belgium on the same issue of supplying coffee pads for the Senseo machines: District Court Antwerp, 20 Feb. 2004, summary in [2004] EIPR N-105.

10. Scharen, a Supreme Court judge, mentions ten cases decided by the Supreme Court alone since 2004, quite a lot when compared to one case in the Netherlands, one in the UK, one in Korea, and one in Japan (see below): Scharen, Die Behandlung der (so genannten) mittelbaren Patent-verletzung in der Rechtsprechung des Bundesgerichtshofes, GRUR 2008, 944. Not all of these cases bear any relevancy for the issue of repair and recycle, though:

    – Federal Supreme Court, 4 May 2004, 36 IIC 963 (2005) – *Flügelradzähler*;
    – Federal Supreme Court, 3 Jun. 2004, GRUR 2004, 845 – *Drehzahlermittlung*;

matter.[11] The relevant provision under German law, section 10(1) Patent Act, is a provision almost identical to section 26 CPC (above). Section 10(2) Patent Act limits liability in cases where 'the means are products generally available in commerce unless the third party consciously instigates the person supplied to act contrary to section 9.2 [commit[s] a direct patent infringement]'.

The cases concerned can be placed into three categories: (1) cases where (essential or non-essential) parts of the invention, or an apparatus for carrying out a process patent, were domestically manufactured, yet subsequently exported (*Abgasreinigungsvorrichtung; Funkuhr II*); (2) issues of damage calculation (*Haubenstretchautomat; Antriebsscheibenaufzug*); or (3) cases concerning the replacement of spare parts (*Flügelradzähler; Pipettensystem; Laufkranz; Coffee Pads*). The first two issues, if not entirely uncontroversial, are relatively clear: where essential parts are exported for a patent infringement to be committed abroad, section 10 will not apply; and although section 10 does not require an act of direct infringement, damages can only be claimed based on a direct infringement as a consequence of the infringing supply. That is an interesting conclusion, and in the case of the coffee pads would lead to a right of injunction without any corresponding right to claim damages, as there was no direct infringement of the patent. Far more problematic have been the spare parts cases.

The leading case in this respect is the above-mentioned case *Flügelradzähler/ Impeller Flow Meter*: where the measuring unit of a patented impeller flow meter was manufactured and sold by the defendant. Since not all elements of the invention were realized by the manufacture of only part thereof, the supply of such parts was no direct infringement. The court thus had to determine, first, whether the measuring capsule was an 'essential element', and, second, whether replacement

---

- Federal Supreme Court, 7 Jun. 2005, GRUR 2005, 848 – *Antriebsscheibenaufzug*;
- Federal Supreme Court, 5 Jul. 2005, – *Abgasreinigungsvorrichtung*;
- Federal Supreme Court, 3 May 2006, GRUR 2006, 837 – *Laufkranz*;
- Federal Supreme Court, 13 Jun. 2006, GRUR 2006, 839 – *Deckenheizung*;
- Federal Supreme Court, 30 Jan. 2007, 38 IIC 607 (2007) – *Funkuhr II/Radio Clock II*;
- Federal Supreme Court, 9 Jan. 2007, GRUR 2007, 679 – *Haubenstretchautomat*;
- Federal Supreme Court, 27 Feb. 2007, GRUR 2007, 769 – *Pipettensystem*;
- Federal Supreme Court, 27 Feb. 2007, 39 IIC 106 (2008) – *Rohrschweißverfahren/Pipe Welding Process*;
- Düsseldorf Appeal Court, 17 Nov. 2005, GRUR-RR 2006, 39 – *Coffee Pads*.

11. Hölder, Mittelbare Patentverletzung und Erschöpfung bei Erschöpfung von Austausch- und Ersatzteilen, GRUR 2005, 20; Keukenschrijver, above, fn. 1, 331; Hölder & Schmidt, Indirect Infringement: Latest Developments in Germany, [2006] EIPR 480; Nieder, Die mittelbare Patentverletzung – eine Bestandsaufnahme, GRUR (2006): 977; Hölder, Ersatzteile und Erschöpfung – Patentschutz für Geschäftsmodelle? GRUR (2007): 96; Rauh, Zur Entbehrlichkeit der subjektiven Merkmale der mittelbaren Patentverletzung, GRUR Int. (2008): 293; Scharen, Die Behandlung der (so genannten) mittelbaren Patentverletzung in der Rechtsprechung des Bundesgerichtshofes, GRUR (2008): 944; Fitzner, Die mittelbare Patentverletzung – quo vadis? Mitteilungen (2008): 243; Fabry & Trimborn, Die mittelbare Patentverletzung – das unterschätzte Geschäftsrisiko, GRUR (2008): 861, 864.

thereof was not covered by the rules of exhaustion explained in the previous chapter. The court held as follows:

1. A means within the meaning of Sec. 10 of the Patent Act refers to an essential element of the invention if this is capable of interacting functionally with one or more features of the patent claim to implement the protected invention. A feature that is completely subordinate for the technical teaching of the invention can be ignored as a non-essential element of the invention.
2. The answer to the question when the replacement of parts of a device is the equivalent of making the device requires a balancing of the protectable interests of the patent holder in the commercial exploitation of the invention on the one hand, and those of the purchaser in the unrestricted use of the patented device put into circulation on the other hand, while taking into account the nature of the patented product.

Although the second issue concerns the distinction between permissible repair and impermissible reconstruction already discussed in the previous chapter, the first issue is a specific interpretation of what constitutes an 'essential element' of the invention. With respect to the exchange of spare parts, both of the above issues were further defined in subsequent decisions.

The *Laufkranz* decision dealt with the question of permissible repair in the case of a patented rail vehicle wheel where the flanged tyre was replaced. The tyre was part of the patent claim, yet represented a part that would typically wear out quickly and could therefore qualify as a 'replacement part'. In these circumstances, the court held:

> The rights of a purchaser of a patented apparatus to use the latter in accordance with its function in principle also extend to the exchange of a part that during the ordinary lifespan of the apparatus will regularly be replaced due to wear and tear or for other reasons, unless the technical effect manifests itself especially in the very part that is to be exchanged.

The whole issue was revisited in *Pipettensystem*, where the headnotes read:

1. A feature of a claim may be regarded as non-essential in the sense of Sec. 10 Patent Act if it does not contribute to the achievement of the invention, that is, to the solution proposed by the patent in order to solve its underlying technical problem.
2. In order to distinguish between purpose-related use and reconstruction of a patented product, it is decisive whether the measures that were undertaken preserve the identity of the patented product already put into circulation or whether this would equal the manufacture of a new product, taking account of the specific characteristics, effects and advantages of the invention.
3. The exchange of parts that is common in such type of apparatus may amount to a reconstruction of the same if the technical effect of the invention manifests itself particularly in the part that is exchanged, because the invention has an influence on its manner of use or lifespan.

4. It would not be correct to assume a reconstruction where the exchanged part is only an object of the improved functioning of the whole apparatus.

The above principles are rather difficult to interpret because of the interaction between 'essential part', exhaustion and implied consent to use:

- The definition of 'essential part' is rather broad and extends to all parts mentioned in the claim other than those that are clearly unnecessary or of only marginal importance to use the invention.
- The definition does not require any inventive contribution, yet requires a technical effect to which the essential part contributes. 'Essential' should thus be interpreted as a technical quality.
- Even where the part is considered to be essential, it is permissible to replace parts of ordinary wear and tear as a consequence of the exhaustion doctrine.
- This permissibility would apply unless 'the technical effect of the invention manifests itself particularly in the part that is exchanged', as this would then amount to a reconstruction rather than a repair.
- Still, even for such technically essential parts of wear and tear, the patentee might have given an implied consent to exchange.[12]

Unfortunately, the above criteria are not particularly useful in order to determine *ex ante* which acts may infringe, and which not. There are several reasons for this:

First, the definition of an 'essential part' almost amounts to squaring the circle: the part need not be in any way different from the state of the art (as section 10 Patent Act may also apply where all parts individually may form state of the art, yet the inventive merit lies in the new and inventive assembly), needs to make a technically important contribution and yet must not qualify as a staple product under section 10(2). When looking at the case law, it seems that the decisions *Laufkranz* and *Pipettensystem* were attempts to contain a definition of indirect infringement that in *Flügelradzähler* was construed far too generously.[13] The provision as interpreted by the courts has become a 'business risk',[14] not least because the amalgamation of insufficiently defined objective elements with some subjective requirements (not further discussed here) and the independence of the provision from any act of direct infringement makes it almost impossible to make a purposive construction thereof.[15]

Second, although it is frequently stressed that the provision does not broaden the scope of patent protection,[16] it cannot be denied that when

---

12. This was so held in *Rohrschweißverfahren* (above, fn. 10) for a process covering several steps where the patentee himself had furnished data that allowed the recipient to initialize the process. The court found that this was an implied consent to use the protected process as intended.
13. In essence, essential parts seem to be all those that relate to elements of the claim.
14. Fabry & Trimborn, Die mittelbare Patentverletzung – das unterschätzte Geschäftsrisiko, GRUR (2008): 861, 864.
15. Fitzner, above, fn. 11, 249.
16. E.g., Keukenschrijver, above, fn. 1, 336.

compared to the case law prior to the enactment of section 10,[17] the scope of permissible repair/refill seems to have shrunk considerably.[18]

The *Coffee Pad* decision rendered by the Düsseldorf Appeal Court is a good example to highlight the above two difficulties. Different from the courts in the Netherlands and Belgium, both the District and the Appeal Court Düsseldorf found the sale of coffee pads an infringement of the apparatus patent. The Appeal Court in *Coffee Pads* held:

> If a filter pad and a coffee filtering machine in their interaction make out the apparatus protected as an invention, and such apparatus is designed for the exchange of filter pads, the economic core of the invention lies in particular in providing the supply of replacement filter pads. Where each time a filter pad is exchanged the apparatus is newly reconstructed, there is no room for the assumption that the benefits allocated to the patentee could already be reaped by the initial supply of the apparatus.

The 'essential part' is defined by the court in economic terms, an approach that (at least in Europe) is usually avoided when interpreting patent claims. It is also inconsistent with the subsequent decisions *Laufkranz* and *Pipettensystem* (as above), and would run the risk of essentially protecting non-technical features of technical rights.[19] But even under the more narrow definition of the *Pipettensystem* case, the coffee pad may qualify as an essential part of the claim: although not distinguishable over prior art, it is essential for making what the apparatus is meant to do. But since the apparatus has to be 'fuelled' with the pads, they may well qualify as staple products (this angle finds no mention in the decision), leading to the second question of exhaustion. And here the court holds that '[E]very time a user puts a new pad into the apparatus, the latter is reconstructed.' This, with the greatest respect, cannot be reconciled with common sense. The Federal Supreme Court had no opportunity to review these findings in light of its latter decisions due to the fact that Sara Lee's patent in August 2005 was revoked by the European Patent Office's Boards of Appeal.

For a further analysis, see below Section III.

4.   The UK

Section 60(2) of the 1977 Patent Act codifies indirect infringement in essentially the same terms as the CPC, yet no decisions as to the issue of what may constitute an 'essential element' seem to have been rendered so far. It is suggested that – different from previous case law – not the difference over prior art, but the necessity for putting the invention into effect should be the relevant criterion.[20] The only

---

17. See in this respect Kowal-Wolk & Schuster, Patentverletzung im Reparatur-, Ersatzteil- und Altteilgeschäft (Festschrift F.K. Beier, 1996), 87.
18. Apparently in the same vein Hölder, GRUR (2005): 22 (above, fn. 11).
19. Hölder, GRUR (2007): 97 (above, fn. 11) likens this to the protection of a business model.
20. *Terrell on Patents*, 15th edn (Sweet & Maxwell, 2000), 8.33.

case law, just as in Japan, concerns the furnishing of parts abroad.[21] A recent Australian decision, however, has shed some light on the definition of 'staple products'. The case concerned the supply of millable timber that was used by the direct infringer to produce cypress oil by a protected process. The High Court of Australia (although in four different judgments) identified millable timber as a staple product suitable for use in a variety of applications for which timber is usually used. Thus, the court did not try to analyse the market for the product or for the potential applications thereof, but limited the analysis to the question whether the product was suitable for a variety of uses.[22]

B.   ASIA: JAPAN AND KOREA

1.   Japan

Japan actually has two provisions on indirect infringement, section 101(1) and (2). Subsection (2) corresponds to Article 26 CPC, with the subjective requirement that the supplier knew or should have known the infringing use of the products, and the limitation for staple products. The provision was introduced in 2003 and complements the provision of subsection (1) that prohibits the supply of part that can *exclusively* be used for the manufacture of an infringing product.

Section 101 Japanese Patent Act prohibits:

(1) In the case of a patent for an invention of a product, the commercial manufacture, transfer, lease, importation or offer for sale for the above purposes, of articles that can exclusively be used for the manufacture of such product.

(2) In the case of a patent for an invention of a product, acts of manufacturing, assigning, etc. of, in the course of trade, articles to be used for the manufacture of the product (excluding those which are generally distributed in Japan) and indispensable for solving the problems through the invention concerned, knowing that the invention is a patented invention and that the articles are to be used for the working of the invention.

The leading case in this respect concerned the patent for a user interface for explanatory notes on certain icons on the screen. The defendant manufactured and sold computer programs that, according to the court, could be considered an indirect infringement of the protected 'information processor', as the software sold by the defendant could be used to produce the protected interfaces.[23]

---

21. English Court of Appeal, *Menashe Business Mercantile v. William Hill* (2003) All E. R. 279. The case concerned a computer network for which parts were supplied abroad. The court regarded the 'effect' of the infringement to occur in the UK and therefore held that such supply was infringing.
22. Australian High Court, 16 Oct. 2008, *Northern Territory v. Collins*.
23. Tokyo High Court, 30 Sep. 2005, reported in Patents & Licensing 2005 issue 6, 38.

The other case concerns the supply of parts for infringement abroad. Here, the court held that 'manufacture' in subsection (1) referred to the Japanese market and dismissed the case.[24]

One reason why the Japanese spare parts cases as mentioned in the previous chapter may not have been argued under the angle of indirect infringement could be the fact that the spare parts were staple products (ink in the case of the toner cartridges, and film in the case of the disposable cameras), and that the direct infringer had purchased these refill items on the market without any specific supplier being identifiable.

2.   Korea

Section 127 Patent Act provides that any commercial activity of production, transfer, lease, import, or offer, for sale or lease of articles used exclusively for the production of an infringing article or for the practice of the patented process constitutes a patent infringement, and thereby corresponds to section 101(1) Japanese Patent Act. This type of infringement is generally referred to as 'indirect infringement', but the infringer does not need to know that a particular component was especially made or adapted for use in the infringement of a patent, which is different from the concept of contributory infringement under US patent law (see below). In the case of *Samsung Electronics v. Sung-Kyu Cho*,[25] the Supreme Court found a toner cartridge of a laser printer an article used exclusively for the production of the patented laser printer, even though such toner cartridges were expendable supplies, and held: (1) the cartridge is an important part of the subject matter of the patent, (2) it is not generally used for any other purpose, (3) future replacement of the cartridge is inevitably expected, and (4) the cartridges have been separately manufactured and sold only by the patentee.

C.   The US

US law distinguishes two kinds of indirect infringement: inducement and contributory infringement.

1.   Inducement

The difference between these two forms of infringement is the following:

> Section 271(b) provides that 'Whoever actively induces infringement of a patent shall be liable as an infringer.' At the outset, we feel that it is necessary to make clear the distinction, often confused, between active inducement of infringement under § 271 (b) and contributory infringement under § 271 (c).

---

24. Tokyo District Court, 27 Feb. 2007, 40 IIC 106 [2009].
25. Supreme Court, 7 Nov. 1996, 96 Ma 365.

Prior to the enactment of the Patent Act of 1952, there was no statute which defined what constituted infringement. However, infringement was judicially divided into two categories: 'direct infringement', which was the unauthorized making, using or selling of the patented invention, and 'contributory infringement', which was any other activity where, although not technically making, using or selling, the defendant displayed sufficient culpability to be held liable as an infringer...Such liability was under a theory of joint tortfeasance, wherein one who intentionally caused, or aided and abetted, the commission of a tort by another was jointly and severally liable with the primary tortfeasor.

The most common pre-1952 contributory infringement cases dealt with the situation where a seller would sell a component which was not itself technically covered by the claims of a product or process patent but which had no other use except with the claimed product or process. In such cases, although a plaintiff was required to show intent to cause infringement in order to establish contributory infringement, many courts held that such intent could be presumed because the component had no substantial non-infringing use.

The legislative history of the Patent Act of 1952 indicates that no substantive change in the scope of what constituted 'contributory infringement' was intended by the enactment of § 271...However, the single concept of 'contributory infringement' was divided between §§ 271 (b) and 271 (c) into 'active inducement' (a type of direct infringement) and 'contributory infringement', respectively. Section 271 (c) codified the prohibition against the common type of contributory infringement referred to above, and made clear that only proof of a defendant's knowledge, not intent, that his activity cause infringement was necessary to establish contributory infringement.[26]

Thus, active inducement as codified in section 271(b) requires a direct infringement and an intent. The latter must be more than mere knowledge and requires, e.g., assistance in preparing instructions for the infringing use:[27]

It must be established that the defendant possessed specific intent to encourage another's infringement and not merely that the defendant had knowledge of the acts alleged to constitute infringement. The plaintiff has the burden of showing that the alleged infringer's actions induced infringing acts and that he knew or should have known his actions would induce actual infringements.[28]

Of particular interest in connection with cases of repair and refill is the sale of staple items under the specific exemption of section 271(c) below. It is questionable if the sale of staple items can amount to active inducement, e.g., by advertising, instruction, etc.

---

26. *Hewlett Packard Company v. Bausch & Lomb*, 909 F.2d 1464 (Fed. Cir. 1990).
27. *Water Technologies Corp. v. Calco*, 850 F. 2d 660 (Fed. Cir. 1988).
28. *Manville Sales Corp. v. Paramount Systems, Inc.*, 917 F. 2d 544 (Fed. Cir. 1990).

2.   Contributory Infringement

Section 271(c) concerns contributory infringement and was codified in 1952 in accordance with prior case law (see above). The provision reads as follows:

> Whoever offers to sell or sells within the United States or imports into the United States a component of a patented machine, manufacture, combination, or composition, or a material or apparatus for use in practicing a patented process, constituting a material part of the invention, knowing the same to be especially made or especially adapted for use in an infringement of such patent, and not a staple article or commodity of commerce suitable for substantial non-infringing use, shall be liable as a contributory infringer.

The justification for finding contributory acts infringing is this:

> It cannot be that, where a useful machine is patented as a combination of parts, two or more can engage in its construction and sale, and protect themselves by showing that, though united in an effort to produce the same machine, and sell it, and bring it into extensive use, each makes and sells one part only, which is useless without the others, and still another person, in precise conformity with the purpose in view, puts them together for use. If it were so, such patents would, indeed, be of little value. In such case, all are tort-feasors, engaged in a common purpose to infringe the patent, and actually, by their concerted action, producing that result. . . . [29]

In order to be applicable, the provision requires:

(1) An act of direct infringement:

> It is plain that § 271 (c) – a part of the Patent Code enacted in 1952 – made no change in the fundamental concept that there can be no contributory infringement in the absence of a direct infringement. That section defines contributory infringement in terms of direct infringement – namely the sale of a component of a patented combination or machine for use 'in an infringement of such patent'. [30]

(2) Knowledge of intent to contribute to direct infringement:

> § 271 (c) does require a showing that the alleged contributory infringer knew that the combination for which his component was especially designed was both patented and infringing. [31]

(3) Not a staple article or commodity of commerce suitable for substantial non-infringing use.

---

29. *Wallace v. Holmes*, 29 F. Ca. 74 (C.C.D. 1871).
30. *Aro Manufacturing Co. Inc. v. Convertible Top Replacement, Inc*, 365 U.S. 336 (1961).
31. *Aro Manufacturing Co. Inc. v. Convertible Top Replacement, Inc.*, 377 U.S. 476 (1964).

III.   ANALYSIS

It seems that patentees in some countries were more successful than in others in order to protect their invention against acts of repair or refill when basing their arguments on indirect infringement. Particularly the German courts have lent patentees a willing ear in this respect. Yet, as the following very brief considerations make clear, indirect infringement should not be a cause of action to broaden the patented scope against such acts that would not infringe when considered under the rules of direct infringement. In other words, separating direct from indirect infringement, as is the law in Germany and has been proposed under the CPC, may unwittingly have led the courts to broaden the patent scope when faced with acts of repair or recycle. The issue is not helped by the fact that the provisions on indirect infringement often use terms that are difficult to define within the framework of patent law, unless (as is advocated here) one takes the purpose of patent law into account.

A.   Essential Element versus State of the Art

The law in many countries requires the supply of an 'essential element' in order to commit an act of indirect infringement. While the US courts have defined this as patent-specific (essential is what distinguishes the invention from prior art), the German Supreme Court attempts a definition that is product-specific, yet ends up with including all parts that are not completely irrelevant for the protected product in question. As mentioned above, it appears preferable to interpret 'essential' in terms of patent law rather than product specification. Essential should be what distinguished the invention over prior art and what makes out the contribution of the invention to society. One other argument may also speak in favour of this interpretation: the actual product the patentee brings on the market may not always conform to the patent specification. The danger is thus that the courts may interpret the essentiality of an element in light of a product that may not be identical to the patent teaching, or may not even have been around at the time of patent application and should therefore not be used to interpret the patent. The same problem occurs for the question of direct infringement when the courts try to determine whether consumers regard the product as one that may be refilled or recycled, an approach taken by the Tokyo High Court in the *Canon* decision (see the previous chapter). Even for the approach that is favoured here, the distinction is not always clear-cut. In the Senseo case mentioned above, the coffee pads as such were state of the art and therefore did not directly contribute to the advantages of the invention over prior art. Yet, according to the Düsseldorf Appeal Court, the coffee pad in its concrete dimensions did contribute to the realization of the advantage that the shortened grooves could confer. Only a tight-fitting coffee pad in its interaction with the modified bottom could prevent hot water from flowing around the pad and directly into the cup instead of being pressed through the pouch. In the end of the day, this does make the pad essential in the patent sense: Also, fuel may be essential for realizing the advantages of an improved injection system without making the fuel 'essential' in the patent sense.

B.   STATE OF THE ART AND STAPLE PRODUCTS

When interpreting the 'essential element' as patent-specific, the exception for staple products will not be of much relevance: staple products are regularly those that are state of the art and do not incorporate those advantages that distinguish the invention from the state of the art. If, on the other hand, the 'essential element' is interpreted as product-specific, the exception for staple products will become of greater importance. After all, a good number of products are 'suitable for a variety of uses', as some of the Australian judges interpreted staple products. But, to take two examples from the above cases, what about ink, coffee pads, or film? While the use of these products is fairly well defined, the precise product for which the use is meant is not. There may be a huge variety of toner cartridges for which the ink may be suitable, a variety of coffee machines into which the coffee pads may be inserted, or a number of different types of cameras for which the film is suitable. One approach to this problem may be to interpret 'staple products' as those that, when meant as spare or replacement parts, have significant non-infringing uses,[32] a fact that should be proven by the supplies of such products, however. In other words, if the supplier can demonstrate that the supplied products have been used as spare or replacement parts for products different from the one covered by the patent, staple products would then be those that are not product-specific. This would make film and ink staple products, while in the coffee pad case, it would incumbent on the supplier of the pads to show that pads in the concrete dimensions can in fact also be used in other coffee machines already on the market.

C.   OBJECTIVE LIMITS (EXHAUSTION) AND IMPLIED PERMISSION

Indirect infringement cannot serve as a circumvention of the patent limits under the exhaustion doctrine. This is clear in principle (if the replacement of a certain part does not alter the identity of the product and therefore does not amount to a new manufacture, the supply of the respective spare part cannot be an indirect infringement, either), yet the German cases have shown that there has been a de facto shift to limit the exhaustion doctrine.[33] One doctrinal issue in connection with exhaustion is the interesting fusion between the doctrines of exhaustion and implied license: the distinction between repair and new manufacture is important in connection with exhaustion; the act of manufacture can never exhaust, and in this

---

32. This criterion has been used in a related context when determining whether the supply of products such as copying machines amounts to a contributory infringement of copyright: US Supreme Court, *Sony Corporation of America v. Universal City Studios*, 464 U.S. 417 (1984).
33. This has been convincingly argued by Hölder, Ersatzteile und Erschöpfung, above, fn. 11.

respect, the English courts have applied a concept that was originally developed by Josef Kohler for German law. On the other hand, the concept of exhaustion may not be sufficient to determine direct or indirect infringement due to the fact that in some cases, the purchaser of products may buy these in the legitimate expectation that the aftermarket is not tied to the manufacturer of the original product, and that certain acts of repair or recycle have implicitly been consented to by the patentee. The purchase of a coffee machine may be such a case. If, as was argued by the Düsseldorf courts in the Senseo case, the replacement of a coffee pad would indeed amount to a reconstruction of the machine, with the consequence that the patentee could indeed prohibit such exchange (leaving aside the fact that when undertaken by a consumer, this would be exempt as private use), one may ask if this conforms to the legitimate expectation of the purchaser of such a product. In other words, would anyone be willing to purchase a coffee machine with the knowledge that it could only be used once. In such case, one should reasonably infer that the patentee has consented to the replacement of the pads, and it is questionable whether such implied consent for replacement can be limited to replacement parts by the manufacturer, if there is free competition in the market for replacement parts. Thus, in some cases of repair or replacement, implied consent by the manufacturer may prevent the latter from arguing infringement, although the exhaustion doctrine would not apply.

D.   Separation of Direct and Indirect Infringement

While the US legal system has remained true to the idea that indirect infringement must indeed be contributory, and that only the contribution to an actual infringement is actionable, this connection has been separated under the CPC and in the patent laws of most European countries modelled after the CPC. The interpretative difficulties with indirect infringement make the wisdom of such separation questionable.[34] In fact, some authors have openly advocated that the provision be abolished outright.[35]

E.   Conclusion

The above analysis has shown that ultimately, the approaches taken in order to determine indirect infringement cannot contribute to the solution of how repair and

---

34. This chapter has only analysed the objective requirements of indirect infringement. The subjective elements such as positive knowledge pose additional problems not further addressed here. Also, procedural questions such as the amount of damages that may be claimed from an indirect infringer (none, really, according to the German Federal Supreme Court decisions of 7 Jun. 2005 and 9 Jan. 2007, above, fn. 10), and the way injunctive orders should be worded (according to the Düsseldorf Appeal Court in the Senseo case [above, fn. 10], the supplier had to state on his goods that these were not suitable for Senseo coffee machines, which quite objectively was not true) have not been addressed here.
35. Fitzner, above, fn. 11.

reconstruction should be distinguished. If commercial repair or replacement of a part does not amount to a direct patent infringement, the supply of the relevant part cannot be considered an act of indirect infringement either. Unfortunately, though, lawsuits for indirect infringement may have contributed to a blurring of the line between permissible repair and impermissible reconstruction.

Part 3
Issues under Copyright Law

Chapter 5

Blocking Repair or Fair Use of Software? The U.S. Perspectives on Anticircumvention

Andy Y. Sun

I. INTRODUCTION

In 1994, witnessing that the use of the Internet began to take off (and perhaps explode), the U.S. copyright industries also saw a growing and widespread availability of devices and/or measures used to circumvent the technical measures they have employed for the protection of their copyrighted work online. Thus, the industries began lobbying the U.S. Congress to pass legislation banning the circumvention of these technical measures and the sale of 'circumvention devices.' When Congress failed to act, the industries succeeded, instead, in convincing the Executive Branch, especially the Office of the U.S. Trade Representative, to move forward with an international treaty mandating such protection. On 20 December 1996, the World Intellectual Property Organization (WIPO) successfully concluded two international 'Internet Treaties,' that is, the WIPO Copyright Treaty (WCT) and the WIPO Performances and Phonograms Treaty (WPPT).[1] Suddenly pressure

---

1. World Intellectual Property Organization (WIPO) Copyright Treaty, adopted in Geneva on 20 Dec. 1996, 36 I.L.M. 65 (1997); WIPO Performances and Phonograms Treaty (WPPT), adopted in Geneva on 20 Dec. 1996, 36 I.L.M. 76 (1997). Note that WCT entered into force on 6 Mar. 2002, *see* WIPO Copyright Treaty Notification No. 32 (6 Dec. 2001); whereas WPPT

Christopher Heath, Anselm Kamperman Sanders (eds.), *Spares, Repairs and Intellectual Property Rights*, pp. 105-123.
© 2009 Kluwer Law International BV, The Netherlands.

began to mount on the U.S. Congress to act quickly so that hopefully both the momentum and a 'bandwagon effect' can be created for other nations to act accordingly and quickly, which will certainly accelerate both treaties to enter into force.[2]

On 20 October 1998, the Digital Millennium Copyright Act (DMCA) in the United States was enacted.[3] Title I of the DMCA is designed to implement the WCT and WPPT. Article 11 of the WCT and Article 18 of the WPPT both specifically require all Contracting Parties to 'provide adequate legal protection and effective legal remedies *against the circumvention of effective technological measures that are used*' by authors, performers, or producers of phonograms '*in connection with the exercise of their rights*' under either treaty or the Berne Convention and that 'restrict acts, in respect of their works, which are not authorized by the authors concerned or permitted by law'[4] (emphasis added). As a result, section 103 of the DMCA creates a new Chapter 12 to the existing Copyright Act, with section 1201 being added to Title 17 of the United States Code, designed specifically to regulate protective technical measures in connection with the protection of copyrighted works.

Since its inception, these anticircumvention provisions have proved to be highly controversial. At the international level, just what exactly does 'effective technical measures' mean? Is it supposed to be an objective or a subjective standard? What may be considered 'ineffective technical measures,' and what is the consequence for that? For instance, should an obsolete software still be considered as an 'effective technical measure,' since the program may still function the way it was designed to be? Is it supposed to be a separate right from the copyright it is intended to cover? These issues naturally spill over to any and all of the domestic legislative regimes that need to comply with their treaty obligations.

In the United States, with the introduction of anticircumvention statutes, its copyright law touches on the regulation of technology itself for the first time, instead of focusing on the protection over expression of creative ideas. It follows that the anticircumvention provisions inevitably reignite the debate on what exactly should be the scope of copyright. Should protection over technical measures be treated separately from the copyrighted work it intends to cover? What may be the

---

entered into force on 20 May 2002; *see* WIPO Performances and Phonograms Treaty Notification No. 32 (20 Feb. 2002).

2. Both treaties require thirty Contracting States to ratify before entering into force. The actual effective date is three months since the depository of the thirtieth instrument with the WIPO. *See* WCT, Art. 20; WPPT, Art. 30.

3. Pub.L. No. 105-304, 112 Stat. 2860 (1998). This legislation marks the most sweeping reform of the U.S. copyright regime since the enactment of the Copyright Act of 1976. *See* Pub.L. No. 94-553, 90 Stat. 2541 (1976). DMCA is the result of prolonged negotiations among various interested groups and individuals. While most of the issues were ironed out by mid-1997, an unexpected issue, the liability of Internet service providers, which is not addressed at all in the WCT and WPPT, popped up and turned out to be the most difficult sticking point. It took another year before all sides eventually agreed on the so-called 'notice and take-down' principle. Once a compromise was finally reached on 1 Apr. 1998, however, the bill moved smoothly through the legislative process.

4. The theory behind the WCT and WPPT is that technological protections encouraged copyright owners to make digital content widely available, and circumvention of technological measures reduced that benefit. *See also* House Rep. 105-551, Part 2, at 63 (Jul. 22, 1998).

socio-economic impact if indeed that is the case? Should there be a separate 'right' for public access or fair use 'right' (which has traditionally been considered as a mere affirmative defense in litigation) as opposed to the enumerated exclusive rights of the copyright holders? Courts in the United States have been confronted with these challenges and are still in the process of crafting out rules and reshaping the future of electronic commerce. This article intends to survey the current landscape of the copyright regime in relation to anticircumvention. This article will also discuss critical cases to showcase the controversies and challenges confronting the courts.

II.   THE LEGISLATIVE STRUCTURE

A.   Types of Prohibitions

Section 1201 of the Copyright Act prohibits three types of circumvention:

(1) gaining unauthorized access to a copyrighted work by circumventing a technological protection measure put in place by the copyright owner, that is, the *act of circumvention itself*, such as decryption and descrambling technologies;[5]

(2) manufacturing and/or making available devices, technologies, or services used to defeat technological protection measures put in place by the copyright owner to prevent unauthorized access to a copyrighted work, that is, *providing means for access*; and

(3) manufacturing and distributing means or devices for circumventing technological measures put in place by the copyright owner to prevent unauthorized copying, that is, *providing means for copying*.

In other words, the statute distinguishes between access control (antitrafficking) and copy technologies and treats them differently, with *direct prohibition* on the act of circumvention being imposed with respect to access control technologies only.[6]

Note that with regard to the prohibition against circumvention devices, it is applicable *only* to devices or services that are primarily designed or produced for circumvention (*primary purpose test*); that have only limited commercially significant purposes or uses other than circumvention (*significant purpose test*); *or* that are marketed for use in circumvention. With a few exceptions, section 1201 does *not* require consumer electronics, telecommunications, or computing equipment manufacturers to design their products to respond to any particular technological measure taken by a copyright owner.[7] As a result, normal household devices

---

5. This portion of the statute became effective as of 28 Oct. 2000, whereas the other forms of prohibition became effective immediately since DMCA entered into force.

6. 17 U.S.C. § 1201 (a)(2)(2000 Supp. II).

7. These exceptions are – for consumer (not professional) analog VCRs and camcorders – they must comply with: (1) 'automatic gain control technology' (which causes distortion in the images upon playback), or (2) 'color stripe copy control technology' (which causes distracting visible

such as videocassette recorders or personal computers do not qualify, since they are not primarily designed to circumvent technological protections granting access to copyrighted works.[8]

B.   LIABILITIES

Violations of this section may result in civil and/or criminal liabilities. Section 1203 gives federal courts power to grant civil damages, an injunction, costs, attorney fees, and even the impounding, modification, or destruction of the devices or products involved in the violation. The court also has discretion to award *treble damages against repeat offenders*, and to *limit damages for innocent violations* (where the defendant proves he/she was not aware and had no reason to believe his/her acts constituted a violation).

In addition, criminal penalties may be available if the violation of section 1201 is done *willfully* and for purposes of commercial advantage or private financial gain. Section 1204 provides for fines up to USD 500,000 or up to five years imprisonment for the first offense, and fines up to USD 1,000,000 or up to ten years imprisonment for subsequent offenses. Note, however, that these penalties are *not* applicable to non-profit libraries, archives and educational institutions.

To clarify potential overlapping liabilities, section 1201 expressly provides three 'savings clauses,' stipulating that no direct copyright infringement, secondary infringement (vicarious and contributory), rights of free speech or the press using consumer electronics, telecommunications or computer products will be affected. In other words, anticircumvention is treated as an independent cause of action separated from all other existing infringement actions.[9]

C.   EXEMPTIONS

Legislative exemptions. During the legislative process of DMCA, many concerns were raised between the addition of this new cause of action and fair use. As a result, Congress was mindful about this issue and the statute itself eventually incorporated seven categories of exemptions to potential circumvention liabilities. They are:

(1) Security exemption: A general exception for law enforcement, intelligence, and other governmental activities.
(2) Educational exemption: For non-profit library, archive, and educational institutions, circumvention is permitted for the sole purpose of making a

---

color stripes to appear through portions of the viewable picture in normal viewing mode) within *eighteen months* since the enactment of DMCA. *See* 17 U.S.C. § 1201 (k) (2000 Supp. II).
8.   *See* House Rep. 105-551, Part 1, at 10 (22 May 1998).
9.   17 U.S.C. § 1201 (c)(2)-(4)(2000 Supp. II).

good faith determination as to whether they wish to obtain authorized access to the copyrighted work.

(3) 'Reverse engineering' exemption: Circumvention is permitted for software developers of a lawfully obtained computer program to identify the elements necessary to achieve *inoperability* of an independently created computer program with other programs.

(4) 'Encryption research' exemption: Circumvention is permitted for access control measures, and the development of the technological means to identify flaws and vulnerabilities of encryption technologies.

(5) 'Minors protection' exemption: This allows a court to consider the necessity for the incorporation of circumvention in technology that prevents access by minors to material on the Internet (i.e., parental control).

(6) 'Personal privacy' exemption: Circumvention is permitted when the technological measure, or the work it protects, is capable of collecting or disseminating personally identifying information about the online activities of a natural person (e.g., 'cookies'). It is available *only if* the user is *not* provided with adequate notice that his online activity is being collected, and the circumvention has no other effect on the ability of the user to gain access to the work.

(7) 'Security testing' exemption: This is the permission of circumvention over access control measures, and the development of technological means for such circumvention, for the purpose of testing the security of a computer, computer system or computer network, with the authorization of its owner or operator.[10]

Administrative exemptions. Recognizing that the statute may not be able to catch up with and reflect on ever-changing technological developments, in addition to the above-listed legislative exemptions, DMCA authorizes the Librarian of Congress (but in fact with recommendations from the Register of Copyrights and the Assistant Secretary for Communications and Information at the U.S. Department of Commerce) to periodically review and grant exemptions to certain classes of works so that the antitrafficking provision shall not apply to persons who engage in non-infringing uses of those particular classes of works.[11]

The Librarian of Congress has determined that, between 28 October 2003 and 27 October 2006, persons who engaged in non-infringing use of the following four classes of copyrighted works are not liable for circumvention:[12]

(1) 'Censorware' applications, that is, lists of Internet locations or websites blocked by commercial filtering software applications intended to prevent

---

10. 17 U.S.C. § 1201 (d)-(j)(2000 Supp. II).
11. 17 U.S.C. § 1201 (a)(B) and (C)(2000 Supp. II). Since the effective date of this provision (28 Oct. 2000), the reviews and recommendations take place each succeeding three-year period.
12. 17 C.F.R. § 201.40 (2004), which codifies Exemption to Prohibition on Circumvention of Copyright Protection Systems for Access Control Technologies. 68 Federal Register 62011 (31 Oct. 2003) and 65 Federal Register 64555 (Oct. 30 2000).

children and other users from viewing objectionable materials while online. Note that the rule tries to emphasize its focus on 'blocking' rather than 'accuracy.' In order to calm critics over excessive blocking, this exemption specifically excludes software designed to protect against damage to computers or networks, such as firewalls, antivirus and anti-spam software programs).

(2) 'Dongles' or hardware locks. But this is only limited to the computer program being used, that is, the exempted class includes *only* the software that actually cannot be accessed due to a damaged or malfunctioning dongle, and only when the dongle cannot be replaced or repaired.

(3) Computer programs and video games in obsolete format or medium.

(4) 'Special format' for the blind and visually impaired in gaining meaningful access to literary works distributed as e-books.[13]

As can be seen, the second and third class of exemptions deal primarily with obsolete software. 'Obsolete' means the machine or system necessary to render perceptible a work stored in that format is no longer manufactured or reasonably available in the commercial marketplace.[14] Note that in order to make a *prima facie* case of exemption, proponents must bear the burden to prove, by a preponderance of 'real, verifiable and reasonable' evidence, that there has been or is likely to be a *substantial adverse effect* and *actual harm* on non-infringing uses by users of copyrighted works.[15] *De minimis* problems, isolated harm, or mere inconveniences are insufficient.[16]

---

13. 17 U.S.C. § 121 (2000 Supp. II).

14. 17 U.S.C. § 108 (c)(2000 Supp. II).

15. See above, fn. 12 also 68 Federal Register at 62,102. Note that the 'actual harm' standard requires the showing of 'actual instances of verifiable problems.' In addition, the Copyright Office interprets the term 'classes of works' under 17 U.S.C. § 1201 (a)(1) as 'attributes of the works themselves, and not by reference to some external criteria such as the intended use or users of the works.' *Ibid.*, at 57,529. These legal standards have generated controversies between proponents and opponents for exemptions in the 2006 review cycle. Proponents argue that the standards are simply too rigid to bear and in effect narrow the scope of fair use. *See*, Library Copyright Alliance and Music Library Association, 'In the Matter of Exemption to the Prohibition of Circumvention of Copyright Protection Systems for Access Control Technologies' <www.copyright.gov/1201/2006/comments/band_LCA.pdf> (1 Dec. 2005). Note that this lobbying group consists of the American Association of Law Libraries, American Library Association, Association of Research Libraries, Medical Library Association, Music Library Association, Special Libraries Association and Jonathan Band, the group's legal counsel. The rights holders lobbying, however, countered with the argument that the 2003 exemption review has never implied a 'rigid' standard in the application of 'substantial adverse effect,' nor is first-hand knowledge required, although actual knowledge is much preferred in the evaluation of a proposed exemption. Citing evidence on the prevalence of DVD players and online music services, among other things, they further argued that the use of access control had the effect of rapid increase in the public availability of all kinds of copyrighted material in digital formats, thus showing no signs of adverse effects. *See*, S. J. Matalitz, 'Joint Reply Comments of Fourteen Organizations,' <www.copyright.gov/1201/2006/reply/11metalitz_AAP.pdf>.

16. See above, fn. 12.

During the 2003 review cycle, at least twenty-five proposed classes of exemptions were turned down by the Register of Copyrights. Examples include, among other things, 'legitimate research projects' that need to be carried out over musical recordings and audiovisual works protected by access control mechanisms; malfunction, damage or obsoleteness to media that render inaccessible audiovisual works embodied in that media (e.g., digital video/versatile disks (DVDs) backup); as well as literary works (especially e-books), sound recordings and audiovisual works protected by access controls that prevent post-sale uses of works, or 'tethered' works (i.e., works that cannot be copied to and used on other devices). With regard to the proposed DVD backup exemption, the evidence was found to be insufficient to prove the fragility of DVDs; with regard to 'legitimate research projects,' the proposal was denied since the proposed class is defined largely in terms of the purpose of the circumvention, and the scope is too broad by virtually covering the entire spectrum of audiovisual works. With regard to proposed 'tethered' works or the e-book exemption, it was denied on the ground that the consumer often has choices between various e-book formats. Alternative formats are also available. Thus 'tethered' works result in a user's inconvenience at best, as long as such alternatives are available.

In January 2006, the Copyright Office began its third round of rulemaking process on the proposed exemptions to prohibition on anticircumvention. As of 3 April 2006, three hearings were conducted; seventy-four comments and thirty-five reply comments were submitted for review. These materials, following consultation with the Assistant Secretary for Communications and Information, will form the basis of the Librarian of Congress' final exemption determination for the next three years, expected to be made on or before 28 October 2006.[17] Once again, as in previous two rounds, proponents (user groups such as libraries) and opponents (rights holder groups) of existing and new exemption proposals clashed with each other literally every step of the way. While the overall environment for the usage of access control seems to be far less lucid this time around and the related technology arguably is getting more mature than the 2003 review process (such as the ongoing expansion of broad bandwidth Internet access and the yet-to-be-resolved peer-to-peer piracy issues at the time), what is similar, though, is that a consensus is still way too far and too difficult to reach.[18] On 25 October 2006, the

---

17. Based on the opinions filed thus far, there are nine exemptions being proposed: access controls that threaten privacy or critical infrastructure (security), software locks for mobile phone reprogramming (firmware), digital audio-visual clip compilation for educational uses, format/platform-shifting type of personal fair use (space- or time-shifting), works tethered to certain operating systems, obsolete software or hardware, back up copies, public domain DVD materials, and several other miscellaneous exemptions. Some of these were identical to what were proposed but denied in 2003. *See* above, fn. 16.

18. Incidents nevertheless occur and, given the widespread usage of such technology, can potentially have a significant impact on everyone involved in the market. A recent high-profile yet notorious example is the Sony BMG CD distribution. See *In re Sony BMG CD Technologies Litigation*, No. 05-CV-09575 (NRB)(S.D.N.Y. 2005). Since 1 Aug. 2003, Sony BMG began to sell some of its musical CD titles with the so-called 'content protection software' being packaged in. Specifically, Sony BMG adopted the MediaMax and 'extended copy protection,' or

Librarian of Congress issued an interim rule, extending the classes of exemptions being granted since 2003 while pending a final rule to be issued later on for the period ending 27 October 2009. On 20 November 2006, the Librarian of Congress issued the latest rulings, which exempt the following works:

(1) audiovisual works included in a college film or media department's library used for educational use in the classroom by that department's professors;

(2) obsolete computer programs or video games for archival reproduction or preservation usage;

(3) damaged or malfunctioning 'dongles';

(4) literary works distributed in e-book format that prevent specialized format for handicapped individuals (such as read-aloud, or screen readers);

(5) firmware used to lawfully connect a wireless telephone handset with a communication network; and

(6) sound recordings and audiovisual works in Compact Disk (CD) format that create or exploit security flaws or 'vulnerabilities' that compromise the security of personal computers.[19]

As can be seen, 'censorware,' which has been on the list since 2000, is no longer considered exempted. This is consistent with the Copyright Office position that all such exemptions are 'rare administrative exceptions,' and should, therefore, be narrowly construed. If and when anyone feels a certain category of works deserve a longer term of exemption from the anticircumvention rule, then he/she should go before Congress and seek legislative exemption as such. However, as far as different stakeholders are concerned, this is likely to set the stage for more anticircumvention-related battles and perhaps litigation down the road, at least in the foreseeable future.

XCP software in those CDs which only allows users to make a limited number of copies from the disk and also rip the music into a digital format to be used by a computer or portable music player. When an XCP CD is inserted into a computer, for example, an End User License Agreement (EULA) appears automatically on the screen and the XCP software installs itself on the user's computer. Allegedly this software contains a potentially harmful 'rootkit' which monitors the user's activities and signals back to the manufacturer. It, therefore, opens up the computer's 'backdoor' and render it much more vulnerable to third party hacking (either with 'malware,' 'spyware,' 'Trojan horses' or other types of hacking devices/software). Sony BMG eventually identified fifty-two titles using the XCP software and more than 20 million CDs have been recalled. Settlement negotiations have been under way with various class action parties as well as state and federal government agencies. For a detailed description of this incident, see Wikipedia, '2005 Sony CD Copy Protection Scandal', <http://en.wikipedia.org/wiki/2005_Sony_CD_copy_protection_controversy> (2005).

19. For the interim rule on extension, *see* Exemption to Prohibition on Circumvention of Copyright Protection Systems for Access Control Technologies, 71 Fed. Reg. 63,247 (Interim Rule 25 Oct. 2006). Apparently one of the reasons for this delay is because of the difficult challenges posed by the firmware or software locks over mobile phones reprogramming. For the final rules issued on 20 Nov. 2006, *see* 71 Fed. Reg. 68,472 (27 Nov. 2006).

III.   THE JUDICIAL INTERPRETATIONS

So far several federal circuit courts have already had the opportunity to interpret and refine what section 1201, especially the antitrafficking provision, really means and covers (or does not cover) since the enactment of DMCA. Inevitably the discussions touched on or reopened debates over some of the most fundamental copyright principles. The U.S. Supreme Court, however, has not had the opportunity to offer its opinions over the debates.

A.   *UNIVERSAL CITY STUDIOS, INC. v. CORLEY*[20]

This is the first case concerning the constitutionality of the anticircumvention statutes. The Content Scramble System (CSS) is a technology created to control access to the contents of DVDs or video compact discs (VCDs).[21] In 1999, a then-16-year-old Norwegian by the name Jon Johansen managed to reverse-engineer and circumvent the CSS lock key. He then released his code-cracking software on the Internet and dubbed it 'DeCSS.' As a result, users can play a very large video computer file on a non-CSS-compliant player as well as copy, manipulate, and transfer that file just like any other computer file.[22] Eric Corley, the defendant in this case, picked up this story and published the entire source code of DeCSS on his website and magazine geared primarily for the so-called hacker community. This was one of the many other websites that published DeCSS at the time. The plaintiffs, the eight major movie studios of Hollywood, brought suit and sought injunction against Corley under the DMCA antitrafficking provision after he refused to comply with the movie studios' cease-and-desist letter by removing DeCSS.

The U.S. Court of Appeals for the Second Circuit affirmed the district court's decision to grant injunction. The court declared that the DMCA:

> targets the *circumvention* of digital walls guarding copyrighted material (and trafficking in circumvention tools), but does not concern itself with the *use* of those materials after circumvention has occurred. Subsection 1201(c)(1) ensures that the DMCA is not read to prohibit the 'fair use' of information just because that information was obtained in a manner made illegal by the DMCA.[23]

On the constitutionality of anticircumvention and antitrafficking statutes, having concluded that computer code conveying information is 'speech' within the meaning

---

20. 273 F.3d 429 (2nd Cir. 2001).
21. First introduced in 1996, CSS was jointly developed by Matsushita and Toshiba, later adopted by the movie studios as the standard to divide the world into eight respective 'zones' or regions for better control of DVD market distribution. CSS is not a copy-protection system per se; rather it is an access control system in the hope to achieve copyright protection: it prevents the playback of discs on unauthorized devices. Therefore, a DVD from one zone may not be played by a device from another zone, even though both are legitimate products.
22. See above, fn. 20, at 437, 438.
23. *Ibid.*, at 443.

of the First Amendment, the court nevertheless concluded that the defendant's constitution challenge that the lower court's DMCA injunction over posting and linking
hindered freedom of expression was premature and speculative. The court held that
intermediate scrutiny, with the showing of a legitimate government interest, was the
appropriate review standard. Being content-neutral in nature, both the anticircumvention and antitrafficking provisions under the DMCA were held to meet that
standard.[24]

In sum, section 1201(c)(1) prohibition (no encroachment on fair use) applies
to the manufacturing, trafficking in and making of devices that would circumvent
encryption technology, not to the users of such technology. It is the technology
itself, rather than the uses of the copyrighted material, that is at issue.

B.   *The Chamberlain Group, Inc. v. Skylink Technologies, Inc.*[25]

Where *Corley* concerned only with the constitutionality issues, the *Chamberlain*
case provided the first opportunity for a court to construe the full boundaries of the
anticircumvention and antitrafficking provisions under the DMCA.

This case concerns alleged circumvention of copyrighted computer software
embedded in the garage door opener (GDO) system. The plaintiff, Chamberlain
Group, adopted the so-called 'rolling code' software program that constantly changes
the hand-held transmitter signals needed to synchronize with the codes in the GDO
motor to open the garage door. The defendant, Skylink, is a competitor of the plaintiff. It made a model (called a 'universal transmitter') to interoperate with general
GDOs, including the plaintiff's models, even though it did not use rolling codes.

Chamberlain initially sued Skylink for both patent infringement and anticircumvention. After the patent claim was dismissed and the motion for summary
judgment under DMCA was declined, only the latter issue was brought before the
Federal Circuit.

From the outset, the Federal Circuit acknowledged that this was a case of first
impression and there was no binding precedent governing the substantive issue of
this case. The court then construed the statute by first making distinction between
property and liability. The court declared that sections 1201(a) and (b) establish
causes of action for liability only; they do not establish a new property right.[26] Such a
distinction was critical because it went straight to the *authorization* issue, upon

---

24. The court noted that while the initial use of DeCSS to gain access to a DVD movie created no
     loss to the movie producers because the initial user must purchase that DVD, once the DVD was
     purchased, however, DeCSS enabled the initial user to copy the movie in digital (and technically
     'perfect') form and transmitted it instantly in virtually limitless quantity, thereby depriving the
     movie producer of sales. 'The advent of the Internet creates the potential for instantaneous
     worldwide distribution of the copied material.' *Id.*, at 453.
25. 381 F.3d 1178 (Fed. Cir. 2004).
26. 'The circumvention provisions convey no additional property rights in and of themselves; they
     simply provide property owners with new ways to secure their property ... Contrary to Cham-
     berlain's assertion, the DMCA emphatically *did not* "fundamentally alter" the legal landscape

which the district court's summary judgment was based. In copyright infringement, a plaintiff only needs to show that the defendant has used the copyrighted work; the burden of proving that the use was authorized falls squarely on the defendant.[27] Under the DMCA, however, since section 1201(a)(3)(A) defines circumvention as an activity undertaken 'without the authority of the copyright owner,' it follows that the plaintiff alleging circumvention or trafficking must bear the burden to prove that the defendant's access was unauthorized. Therefore, with the basic assumption that access is permissible unless prohibited, the defendant must prove authorized copying and the plaintiff must prove authorized access.

The *Chamberlain* court completely rejected the plaintiff's arguments on statutory construction. Recognizing that its ruling could create uncertainties down the road, the court nevertheless concluded that the anticircumvention provisions prohibit only forms of access that bear a reasonable relationship to the protections that the Copyright Act otherwise affords copyright owners.

In sum, the court held that a plaintiff alleging a violation of section 1201(a)(2) must prove: (1) ownership of a valid *copyright* on a work, (2) effectively controlled by a *technological measure*, which has been circumvented, (3) that third parties can now *access* (4) *without authorization*, in a manner that (5) infringes or facilitates infringing a right *protected* by the Copyright Act, because of a product that (6) the defendant either (a) *designed or produced* primarily for circumvention; (b) made available despite only *limited commercial significance* other than circumvention; or (c) *marketed* for use in circumvention of the controlling technological measure. Failure to prove any of one of elements one through five would have failed to prove a *prima facie* case of circumvention. A plaintiff capable of proving those five elements need prove only one of (6)(a), (b) or (c) to shift the burden back to the defendant. At that point, the various affirmative defenses under section 1201 become relevant.[28]

The court concluded that the district court was correct by narrowly focusing on Skylink's behavior, intent, and product within the context of industry expectations. The court pointed out that in addition to failing to prove the fourth element (lack of authority), plaintiff neither alleged copyright infringement nor explained how the access provided by defendant's product facilitated the infringement of any right that the Copyright Act sought to protect. Therefore, the plaintiff failed to demonstrate the nexus between access and protection and the district court was correct in denying its motion for summary judgment.[29]

---

governing the reasonable expectations of consumers or competitors; *did not* "fundamentally alter" the ways that courts analyze industry practices; and *did not* render the pre-DMCA history of the GDO industry irrelevant.' *Id.*, at 1192-94.

27. 'The premise underlying this initial assignment of burden is that the copyright laws authorize members of the public to access a work, but not to copy it. The law therefore places the burden of proof on the party attempting to establish that the circumstances of its case deviate from these normal expectations; defendants must prove authorized copying and plaintiffs must prove unauthorized access.' *Id.*, at 1193.

28. *Id.*, at 1203.

29. *Id.*, at 1203-1204.

C.   *LEXMARK INTERNATIONAL, INC. v. STATIC CONTROL COMPONENTS, INC.*[30]

Just a couple of months after the Chamberlain decision, the U.S. Court of Appeals for the Sixth Circuit came down with its decision concerning the antitrafficking provision of the DMCA. In this case, plaintiff Lexmark International, a world renowned manufacturer of computer printers and related accessories, sued its competitor for selling compatible, remanufactured products, thereby circumventing the built-in control measure that was placed within the plaintiff's own toner cartridges. The software program and the microchip in each Lexmark printer were designed to authenticate the source of refilled or replacement toner and only the plaintiff's own toner cartridges would be accepted. To compete with the plaintiff, the defendant copied the plaintiff's code in its own microchips so that its refilled toner cartridges are interoperable with that of plaintiff's but sold at a much lower price.

Lexmark sued on the ground that the unauthorized reproduction of the microchip code constituted copyright infringement, and that the interoperable product violated the anticircumvention provisions under the DMCA. The district court granted the motion for preliminary injunction. The defendant appealed.

The Sixth Circuit vacated and remanded the case to the district court on the ground that the plaintiff failed to demonstrate likelihood of success on the merits. The court first examined the copyrightability of the computer program (the 'Toner Loading Program' (TLP)) in question. Drawing from the idea-expression dichotomy, the court held that the TLP, designed primarily to achieve the function of blocking out other name brand products, was not copyrightable – 'lock-out' codes, in general, fell on the function-idea rather than the original-expression side of the copyright line.[31] Furthermore, the court held that when external factors constrained the choice of expressive vehicle, the doctrine of *scènes à faire*, that is, scenes that must be done, precluded copyright protection. In the computer software context, the doctrine meant that the elements of a program dictated by practical realities (such as hardware standards, mechanical specifications, and compatibility requirements) may not obtain copyright.[32] To the extent compatibility required that a particular code sequence be included in the component device to permit its use, the merger and *scènes à faire* doctrines generally preclude the code sequence from obtaining copyright protection.[33]

---

30.   387 F.3d 522 (6th Cir. 2004).
31.   'Lock-out codes' are described as a 'security system [employed by manufacturers] to bar the use of unauthorized components.' *Id.*, at 536.
32.   *Ibid.*, at 535.
33.   Merger doctrine in the copyright context means if an idea and the way to express it are so intricately tied that the ways of expression of that idea have little possible variation, there is no copyright infringement. Citing *Sega Entertainments, Ltd. v. Accolade, Inc.*, 977 F.2d 1510 (9th Cir. 1992), here the court, in turn, quoted the CONTU Final Report: 'When specific instructions, even though previously copyrighted, are the *only and essential means of accomplishing a given task*, their use by another will not amount to infringement.' *Ibid.*, 536; see also, Final Report of

Having concluded that the computer program in question was not copyrightable, the fair use issue was naturally moot. The *Lexmark* court, for the sake of further proceedings, however, nevertheless chose to comment on the district court's fair use interpretation under section 107 of the U.S. Copyright Act.[34] With regard to the first factor listed under section 107 (purpose and character of the use), the court distinguished between mere profit-making and profiting from the exploitation of the copyrighted material without paying the customary price charged by the copyright owner. The court found the defendant copied the computer program for the purpose of achieving interoperability (a particular function), not for the exploitation of plaintiff's expressions. Thus, this factor may not necessarily tilt in plaintiff's favor. On the fourth factor (effect on the potential market), the court put its emphasis not on the toner cartridge market, but on the market of the computer loading program itself. Given that neither party provided any evidence on the adverse effect to the market of the toner loading software program, the court was reluctant to hold this factor in plaintiff's favor either.[35] As a result, even if the computer program were copyrighted work, fair use may be in store for the defendant to claim.

On the plaintiff's DMCA claims, Plaintiff Lexmark argued that the defendant's microchips that contained the TLP 'lock-out' code was a 'device' used to circumvent the 'technical measures' that 'effectively controls access' to plaintiff's 'Printer Engine Program,' (PEP), which is copyright-protected and embedded inside each printer itself. The Sixth Circuit disagreed.[36] The court pointed out that it was not Lexmark's authentication sequence that 'controls access' to the PEP; rather it was the purchase of Lexmark's printer that allows 'access' to the program. Because there was actually no security device to protect access to the PEP, there was nothing to be circumvented. In other words, anyone who purchased a Lexmark printer might read the literal code of PEP directly from the printer memory, with or without the benefit of the authentication sequence, and the data from the program might be translated

---

the National Commission on New Technological Uses of Copyrighted Works, at 20 (31 Jul. 1978).

34. The Copyright Act provides:

Notwithstanding the provisions of ss 106 and 106A, the fair use of a copyrighted work, including such use by reproduction in copies or phonorecords or by any other means specified by that section, for purposes such as criticism, comment, news reporting, teaching (including multiple copies for classroom use), scholarship, or research, is not an infringement of copyright. In determining whether the use made of a work in any particular case is a fair use the factors to be considered shall include – (1) the purpose and character of the use, including whether it is of a commercial nature or is for nonprofit educational purposes; (2) the nature of the copyrighted work; (3) the amount and substantiality of the portion used in relation to the copyrighted work as a whole; and (4) the effect of the use upon the potential market for or value of the copyrighted work. The fact that a work is unpublished shall not itself bar a finding of fair use if such finding is made upon consideration of all the above factors. 17 U.S.C. § 107 (2000 Supp. II).

35. See above, fn. 30, at 544.
36. *Ibid.*, at 546.

into readable source code. Then copies could be freely distributed. Thus, DMCA is inapplicable to readily accessible copyrighted works.[37] In sum, circumventing a 'secret handshake' between a toner cartridge and a printer does not violate the DMCA because the handshake does not 'effectively' control access to a copyrighted work. Rather, the purchase of the printer gives the owner access to the printer code.

D.   STORAGE TECHNOLOGY CORP. (A/K/A STORAGETEK) V. CUSTOM
            HARDWARE ENGINEERING & CONSULTING, INC.[38]

This case presents a similar fact pattern to that of *Lexmark*, but with a twist. Plaintiff StorageTek is the manufacturer of automated data storage machines (or digital libraries). In these machines, two sets of copyrighted codes are used to control and manage the operation of two respective units within: one is called the Management Unit and the other is called the Maintenance Unit. StorageTek claimed that the defendant Custom Hardware Engineering (CHE), an independent repair business specialized in StorageTek machines, infringed on its copyright when CHE rebooted and reconfigured StorageTek's Management and Maintenance Units in a repair process. Alternatively, StorageTek argued that CHE violated the DMCA when it circumvented certain passwords to force the plaintiff's machine to respond and transmit certain messages or codes concerning the potential errors in the system. StorageTek also alleged trade secrets misappropriation against CHE. CHE, on the other hand, alleged that StorageTek committed various antitrust violations.

The U.S. District Court for the District of Massachusetts granted an injunction against CHE and its president, but the Federal Circuit vacated and remanded that judgment. The Federal Circuit, as an issue of first impression, decided that it needed to first interpret the meaning of section 117(c) of the Copyright Act (the safe-harbor rule for the making of a computer program) before heading into the area of circumvention.[39] Having pointed out that Congress enacted this provision

---

37. For an excellent analysis of these recent anti-circumvention cases, see Zohar Efroni, 'A Momentary Lapse of Reason: Digital Copyright: The DMCA and A Dose of Common Sense,' *Columbia J. L. & Arts* 28 (2005): 249.
38. 421 F.3d 1307 (Fed. Cir. 2005).
39. The Copyright Act provides:

    It is not an infringement for the owner or lessee of a machine to make or authorize the making of a computer program if such copy is made solely by virtue of activation of a machine that lawfully contains an authorized copy of the computer program, for purpose only of maintenance or repair of that machine, if – (1) such new copy is used in no other manner and is destroyed immediately after the maintenance or repair is completed; and (2) with respect to any computer program or part thereof that is not necessary for the machine to be activated, such program or part thereof is not accessed or used other than to make such new copy by virtue of the activation of the machine. 17 U.S.C. § 117(c)(2000, Supp. II).

    Note that this provision was added by the DMCA in 1998.

'to ensure that independent service organizations do not inadvertently become liable for copyright infringement merely because they have turned on a machine in order to service its hardware components,'[40] the majority opinion held that 'Congress sought to protect the class of companies that fix and maintain computer systems, as opposed to those that would make other commercial use of copyrighted material.'[41] As a result, the statutory requirement that copies of the maintenance or repair software 'be destroyed immediately after the maintenance or repair is completed' was *not* to create artificial restraints on companies so long as their only reason for copying the software was to fix and maintain the machine on which the software was running.

On the other hand, the majority opinion also pointed out that separate 'free-standing programs' that load into a computer's random access memory (RAM) upon start clearly are not within the scope of the safe-harbor rule under section 117(c)(2), as they are *not* 'necessary for the machine to be activated' (because they do not 'need to be so loaded in order for the machine to be turned on').[42] Here, the court believed that CHE's entire purpose was to diagnose and repair the computer library system and held that CHE was likely to prevail on the merits of safe-harbor rule arguments.

Separately, the court applied the implied license doctrine to counter Storage-Tek's argument that its licenses do not extend to third parties and CHE's use of its system clearly exceeded the scope of the license and thus constituted copyright infringement. The court stressed the principle that 'uses' that violate a license agreement constitute copyright infringement only when those uses would infringe in the absence of any license agreement at all.[43] Here the majority opinion held that '[B]ecause the whole purpose of the license is to allow the tape library owners to activate their machines without being liable for copyright infringement, such activity by the licensee and its agents is implicitly authorized by the license agreement unless the agreement explicitly prohibits third parties from powering up the machines.'[44]

On StorageTek's DMCA claims, the court reiterated the ruling in *Chamberlain* that Congress chose to create new causes of action for circumvention and for trafficking in circumvention devices, but did not choose to create new property rights.[45] Thus, the DMCA must be read in the context of the Copyright Act, which balances the rights of the copyright owner against the public's interest in having appropriate access to the work. Courts generally have found a violation of the DMCA anticircumvention provision only when the alleged access was intertwined with a right protected by the Copyright Act. To the extent that StorageTek's rights under copyright law were not at risk, the DMCA did not create a new source of liability.[46]

---

40. *See* H.R. Report No. 105-551, pt 1, at 27.
41. See above, fn. 38, at 1312.
42. *Ibid.*, at 1314.
43. *Ibid.*, at 1316.
44. *Ibid.*, at 1317.
45. See above, fn. 25, at 1203.
46. See above, fn. 38, at 1318.

With regard to CHE's use of a device to 'crack' the password of the machine, the court pointed out that the copying of CHE's software into RAM when the Control or Management Units are rebooted takes place regardless of whether any cracking device was used. In other words, the court found no nexus between any possible infringement and the use of the circumvention devices.[47] CHE's circumvention of the password only allowed it to use portions of the copyrighted software that StorageTek wished to protect technologically. While the court recognized that the activation of the maintenance code may have violated Storage-Tek's contractual rights vis-à-vis its customers, those were not the rights protected by copyright law.

IV.   ANALYSES AND COMMENTS

Copyright law is designed to maintain a delicate balance between the private, exclusive rights of an individual of a creative work, with the public interest in accessing that work. As a result, a number of exceptions to the exclusive rights are created, such as fair use, in the hope to achieve that balance. As a result, whether infringement indeed took place requires nuanced analyses in light of the specific facts of each case.

By its very nature, technical protection measures, especially access control (or sometimes interchangeably referred to as digital right management (DRM) measures, are incapable of such nuanced analyses, as they laid down layers of invisible walls between the copyrighted work in its entirety and the outside world. Therefore, there have been concerns that the prevalent usage of access control or DRM measures would seriously jeopardize the copyright exceptions, and eventually encroach upon the fundamental value upon which online knowledge dissemination is based.[48]

These concerns, together with *Chamberlain*, inevitably raise a fundamental issue: whether there is or should be a public 'right' of fair use, or at least some sort of 'public right' to access copyrighted works that derives from the Copyright Clause of the Constitution. Traditionally fair use has been treated as an affirmative defense to the exercise of a copyright holder's exclusive rights.[49] In *Chamberlain*, though, the court strongly hinted, if not outright admitted, that such a public right of access did exist and should be used to balance against the copyright holder's enumerated exclusive rights.[50] Such a reading of the copyright statute, however,

---

47. *Ibid.*, at 1319.
48. See B. G. Joseph, 'Copyright Issues on the Internet, the DMCA and Technological Protection,' *PLI/Pat.* 830 (2005): 483 (Advanced Seminar on Copyright Law, 2005).
49. See *Campbell v. Acuff-Rose Music, Inc.*, 510 U.S. 569, 590 (n. 20)(1994). The Second Circuit further elaborated: '[W]e note that the Supreme Court has never held that fair use is constitutionally required, although some isolated statements in its opinions might arguably be enlisted for such a requirement.' *See* Corley, above, fn. 20, at 458.
50. For example, the *Chamberlain* court stated specifically: 'The DMCA does not create a new property right for copyright owners. Nor, for that matter, does it divest the public of the property rights that the Copyright Act has long granted to the public.' See above, fn. 25, at 1204.

is still a minority view in the U.S. at the present stage.[51] A case in point is *StorageTek*. While citing *Chamberlain* for guidance, the same Federal Circuit apparently has carefully backed away from the broad assertion in *Chamberlain*.

On the other hand, there are scholars who proposed that as an integral part of the copyright system, there should be an exclusive 'access right' for the copyright holder in today's digital environment.[52] This is because in the digital environment, physical copies play a secondary role as exploitation quickly shifts to the 'experiencing' of works online. When access equals experiencing, copyright law must be relevant and integrated with this newly developed exclusive right, otherwise it will be unrealistic. This proposition, if adopted, naturally leads to the issue of what impact it may have on the traditional 'first sale' or exhaustion doctrine, now that the copyright holder may virtually obtain full access control. Does it mean the copyright holder will be granted full control over the 'tethered' works? No one seems to know the answers at the present time.[53]

While *Lexmark* made it clear that accessing of a set of codes for the purpose of interoperability ('secret handshake') did not in and of itself render the act a violation under the DMCA, the court still did not provide clear guidelines on what computer program should be copyrightable. The idea/expression dichotomy certainly does not help for those who intend to develop a certain software program without knowing whether that program will indeed come under the realm of copyright protection. Nor will others who intend to access the information know for sure whether that access will result in DMCA violation. In other words, *Chamberlain*, *Lexmark*, and *StorageTek* may have created more confusions and uncertainties than answers to the control access and anticircumvention issues (especially in the antitrafficking area). This can, in turn, have a significant impact on licensing practices and competition as well.

Scholars have suggested that if there should be any fault of the anticircumvention and antitrafficking provisions, it did not rest with enforcement agencies or courts, but the blame should squarely fall in the statute, hence Congress itself.[54] As far as enforcing agencies are concerned, given that there is such a huge gap between rights holders and users, and a consensus is far from reality, the Register of Copyrights is basically left with no real meaningful tools to balance the interests at stake, but is trying to be as 'cautiously creative' as possible yet not to overstep the boundaries to unduly influence the market or technological developments. Courts are equally forced to interpret the statutes with the most reasonable and perhaps best possible outcome while their hands are tightened up with the statutory language. But one thing is clear from the lines of cases thus far: American courts

---

51. See *Bateman v. Mnemonics, Inc.*, 79 F.3d 1532, 1542 (fn. 22) (11th Cir. 1996).
52. See J. C. Ginsburg, 'Essay: From Having Copies to Experiencing Works: The Development of an Access Right in U.S. Copyright Law,' *J. Copyright Soc'y U.S.A.* 50 (2003): 113, at 116.
53. For another excellent article on the subject, see Hsien-chen Li, 'A Case Analysis of the DMCA Anti-circumvention Provisions from Aspects of Fair Use and Competition,' *NCCU Intellectual Property Rev.* 2 (2004): 134 (Taiwan).
54. See above, fn. 37.

may not have much tolerance if any potential plaintiff intends to use DMCA as a tool to restrict competition.

Yet from the policy perspective, before Congress can act prudently, more detailed and thorough empirical studies on the impact of access control or DRM are necessary. While initial data seems to suggest that the public access to copyrighted materials has increased in recent years along with the ever-increased uses of access controls, such as the availability of online digital audio-visual works and services (including distribution channels), entertainment software, digital text and database products, and business software applications or delivery mechanisms, we do not know for sure whether this parallel growth is exclusively co-related between the two or DRM may turn out to be a major hindering factor for the market need of interoperability, and, therefore, prolonging piracy in the long run.[55] Also not clear is whether this is just a phenomenon in the United States alone or it is prevalent throughout the world. The concern has always been the ever-widening fall line between the haves and the have-nots, or the so-called 'information divide.'[56]

V.   CONCLUSION: THE GOOD, THE BAD, AND THE UGLY

The passage of anticircumvention provisions in the DMCA ushered the entire copyright system into unfamiliar territory. Instead of a nuanced, unfettered, yet cautiously balanced maneuver between copyright holders and the public in the past, courts now must still do the same under the DMCA, still standing on a tightrope, but with both hands tightened. The right of 'access control' may have indeed changed the copyright fundamentals for the first time in many years and we the human being, while enjoying the coming of the online digital era and the wider spread of information or knowledge dissemination, do not seem to be ready for all the potential consequences, some of which may potentially and seriously hinder the very progress of e-commerce. Perhaps only time will tell, but in the meantime,

---

55. For data concerning the growth of public access and widespread use of control access, see Metalitz, above, fn. 15. For initial empirical studies suggesting that current DRM technology is actually hindering the market need for interoperability and, therefore, becoming a market barrier and may be actually hurting the audio-visual industry as a whole and prolonging piracy, see iSuppli Corporation, 'Digital Rights Management and Conditional Access: Keys to the Digital Content Kingdom,' <www.isuppli.com/whitepapers/pdf/MMCS.pdf> (2006): at 6-7; see also A. Bruno, 'iTunes at Center of Digital Rights Protest,' *Reuters/Billboard* (16 Jun. 2006).

56. The United Nations studies have consistently pointed out that huge disparities exist in the access and use of information technologies, and that these disparities are not likely to be removed in the near future unless a concerted action is taken at the national, regional, and the international levels. See U.N. Department of Economic and Social Affairs (DESA), Division for Public Administration and Development Management, 'United Nations Global E-government Readiness Report 2005: From E-government to E-inclusion,' UNPAN/2005/14, <http://unpan1.un.org/intradoc/groups/public/documents/un/unpan021888.pdf> (2005). See also S. Basu, 'E-government and Developing Countries: Role of Technology and Law,' <www.digitaldivide.net/articles/view.php?ArticleID=601> (2006).

whether the American DMCA model offers the best possible solution remains to be seen. Although the jury is still out, the initial verdict is already in: given that both WCT and WPPT do require each Member State to comply with the rules on anticircumvention, the practical effect is that all nations must sooner or later adopt relevant anticircumvention standards and balance these against fair use.

So at least for now, when dealing with anticircumvention and access control issues, we may be witnessing a landscape of the good, the bad, and the ugly. The good is that there is finally some governance over the use of technical measures and their relationship with the existing copyright regime. The bad, though, is that it is still a developing gray area filled with vagueness. Arguably the quality of DRM or access controls has not reached the level of interoperability where users can seamlessly operate on various devices. On the contrary, the negative perception by the end users is likely to enable piracy to continue longer. This can be quite a nightmare for those who have anything to do with legitimate repair and/or re-tooling business to manage and to compete. The ugly is that such uncertainties may provide the opportunities to invite more corporate intimidation and litigation.[57] We must be mindful that experiences have demonstrated, time and time again, that technological measures simply will not provide the final solution to piracy, although it will indeed slow the spread of piracy at best, causing more inconvenience along the way, particularly for legitimate users. Thus, anticircumvention provisions alone will not lead to a more pro-competitive global society and provide effective contours for knowledge and information dissemination, particularly to the poor. A more coherent and comprehensive strategy involving more than mere legal solution is needed to combat piracy. Given the complexity of this area, it does take the wisdom of all to craft up a better and more effective, balanced, and harmonized copyright system involving multi-facet approaches that encompass and combine legal, management, and technological tools. Only a strong enough international and domestic intellectual property enforcement mechanism as well as an effective licensing regime will render future addition of access control measures unnecessary both in terms of cost and effectiveness. International harmonization and interoperability are the two ultimate objectives for this strategy to work, and this is a long-term job for all, not just the users or copyright holders alone, to commit and to accomplish.

---

57. An example is the legal battle between Edward W. Felten, a famed cryptographer and a professor at Princeton University, and the Recording Industry Association of America (RIAA), over the publication of Felten's and his team members' successful decoding of RIAA's digital copyright protection scheme challenge. See J. Black & P. O'Connell, 'A "Speed Bump" v. Music Copying: Master Cryptographer – and Code Cracker – Edward Felten Says Technology Isn't the Answer to Digital Copyright Violations,' *BusinessWeek*, <www.businessweek.com/bwdaily/dnflash/jan2002/nf2002019_7170.htm> (9 Jan. 2002). See also H. Green, 'Are the Copyright Wars Chilling Innovation?,' *BusinessWeek*, <www.businessweek.com/bwdaily/dnflash/jan2002/nf2002019_7170.htm> (11 Oct. 2004): 210.

Part 4

Issues under Trade Mark and Design Law

Chapter 6

Trademarks and Reconditioned Goods in Greater China and at Common Law

Michael D. Pendleton

I.   INTRODUCTION

This chapter deals with the vexed question of reconditioned or spare parts and trademark law in Hong Kong and China. The question seems vexed in most jurisdictions and extends to other intellectual property (IP) causes of action as we will see in the other chapters of this book. IP protection for spare parts across the various IP causes of action is often cumulative, that is, one must address the trademark, patent, copyright, and other cause of action issues in relation to the same spare part.

It is important to note, and has been highlighted in the first two chapters, that the issue of reconditioned or spare parts and IP often puts consumer and competitor interests at variance with originator interests. Of course, these are always at variance in the context of IP, but in the context of spare parts are more aggravated because of the distinction between the justifications for IP rights on the one hand and how they should be allowed to be exercised on the other. In many jurisdictions the question of how IP rights are allowed to be exercised is addressed by competition law, yet in Hong Kong, sadly we have never had a competition, trade practices, or antitrust law. A recent attempt to submit a Private Members Bill in the Hong Kong Legislative Assembly for a competition law was defeated. Hong Kong

Christopher Heath, Anselm Kamperman Sanders (eds.), *Spares, Repairs and Intellectual Property Rights*, pp. 127-145.
© 2009 Kluwer Law International BV, The Netherlands.

must be one of the few economically developed economies in the world without a competition law. It is openly acknowledged that the reason for the opposition to a competition law in Hong Kong is due to lobbying by the small number of families that are allowed to bid for the release of new land by the government. China has recently introduced an anti-monopoly law, and certain restrictive trade practices are also addressed in the Unfair Competition Act.

II.   HONG KONG

A.   TRADE MARKS ORDINANCE (CAP 43) LHK

On 4 April 2003, a new Trade Marks Ordinance (Cap 559) ('the new TMO') came into operation.[1] The new TMO is based closely on the United Kingdom Trade Marks Act 1994, which in turn was enacted as part of the harmonization process for the trademark laws of European Union members.[2] The new TMO is therefore modelled on the trademark laws of the countries of the European Union; the decisions of the United Kingdom courts and tribunals and of the European Court of Justice (ECJ), although not binding, will no doubt be of persuasive authority in its interpretation.[3]

1.   Refilling, Repackaging, and Repair

Repackaging, refilling, repair, making a new product – these are fine distinctions of fact and degree and for what purposes the distinction is made. The recent Hong Kong decision in *KPSS Kao Professional Salon Services GMBH v. Southern Group Ltd*[4] was about refilling rather than repair, but similar issues arose.

The plaintiff manufactures hair products, including hair gels in respect of which it owns the registered trademarks 'Goldwell'. The plaintiff claimed that the defendant infringed the trademarks and passed off goods sold by reference to signs identical or similar to the trademarks as and for the plaintiff's goods. The main complaint in the plaintiff's evidence is that the label on the jars sold by the defendant was inferior. There is no evidence that the contents of the jars were not genuine.

---

1. Commencement notice L.N. 31 of 2003. The new Trade Marks Rules (L.N. 30 of 2003) as amended by Legislative Council Resolution dated 3 Apr. 2003 (L.N. 97 of 2003) also came into force on the same date.
2. The Trade Marks Act 1994 is the governing legislation in the United Kingdom and came into force on 31 Oct. 1994.
3. The text of the new TMO and of the new Trade Marks Rules (as amended by Legislative Council Resolution) can be seen in the database of the Laws of Hong Kong at <www.justice.gov.hk>. The Trade Marks Registry Work Manual can be seen on the Intellectual Property Department's website at <www.ipd.gov.hk> As to the legal effect of the Works Manual, see *DU PONT Trade Mark* (2004) FSR.
4. (2005) 1749 HKCU 1.

Under the new law, section 14 of the new Ordinance gives the owner of a registered trademark the exclusive rights in the trademark, which rights are infringed by use of the trademark in Hong Kong without the owner's consent. The infringing acts are defined by section 18 of the new Ordinance as follows:

(1) A person infringes a registered trademark if he uses in the course of trade or business a sign which is identical to the trademark in relation to goods or services which are identical to those for which it is registered.

(2) A person infringes a registered trademark if:
   (i)   he uses in the course of trade or business a sign which is identical to the trademark in relation to goods or services which are similar to those for which it is registered; and
   (ii) the use of the sign in relation to the goods or services is likely to cause confusion on the part of the public.

(3) A person infringes a registered trademark if:
   (i)   he uses in the course of trade or business a sign which is similar to the trademark in relation to goods or services which are identical or similar to those for which it is registered; and
   (ii) the use of the sign in relation to the goods or services is likely to cause confusion on the part of the public.

(4) A person infringes a registered trademark if:
   (i)   he uses in the course of trade or business a sign which is identical or similar to the trademark in relation to goods or services which are not identical or similar to those for which it is registered;
   (ii) the trademark is entitled to protection under the Paris Convention as a well-known trademark; and
   (iii) the use of the sign, being without due cause, takes unfair advantage of, or is detrimental to, the distinctive character or repute of the trademark.

The judge decision (in footnote 41) referred to section 21 of the new TMO, which he said makes it possible for a trader to use a competitor's trademarks for the purpose of identifying the latter's goods or services, provided that such use is 'in accordance with honest practices in industrial or commercial matters'.

27. I note that the defence in section 21 is primarily directed at advertising. The learned authors of *Intellectual Property Rights, Hong Kong SAR and Peoples' Republic of China* say at paragraph II [976.1] that it is primarily directed, but not restricted to comparative advertising and 'it may also cover for example repaired or reconditioned goods of the proprietor'.

28. Perhaps my approach is unsophisticated, and it is true that I have no great experience of infringement or passing off cases, but it seems to me that the absence of any evidence that the hair gel was or was not the original hair gel made by the plaintiffs is an important factor. As I have indicated, there is no such evidence. The plaintiff's witness seems to indicate that what the defendant sold was not genuine but that is as far as it goes.

29. Without knowing that the contents were not genuine, it is difficult to go further than suspicion, and say that the re-labelling must have been dishonest. Obviously there is suspicion; if the contents are genuine, why would anyone scrape off the numbers and put on new labels? On the other hand, why does the plaintiff itself scrape numbers on the lids, and cover them with adhesive labels in the first place? Perhaps the answer is that the plaintiff itself puts new gel in old jars. In any event the answer is not so obvious that dishonesty must be inferred.

30. As to whether the quality of the defendant's labels is detrimental to the distinctive character or repute of the plaintiff's trade marks [sic], this seems to me far-fetched. For my own part, I cannot see why the label should matter. The customer gets a plastic stick-on label or a paper stick-on label with the same words and logos and in almost the same shade of blue. One wonders if the average customer cares, one way or the other, what the label looks like, so long as the hair gel does what he or she expects it to do. Perhaps the customer does care; perhaps they will buy the plastic label but will not buy the paper one; but I think that some evidence from customers that it mattered to them, rather than bare assertions by the plaintiff would be necessary to show detriment.

Thus the judge found the use honest and the section 21 defence succeeded.

2.   Establishing Infringement under Section 18 of the Trade Mark Ordinance

Where a person uses a sign in the course of trade[5] or business,[6] the following issues arise on the question of infringement:

(1) whether the sign and the registered mark are identical or similar;[7]

---

5.   'Trade Mark Ordinance' includes a profession: s. 2(1) of the new Ordinance.
6.   The use by the alleged infringer must be in the course of trade or business in Hong Kong: s. 14(1) of the new Ordinance. See also *Beautimatic International Ltd v. Mitchell International Pharmaceuticals Ltd* (2000) FSR 267. The court should consider whether the defendant has any trade in Hong Kong or has any customers buying goods or services for consumption in Hong Kong: *Euromarket Designs Inc v. Peters and Crate & Barrel Ltd* (2001) FSR 288, where Jacob J held that use of a sign on the Internet in a website should not be regarded as a use in every country of the world. It may be different, of course, if the use is directed to customers or potential customers in Hong Kong, or sales to and in Hong Kong result. See also *800-FLOWERS Trade Mark* (2002) FSR 191 (CA) and *Bonnier Media Ltd v. Greg Lloyd Smith and Kestrel Trading Corp* (2002) ETMR 1050 (Ct of Session, Scotland) as to use on the Internet.
7.   Where the registered mark is a word mark, and the defendant's sign consists of that word with other words, United Kingdom decisions are unclear as to whether the mark and the sign is identical, or that they are to be dealt with under the principles set out in para. 926. First instance decisions so far suggest that they are identical: see *British Sugar Plc v. James Robertson & Sons Ltd* (1996) RPC 281; *Aktiebolaget Volvo v. Heritage (Leicester) Ltd* (2000) FSR 253; *AAH Pharmaceuticals Ltd v. Vantagemax Plc* (2003) ETMR 205 (cf *Premier Luggage and Bags Ltd v. Premier Co (UK) Ltd* (2003) FSR 69 at 89). In *Thomson Holidays Ltd v. Norwegian Cruise Lines Ltd* (2003) RPC 586 (CA), the registered mark was the word 'FREESTYLE' and the defendant's use of 'FREESTYLE CRUISING' and 'NCL FREESTYLE CRUISING' was

(2) whether the goods or services in relation to which the sign is used are identical or similar to those for which the mark is registered;[8]

(3) unless there is identity in both issues one and two above,[9] whether the use of the sign in relation to those goods or services is likely to cause confusion on the part of the public.

These questions are separate and are considered further below.

The use must be 'in the course of trade' (old section 27) 'in connection with the provision of any services' (old section 27A) or 'in the course of trade or business' (new section 18).

The wording of old section 27 required that the use of a trademark for goods had to be in the course of *some* trade, as opposed to being for private or domestic purposes. It was unclear, however, whether the infringer had to be actually trading in the goods registered. In *Ravok (M) (Weatherwear) Ltd v. National Trade Press*,[10] Lord Goddard held that it had to be, relying on the definition of trademark in *Aristoc v. Rysta*.[11] More recently, however, infringement was found in two cases where the infringer was not actually trading in the relevant goods, although his field of trade was closely connected. In *Rolls-Royce v. Dodd*,[12] the defendant was a motor engineer who built and used a car bearing a number of Rolls-Royce's marks registered for motor cars. It was common ground that the defendant did not trade in motor cars and that he was merely publicizing his business. Whitford J nevertheless granted an interlocutory injunction on the basis that the defendant had applied Rolls-Royce's marks in the course of his trade as a motor engineer. In a slightly later case, *Ind Coope v. Paine & Co Ltd*,[13] the same judge held at trial that the

---

held to be a use of identical marks. The above should be read in the light of the opinion of the ECJ in *SA Societe LTJ Diffusion v. Sadas Vertbaudet SA* (2003) FSR 608, which has since been followed in the United Kingdom: see the discussion at para. 475.20. The position is also not clear where the defendant's sign consists of the registered word mark plus additional letters making it also a word but one that is different overall. In *Decon Laboratories Ltd v. Fred Baker Scientific Ltd* (2001) RPC 293, where the registered mark was 'Decon' and the defendant used it as the prefix to words, Pumfrey J also considered them to be identical. Cf. *Origins Natural Resources Inc v. Origin Clothing Ltd* (1995) FSR 280, and *IDG Communications Ltd's Trade Mark* (2002) RPC 283 (TM Reg), where a word in the singular was considered not identical to the word in the plural. The same conclusion was reached by the appointed person (Simon Thorley QC) in *REACT Trade Mark* (2000) RPC 285 ('React' and 'Reactor'). See also *NUTRITIVE Trade Mark* (1998) RPC 621 (TM Reg). See also para. 475.20 above. In *Prudential Assurance Co Ltd v. Prudential Insurance Co of America* (2004) FSR 498 (CA), the trade mark 'PRUMERICA' was held to be not identical with 'PRU' or 'PRUDENTIAL'. This latter line of cases would appear to be consistent with the ECJ opinion.

8. Where the mark used is a 'well-known trademark' and the goods or services on which the alleged infringing sign is used on goods or services not identical or similar to those for which the mark is registered, s. 18(4) is applicable.

9. Where confusion is probably inevitable and assumed by the legislature: see *CORGI Trade Mark* (1998) RPC 549 at 557 (the appointed person), citing Art. 16(1) of the TRIPS Agreement.

10. (1955) 1 QB 554; 72 RPC 110.

11. (1945) AC 68; 62 RPC 65.

12. (1981) FSR 517.

13. (1983) RPC 326.

defendant, who sold beer-making kits (and not beer), had infringed the plaintiff's trademark registered for beer. It is submitted that the better view is that the infringer of a trademark for goods could only infringe if he used the mark in the course of carrying out some trading activity. This construction is also consistent with the corresponding part of section 27A. The infringing use had still to be in *relation* to the service registered, but there is no requirement that it was made in connection with the provision of that particular service; it was only essential that it be used in connection with the provision of *some service*. The requirement under the new law is that the alleged infringing sign must be used, 'in the course of trade or business' (section 18), and in this respect the new law should be the same as the old law. Use was confined under the old law by section 2(2)(a) to a printed or other visual representation of the mark. Oral use cannot infringe. Under the new law, use includes any use and is not confined to a graphic representation.

In *Orfevrerie Cristofle SA v. Coway*,[14] the defendant's use of its mark in Hong Kong consisted of keeping watches bearing the mark for reference in relation to its watch trade, using the mark in advertisements for its watches in the Yellow Pages directory and showing watches bearing the mark to a potential customer enquiring into its watches in Indonesia. Deputy Judge Leong held[15] that the above constituted infringement of the plaintiff's mark registered for watches and that usage of the mark in Hong Kong for the purpose of trade in Indonesia could still be infringement even if there was no intention or attempt to sell the goods in Hong Kong.

3.   Section 19(3): Honest Practices in Industrial and Commercial Practices

The new TMO enhances the protection offered to the owners of registered trademarks in a number of ways, as evidenced in section 18, which mirrors the wording of the Relative Grounds in section 12 and broadens the definition of infringement by including the situation of the use of identical or similar marks in respect of *dissimilar* goods or services, and by removing the requirement that the mark be used by the infringer in a trademark sense. On the other hand, comparative advertising is now allowed, provided that the conditions set out in section 21 are satisfied.

4.   Infringement by Use

Under the relevant provisions of the old TMO,[16] a mark is infringed if any person other than its proprietor or registered user uses a similar or identical mark in the

---

14. Deputy Judge J Leong QC, 1 Apr. 1993 – HCA No 2517 of 1992.
15. Relying on *Reuter v. Muhlens* (1954) Ch. 50; 70 RPC 102; *Vac-U-Flex TM* (1965) FSR 176 and *Official Ruling 1944A* (1944) 61 RPC 148.
16. HK Trade Mark Ordinance, ss 27 (infringement of Part A trademarks), 27A (infringement of Part A service marks), 28 (infringement of Part B trademarks) and 28A (infringement of Part B service marks).

course of trade in relation to any goods in respect of which it is registered, such use being either:

(1) use as a trademark; or
(2) use on goods or in advertising material so as to import a reference to some person having the right either as proprietor or registered user to use the mark, or to goods with which such a person is connected in the course of trade.

In *Stichting Greenpeace Council v. Income Team Ltd & Ors*,[17] the plaintiff, an international environmental organization, sued the defendant companies for infringing its mark 'GREEN PEACE', which had been registered in some 120 countries including Hong Kong. One of the issues was whether the use of the name 'GREEN PEACE' on the defendants' hang-tags, shopping bags, sales memos, credit card receipts, business cards, and mailing list application forms constituted 'use as a trademark' under section 27(1)(a) of the old TMO. Notwithstanding that the clothes sold in the defendants' shops bore the overseas manufacturers' marks, the Hong Kong High Court held that the defendants had offered the clothes for sale under and by reference to the mark 'GREEN PEACE', such use being more than sufficient to constitute trademark use.

In an earlier Hong Kong case, *Levi Strauss & Co v. Maruichi Holdings (HK) Ltd*,[18] the provision of sample counterfeit 'Levi 501' jeans followed by a quotation also constituted use of the mark 'Levi 501' in the trademark sense.

Now, section 18 of the new TMO simply refers to the use of a sign 'in the course of trade or business'. Furthermore, section 18(5) expressly provides that a person uses a sign if he:

(1) applies it to goods or their packaging;
(2) offers or exposes goods for sale under the sign;
(3) puts goods on the market under the sign;
(4) stocks goods under the sign for the purpose of offering or exposing them for sale or of putting them on the market;
(5) offers or supplies services under the sign;
(6) imports or exports goods under the sign; or
(7) uses the sign on business papers or in advertising.

Thus, what the defendants did in the *Greenpeace* case will still be infringement under the new TMO.

In the United Kingdom, the question of whether 'use' in the equivalent provision, viz, section 10 of the 1994 Act, should be interpreted as 'use in a trademark sense' was addressed by Jacob J in *British Sugar Plc v. James Robertson & Sons Ltd*[19] as follows:

I see no need to put any gloss upon the language of section 10. It merely requires the court to see whether the sign registered as a trade mark is used in

---

17. (1997) FSR 149.
18. (1992) 1 HKC 419.
19. (1996) RPC 281.

the course of trade and then to consider whether that use falls within one of the three defining subsections.

This was followed in *Philips Electronics NV v. Remington Consumer Products Ltd,*[20] where the Court of Appeal confirmed that section 10 does not require the infringing use to be trademark use.

Given that section 18 adopts the language of section 12, what is said above in relation to similarity of marks, similarity of goods or services, and likelihood of confusion in respect of the Relative Grounds is also relevant to the interpretation and application of section 18. In addition to the opposition cases discussed above, the following United Kingdom infringement cases will also help in our understanding of the requirements for infringement under the new TMO.

In *Wagamama Ltd v. City Centre Restaurants Plc,*[21] Laddie J confirmed that 'classic infringement' in the sense of confusion as to the source or origin of goods or services is applicable to infringement under section 10 of the 1994 Act as it was under section 4 of the 1938 Act. Reference was also made to the approach recently set out by Jacob J in *Origins Natural Resources Inc v. Origin Clothing Ltd:*[22]

> Section 10 of the Trade Marks Act presupposes that the plaintiff's mark is in use or will come into use. It requires the court to assume the mark of the plaintiff is used in a normal and fair manner in relation to the goods for which it is registered and then to assess the likelihood of confusion in relation to the way the defendant uses its mark, discounting external added matter or circumstances. The comparison is mark for [sign].[23]

This is not at all different from the test for likelihood of deception under section 12(1) of the 1938 Act enunciated by Evershed J in *Smith Hayden & Co's Application:*[24]

> Assuming user [sic] of [the opponents' marks] in a normal and fair manner for any of the goods covered by the registrations of these marks (and including particularly goods also covered by the proposed registration of [the applicants' mark]), is the court satisfied that there will be no reasonable likelihood of deception and confusion amongst a substantial number of persons if [the applicants] also use their mark normally and fairly in respect of any goods covered by their proposed registration?[25]

---

20. (2006) EWCA Civ 847.
21. (1995) FSR 713.
22. (1995) FSR 280 at 284.
23. As corrected by Jacob J himself in *British Sugar* (fn. 21 above) at 293.
24. (1946) RPC 97. Fn. 22 above, where the test for s. 11 of the 1938 Act is discussed. Note that Evershed J was cautious in choosing the words for the two tests in order to reflect the difference in their requirements. The test for s. 12(1), which basically requires a comparison of marks, begins with the words 'Assuming user', whereas that for s. 11, which deals with a much broader sense of likelihood of deception, requires the court to 'have regard to the user'.
25. 'User' substituting for 'reputation' as suggested by the House of Lords in *BALI Trade Mark* ((1969) RPC 372).

This test, having been applied in numerous Hong Kong and United Kingdom cases, including those decided under the 1994 Act,[26] will certainly remain relevant to opposition and infringement under the new TMO. Also relevant will be the doctrine of imperfect recollection in relation to which Laddie J in *Wagamama* quoted the following judgment of the Privy Council in *de Cordova v. Vick Chemical Co*:[27]

It is more useful to observe that in most persons the eye is not an accurate recorder of visual detail, and that marks are remembered rather by general impressions or by some significant detail than by any photographical recollection of the whole.

An illustration would be *Portakabin Ltd v. Powerblast Ltd*,[28] an infringement case under the 1938 Act. In this case, in comparing the marks 'Portoblast' and 'Porta', Mummery J had regard to the idea of the marks and said:

The addition of the next five letters, 'blast', in the defendant's mark, does not diminish the resemblance of 'Portoblast' to the registered mark 'Porta' in its essential features or idea.

Upon establishment of infringement of his registered trademark, a plaintiff may be granted relief by way of damages, injunctions, accounts of profits or otherwise[29] (section 22(3) of the new TMO). Besides, he may also apply for orders for delivery up and disposal under sections 23 and 25, respectively. Note that such orders are available not only against infringing goods, but also against infringing material and articles as defined in sections 17(3) and (4).[30]

5. Comparative Advertising

Comparative advertising may often arise in the repair/reconditioning context. The status of comparative advertising was unclear under the old TMO. The expression

---

26. See, for instance, *BALMORAL Trade Mark* ((1998) RPC 297) and *REACT and Device Trade Mark* (1999) RPC 529 (confirmed by the Appointed Person at (2000) RPC 285).
27. (1951) 68 RPC 103, at 106.
28. (1990) RPC 471.
29. In *Portakabin Ltd v. Powerblast Ltd*, the plaintiff was granted, inter alia, an order for obliteration or destruction on oath of references to the mark from articles and advertising material.
30. See also Art. 46 of the TRIPS Agreement:

In order to create an effective deterrent to infringement, the judicial authorities shall have the authority to order that goods that they have found to be infringing be, without compensation of any sort, disposed of outside the channels of commerce in such a manner as to avoid any harm caused to the right holder, or, unless this would be contrary to existing constitutional requirements, destroyed. The judicial authorities shall also have the authority to order that materials and implements the predominant use of which has been in the creation of the infringing goods be, without compensation of any sort, disposed of outside the channels of commerce in such a manner as to minimize the risks of further infringements. In considering such requests, the need for proportionality between the seriousness of the infringement and the remedies ordered as well as the interests of third parties shall be taken into account. In regard to counterfeit trademark goods, the simple removal of the trademark unlawfully affixed shall not be sufficient, other than in exceptional cases, to permit release of the goods into the channels of commerce.

used in section 27(1) is 'importing a reference', the meaning of which depends upon the nature of the mark and the facts in each case. The use of a mark that consists of an invented word, for instance, can easily be treated as 'importing a reference' to its proprietor or his goods as it could scarcely be used except for that purpose.[31]

Section 21 of the new TMO now clarifies the ambiguous legal position and makes it possible for a trader to use a competitor's trademarks for the purpose of identifying the latter's goods or services, provided that such use is 'in accordance with honest practices in industrial or commercial matters'. Although 'use' is not further defined, the explicit heading 'Use in advertising etc.' confirms that comparative advertising is within the ambit of the section.

> In determining whether a use is in accordance with honest practices in industrial or commercial matters, the court may consider such factors as it considers relevant, including:
>
> (a) whether the use takes unfair advantage of the trademark;
> (b) whether the use is detrimental to the distinctive character or repute of the trademark; or
> (c) whether the use is such as to deceive the public.[32]
>
> But any such use otherwise than in accordance with honest practices in industrial or commercial matters shall be treated as infringing the registered trademark if the use without due cause takes unfair advantage of, or is detrimental to, the distinctive character or repute of the trademark.

In the United Kingdom, the parallel provision, section 10(6) of the 1994 Act, has been considered in *Barclays Bank Plc v. RBS Advanta*,[33] *Vodafone Group Plc v. Orange Personal Communications Services Ltd*[34] and *Cable & Wireless Plc v. British Telecommunications Plc*.[35]

In the first case, Barclays Bank sought an interlocutory injunction to restrain RBS Advanta from distributing advertising literature that included a brochure containing a comparative table of fees and interest rates for various credit cards, including the Barclaycard. On the construction of section 10(6), Laddie J said:[36]

> [T]he primary objective of section 10(6) is to allow comparative advertising. As long as the use of the competitor's mark is 'honest', then there is nothing wrong with telling the public of the relative merits of competing goods or services and using registered trade marks to identify them.

---

31. See *Kerly's Law of Trade Marks and Trade Names*, 12th edn (Sweet & Maxwell, 1986), 277, para. 14-27, and the cases referred to therein.
32. Section 21(2). Cf s. 10(6) of the 1994 Act: 'Nothing in the preceding provisions of this section shall be construed as preventing the use of a registered trademark by any person for the purpose of identifying goods or services as those of the proprietor or a licensee.'
33. (1996) RPC 307.
34. (1997) FSR 34.
35. (1998) FSR 383.
36. Fn. 32 above, at 315.

Laddie J then made two observations in relation to the application of the section:

> First . . . the onus is on the registered proprietor to show that the factors indicated in the proviso exist . . .
>
> Secondly, there will be no infringement unless the use of the registered mark is not in accordance with honest practices. Both counsel agreed, rightly in my view, that this test is objective. This part of the proviso simply means that if the use is considered honest by members of a reasonable audience, it will not infringe. The fact that the advertising pokes fun at the proprietor's goods or services and emphasises the benefits of the defendant's is a normal incidence of comparative advertising. Its aim will be to divert customers from the proprietor. No reasonable observer would expect one trader to point to all the advantages of its competitor's business and failure to do so does not *per se* take the advertising outside what reasonable people would regard as 'honest'. Thus mere trade puffery, even if uncomfortable to the registered proprietor, does not bring the advertising within the scope of trade mark infringement.[37]

This was followed in *Vodafone Group Plc v. Orange Personal Communications Services Ltd* and *Cable & Wireless Plc v. British Telecommunications Plc.* In *Vodafone*, Jacob J reiterated Laddie J's criticism that the words 'without due cause takes unfair advantage of, or is detrimental to, the distinctive character or repute of the trademark' added nothing of significance to the requirement of 'in accordance with honest practices'. In *Cable & Wireless*, again a decision of Jacob J, the learned judge emphasized that the test of honesty was an objective one: whether a reasonable trader could honestly have made the statements he made based upon the information that he had. What is said in all these cases should be equally applicable in the interpretation of section 21 in Hong Kong.

6.   Exceptions to Infringement

Section 19(2) of the new TMO provides that a registered trademark is not infringed by the use of another registered trademark in relation to goods or services for which the latter is registered. This corresponds to section 11(1) of the 1994 Act, which is inserted to reinforce the protection offered by the honest concurrent use provisions.

Section 19(3) further provides that the following is not infringement if it is in accordance with honest practices in industrial or commercial matters:

(1) the use by a person of his own name or address or the name of his place of business;

(2) the use of a person of the name of his predecessor in business or the name of his predecessor's place of business;

(3) the use of signs which serve to designate the kind, quality, quantity, intended purpose, value, geographical origin, time of production of

---

37. *Ibid.* The 'proviso' refers to the second paragraph in s. 10(6) of the 1994 Act (fn. 32 above).

goods or rendering of services, or other characteristics of goods or services; or

(4) the use of the trademark where it is necessary to indicate the intended purpose of goods or services (for example, as accessories or spare parts).

This is similar to, but not identical with, section 11(2) of the 1994 Act. In *British Sugar Plc v. James Robertson & Sons Ltd,*[38] Jacob J drew a distinction between using a sign as a trademark and using a sign to describe goods or services, and held that only the latter was covered by section 11(2).[39] In the instant case, looking at the whole context of the use of the word 'Treat', in particular its appearance alongside the maker's name, Jacob J held that the use was within the ambit of section 11(2).

Even under the old TMO, section 27(1) is subject to sections 33 and 34, the former making specific reference to honest concurrent use under section 22, while the latter refers to bona fide use of one's own name[40] and bona fide description of the character or quality of one's goods.

B.   OWNERSHIP OF THE BADGE OF RECOGNITION: MANUFACTURER, DEALER, OR DISTRIBUTOR

Common Law Passing-Off

Passing-off was also pleaded in *KPSS Kao Professional Salon Services GMBH v. Southern Group Ltd,*[41] considered above. You will recall the defendant had refilled with hair gel jars branded with the plaintiff's marks. The plaintiff asserted that the quality of the packaging, including the trademarks, applied to the plaintiff's products was regarded by consumers as significant, and the use of the infringing label, which is of inferior quality, interferes with the original packaging in a way inconsistent with the expectation of the customers. Deputy High Court Judge Muttrie held:

> On passing off, much the same considerations apply. We do not know whether the gel is genuine or not. If it is genuine, there can surely be no misrepresentation and no damage flowing from misrepresentation.[42]

Difficult questions arise where trading activity is conducted solely by a dealer, distributor, or repairer in contradistinction to the innovator, designer, or manufacturer of goods. In *Guangzhou Green-Enhan Bio-Engineering Co Ltd & Sun*

---

38. (1996) RPC 281.
39. *Ibid.*
40. See *Nad Electronics Inc v. Nad Computer Systems Ltd* (1997) FSR 380, where the 'own name defence' was considered under both s. 8 of the 1938 Act and s. 11(2) of the 1994 Act.
41. (2005) 1749 HKCU 1.
42. *Ibid.*, at 3.

Yat-Sen University v. Green Power Health Products Int. Co Ltd & Others[43] there was a dispute as to the ownership of intellectual property between entities in Hong Kong and Southern China. The plaintiff is a division of Sun Yat-Sen (or Zhongshan) University (Plaintiff) in Guangzhou (Canton), concerned with researching Chinese medicine. It developed a technology for denuding or 'cracking' the protective cover of a type of mushroom (lingzhi) spore. This spore was shown by the university's research to be beneficial for general health but many individuals did not have the metabolism to break down the protective covering over the spore and did not benefit. Thus devised, the product required marketing in mainland China and Hong Kong. It appears the plaintiff had very little or anything to do with the brand names, packaging, or other aspects of marketing. The nature of the agreement as to ownership of IP and in what jurisdictions, between the plaintiff and the Hong Kong individuals and companies (Defendants), and the result of the agreement made under Chinese law in terms of ownership in Hong Kong of IP yet to come into existence, was the core issue in the decision. Ultimately, Lam J held that an implied term of contract operated under the law of the contract, that is mainland China, to grant ownership of all IP to the plaintiff.[44]

The situation in the present case was that the parties had agreed (albeit impliedly according to my above analysis) upon the ownership of goodwill to be generated by activities involving both of them in the future. Is there any reason the law should not give effect to such an agreement? In my judgment, the answer is no. It may not be a licensing agreement in the strict sense, it is still an agreement concerning ownership of goodwill that could be enforceable in the eyes of the law.

A number of causes of action were pleaded including passing-off, contract, registered trademarks, copyright, and malicious falsehood.

In respect of the claim in passing-off, Lam J, held that goodwill, which is a condition precedent to a passing-off action, was to come into being in the future in Hong Kong, and belonged to the plaintiff manufacturer by virtue of an implied term of contract pursuant to Chinese contract law (the proper law of the contract). The relevant badge of recognition, aside from the product name, was the get-up of the boxes containing the medication. Ultimately, Lam J appeared to treat get-up as excluding copyright material, registered trademark material, and other material that was the subject matter of other IP causes of action (which he dealt with separately). The get-up, or total appearance, of the product was thus denuded of significant parts of the product's actual appearance. Thus denuded of other materials, the get-up was found to be non-distinctive and incapable of serving as a badge of recognition, the first element of the cause of action for passing-off. This, with respect, seems contrary to established authority and an odd result. IP causes of action are not mutually exclusive of one another but cumulative. An action for registered trademark infringement, copyright, designs, or confidence does not

---

43. Court of First Instance, <http://legalref.judiciary.gov.hk/lrs/common/search/search_result_detail_frame.jsp?DIS=44883&QS=%28%24zhongshan%7Cuniversity%7Cv%7Cgreen%7Cpower%29&TP=JU> 8 Apr. 2005.
44. *Ibid.*, para. 73.

preclude a passing-off action in respect of the self same material, be it a logo, name, or other element or badge of consumer recognition.

On the facts outlined by the judge in this case, it seems the relevant badges of recognition in the compendious sense, which are the basis of the goodwill and reputation, were by and large conceived or coined by defendants. Further, the activities of distribution of the goods under those badges of recognition were activities of the defendants. Lam J draws attention to the distinction between manufacturer's marks and dealer's marks and refers to *Shanahan, Australian Law of Trade Marks and Passing Off.*

104. In *Shanahan, Australian Law of Trade Marks and Passing Off,* 2nd Edition, p. 42-43, a distinction was drawn between two classes of trade marks. The first class is manufacturer's marks, which the learned author described as follows: 'A manufacturer who has applied a mark to goods to indicate that he or she is the "origin" of the goods is most unlikely to be denied proprietorship because of the activities of some dealer in those goods. The evidence in these cases will generally show that in the hands of the dealer, the mark has retained its initial significance as an indication of the manufacturing source of the product. The dealer does not establish proprietorship by showing only that purchasers look to the dealer as the sole supplier of the goods; they might well do that in recognition of the dealer's exclusive selling right, while aware all the while that the mark denotes some manufacturing origin. This is particularly likely where the manufacturer is actually identified by the labels or the goods are clearly of foreign origin.

105. The second class is dealer's mark . . . [T]here is a class of case in which the mark is clearly that of the distributor or importer. Here the dealer has 'selected' the goods. They have been made to the dealer's specifications (to the dealer's 'special order') by a manufacturer (or several manufacturers) who have applied the mark to the goods at the dealer's instigation to indicate that the dealer is connected in the course of trade with those goods. In such cases the dealer will usually have nominated the mark to be used; however, the dealer's proprietorship is not based essentially on that circumstance (though it may well be relevant to the implication of some agreement affecting proprietorship) but on what the mark symbolises, namely, that the goods have been issued under the 'aegis of the dealer.'

106. Without losing sight of what I said earlier that the ownership of goodwill associated with a trade mark is ultimately a question of fact and no single test or factor could be regarded as conclusive, I find these passages from *Shanahan* illuminating. In the present context, bearing in mind how the names had been used (with significant references to the research of FERC as the selling point of the products), the relationship between the parties as reflected in the agreements (in the case of ENHANVOL and ENHANTEA) and other matters I have alluded to, I consider that it is more likely that the consumer public regarded the names [more] as a manufacturer's mark than a dealer's mark.

Shanahan distinguishes manufacturer's marks where the activities of dealers in promoting goods do not deny the manufacturer's proprietorship, and dealer's marks where the manufacturer puts a mark nominated by the dealer on goods to show an association in the course of trade with those goods yet the manufacturer's aegis remains on the goods.[45] But in this case no IP as to packaging including copyright or registered rights such as trademarks had come into existence at the time of the agreement.

Lam J characterized the agreement and the nature of the relationship between plaintiff and defendant as a future assignment of goodwill attaching to badges of recognition to come into existence in the future. Once protectable goodwill has come into existence, the normal rule in passing-off is that one cannot assign badges of consumer recognition such as unregistered trademarks, logos, get-up, and the like without assigning the whole goodwill of the business, which means in effect a sale of the business. Lam J referred to manufacturer and distributor cases. These cases involved packaging and perceptions of the public as to origin and actual control by manufacturer or distributor.[46]

Lam J made the following observation as to the perception of consumers:

> 111. It has become fashionable in some trades to engage a celebrity as a product spokesman or spokeswoman. It is just a marketing technique and from a legal point of view, there is no distinction between that and the design of a get-up or a plot for promotional audio or video footage. For the purpose of ascertaining ownership of goodwill, in particular the competition for owner-ship between the parties in this action, it is not a significant factor. Nowadays, an average consumer in Hong Kong can readily appreciate that the endorse-ment or promotion of a product by a celebrity does not mean that he or she is the trader supplying the goods in question. Nor does it imply that the person who arranged for such endorsement must be the owner of the goodwill. These are all basically commercial arrangements with regard to the marketing of the products. An analogy can also be drawn with an advertising agent engaged by a local distributor for the promotion of an imported product. Even if he paid all the fees of the advertising agency, it would be wrong to suggest that by reason of that the local distributor must be the owner of the goodwill.

In this case it was participation by the dealer far beyond the mere payment of fees. It appeared to involve the entire creation by the defendant of the IP beyond the patents and trade secrets (if any) in relation to the medical technology.

Lam J held in effect that on the basis of the overall relationship between the parties, given the creation of the technology for the medication by the plaintiff, the generation of the IP by the defendants (excluding patents and trade secrets that clearly were owned by the Plaintiffs), the plaintiffs were the rightful owners of this

---

45. Ibid., paras 104-106. See Shanahan, 2nd edn, 42-43.
46. Cheung J, *Guandong Foodstuffs Import & Export Group (Group) Corp v. Tung Fook Wine Co. Ltd* (1982) 3 HKLRD 545.

IP in Hong Kong. Whether this should be the basis for an implied term of contract – especially problematic in mainland Chinese law – or for any other legal device for ascribing ownership, is moot. It illustrates the difficulty of dealing with the manufacturer/dealer/distributor relationship in an area of law that historically developed solely around the interests of manufacturers.

III.   MAINLAND CHINA

The author is not aware of any specific cases of spare parts and reconditioning involving IP claims. The trademark and other IP laws make no specific mention of it. Having said that, the relevant laws are summarized as follows.

A.   TRADEMARK LAW AND IMPLEMENTING REGULATIONS

The *Trademark Law of the People's Republic of China* (the 'Trademark Law') came into effect on 1 March 1983 and was revised on 1 July 1993 and then again on 27 October 2001. The latest version entered into effect on 1 December 2001. The *Implementing Regulations of the PRC Trademark Law* ('Implementing Regulations') entered into effect on 15 September 2002.

1.   Infringement of Registered Trademarks

Under the Trademark Law, the following acts constitute an infringement of the exclusive right to use a registered trademark:

- use of a trademark that is the same as or similar to a registered trademark on the same or similar goods without the permission of the trademark registrant;
- sale of goods that infringe the exclusive right to use a registered trademark;
- forgery or the unauthorized manufacture of representations of another's registered trademark, or the sale of representations of a registered trademark that were forged or manufactured without authorization;
- substituting the trademark of a trademark registrant without his consent and putting goods bearing such substituted trademark back on the market; or
- causing other harm to another party's exclusive right to use a registered trademark.

The Implementing Regulations make it clear that registrations containing generic names, devices, model numbers, or other descriptive elements will not be enforceable against third parties making legitimate use of such elements.

The Interpretation of the Supreme People's Court on Several Issues Concerning the Application of the Law to the Trial of Civil Dispute Cases Involving Trademarks (the 'Trademark Civil Dispute Interpretation'), effective 16 October

2002, also specifies three other circumstances that may be regarded as infringements, namely:

- the use of a registered trademark within a trade name that is used 'prominently' in relation to goods that are similar or identical to those for which the mark is registered;
- the use of a registered trademark that is a reproduction, imitation or translation of a well-known mark for goods that are dissimilar to those for which the mark is registered; and
- the registration and use of a domain name which is similar to a registered trademark where such use is made in relation to goods that are similar to those for which the mark is registered.

Where an act of registered trademark infringement has occurred, the trademark registrant or interested party may pursue administrative or judicial actions. In certain cases, criminal liability may also be pursued.

2. Administrative Actions

Where a foreigner wants to file a trademark infringement complaint with an AIC, it must do so via an official trademark agent. Complaints to AICs may be filed by the registrant of the infringed mark or by an interested party.

3. Criminal Liability for Trademark Counterfeiting

Under the revisions to the *Criminal Code of the PRC* ('Criminal Code') which took effect in October 1997, the following acts of trademark counterfeiting can constitute a crime, provided that the circumstances are 'serious':

- use of a trademark identical to a registered trademark on the same type of goods without the permission of the owner of the registered trademark;
- sale of goods in the knowledge that they bear a counterfeit registered trademark; and
- forgery or manufacture without authorization of representations of the registered trademark of another person or sale of representations of a registered trademark that have been forged or manufactured without authorization.

In general, if the circumstances are 'serious', the defendant can be sentenced to up to three years of criminal detention (which may include prison) and/or be required to pay a fine. If the circumstances are 'exceptionally serious', the defendant must be sentenced to at least three years prison but not more than seven, and is also required to pay a fine.

The Supreme People's Court (SPC) and the Supreme People's Procuratorate (SPP) recently issued a joint interpretation on criminal thresholds in trademark counterfeiting cases, which took effect on 22 December 2004. This new interpretation sets lower criminal threshold amounts which, although still high, should have the effect of making prosecutions much easier to obtain. The new guidelines cut in half the threshold amount for individuals. A case is now 'serious' if the value of the counterfeit product involved is more than CNY 50,000 (USD 6,000). For enterprises, a case is now 'serious' if the value of the counterfeit product involved is more than CNY 150,000 (USD 18,000), a 70% reduction.

B.   UNFAIR COMPETITION ACT

The *Act of the PRC Against Unfair Competition* ('Unfair Competition Act') entered into effect on 1 December 1993 and was formulated 'to ensure the sound development of the socialist market economy, encourage and safeguard fair trade, stop acts of unfair competition, and protect the lawful rights and interests of business operators and consumers.' The scope of the Unfair Competition Act is broad and covers passing-off, the imitation of trade dress, the infringement of trade secrets, the unauthorized use of an enterprise name or personal name, as well as a number of other legal areas that are not necessarily IP related, such as prize sales and false advertising.

Since its entry into effect, the Unfair Competition Act has been supplemented by a number of regulations intended to clarify some of its ambiguities. These include the *Several Regulations on the Prohibition of Acts of Unfair Competition Involving the Passing-off of a Name, Packaging or Trade Dress Peculiar to Well-known Merchandise* ('Trade Dress Regulations'), effective 6 July 1995, and the *Several Regulations on the Prohibition of Acts of Infringement of Trade Secrets* ('Trade Secret Regulations'), effective 23 November 1995.

The Fair Trade Bureau under the SAIC oversees the implementation of the Unfair Competition Act. At local level, AICs are entrusted with carrying out the administrative enforcement of the law and many AICs have a so-called Economic Inspection Section for this purpose, separate from the Trademark Section that has jurisdiction over trademark matters.

There is some overlap between the provisions of the Unfair Competition Act and the Product Quality Act. The Product Quality Act sets out the obligations and liabilities of producers, suppliers and sellers in relation to product quality and contains a number of provisions targeting the production and sale of fake and substandard merchandise.

Passing-off

Among other matters, the Unfair Competition Act prohibits business operators from engaging in the following acts of unfair competition:

- passing-off a registered trademark;
  [There have been reverse or inverse passing-off cases in China. In one case to remove trademarked labels from tee shirts and replace them with the defendant's registered trademarks was held actionable as passing-off the shirts as those of the defendants.]

- making unauthorized use of the name, packaging or trade dress peculiar to or similar to that of well-known merchandise;
- making unauthorized use of an enterprise name or personal name;
- making use of certification marks, marks of fame or marks of excellence that are counterfeit or used without authorization; and
- falsifying the place of origin of merchandise or making misleading and false statements as to merchandise quality.

Under the Trade Dress Regulations, 'well-known merchandise' is defined as merchandise that has achieved a certain level of name recognition in the market and is known to the relevant public. In addition, merchandise may be deemed well-known if the unauthorized use is sufficient to cause purchasers to be mistaken. In practice, trade dress infringement actions are generally only possible where the legitimate owner is able to demonstrate that his or her goods were introduced into the People's Republic of China (PRC) market-place prior to the infringer's goods.

One of the areas where the provisions of the Unfair Competition Act and the Product Quality Act overlap is their prohibition against the falsification of the place of origin of merchandise. One of the effects of this overlap is that rights holders sometimes have the choice of filing an administrative complaint with the local AIC, which has jurisdiction over unfair competition matters, or with the local TSB, which has jurisdiction over product quality matters.

There is also considerable overlap between the provisions of the Unfair Competition Act and the Trademark Act, both of which prohibit the 'passing-off' (i.e., counterfeiting) of PRC-registered trademarks. Because of this overlap, the Unfair Competition Act specifically refers back to the Trademark Act and the Product Quality Act in its provisions dealing with punishment for acts of passing-off registered trademarks, falsifying the place of origin, etc.

Chapter 7

Repairs, Interconnections, and Consumer Welfare in the Field of Design

Alison Firth

I. INTRODUCTION

Repairs frequently involve the use of replacement or 'spare' parts.[1] The spare part must fit the product to be repaired and, if it has an aesthetic aspect, offer a good visual match. The classic case involves spares for cars and other road vehicles.[2] The need for geometric and visual identity with the original part means that it is

---

1. For a cautionary note on the use of the phrase in the context of European design law reform, see J. Straus 'Design Protection for Spare Parts Gone in Europe? Proposed Changes to the EC Directive: the Commission's Mandate and Its Doubtful Execution', *EIPR* (2005): 391 at 393.
2. The European Policy Evaluation Consortium (EPEC) stated in a proposal of the 'spare parts' aspects of EC directive 98/71/EC on the legal protection of designs 'Whilst the provisions of the Directive are generic in their application, they have elicited particular interest in the automotive sector, and cars especially, where the market for replacement parts is substantial. According to this study, no other sectors are specifically concerned.' Impact assessment of possible options to liberalize the aftermarket in spare parts Final Report to DG Internal Market, <http://oami.europa.eu/en/office/pdf/spare.pdf>, 18 Nov. 2003 (last visited 09 Jul. 2007).

Christopher Heath, Anselm Kamperman Sanders (eds.), *Spares, Repairs and Intellectual Property Rights*, pp. 147-180.
© 2009 Kluwer Law International BV, The Netherlands.

difficult to use visual appearance as an indication of origin.[3] For reasons of safety, quality control, and economics, the manufacturers of original products are anxious to control the supply of spare parts, often attempting to keep these supplies within their own distribution networks.[4] On safety, the counter-argument is that such concerns should be addressed by measures other than design law.[5] Furthermore, even within the original manufacturers' distribution network, stocks of spares for obsolete products are costly to maintain and repairers and consumers may have to look elsewhere. Indeed, independent spares manufacturers may make components not offered by the original equipment manufacturer.[6] Repairers in a competitive economy[7] will be looking to cut costs. Independent manufacturers may seek to supply these demands. The legal protection of designs will be relevant to all these issues.

The economics of the aftermarket is key to all the papers in this volume. The interest of a creator in the product's aftermarket has been recognized by the courts in awarding damages for infringement of intellectual property rights. The US case of *King Instrument v. Perego*[8] was identified by Karnell[9] as demonstrating

---

3. In the EC's proposal for a 'repair clause' as new Art. 14 of Directive 98/71/EC of the European Parliament and of the Council of 13 Oct. 1998 on the legal protection of designs, Art. 14(2) imposes an obligation on EC Member States to 'ensure that consumers are duly informed about the origin of spare parts so that they can make an informed choice between competing spare parts'. Arguably, a uniform, EC-wide obligation on suppliers of spare parts and on repairers would be more valuable to consumers.

4. B. Arruñada, L. Garicano & L. Vázquez, 'Contractual Allocation of Decision Rights and Incentives: the Case of Automobile Distribution', *JL Econ & Org* 17 (2001): 257.

5. E.g. Gerhard Riehle of ECAR, an alliance of European organizations representing vehicle parts producers, distributors, repairers and others:

    Safety of spare parts, of course, is a high-ranking public good. When and where needed, however, safety is effectively and finally dealt with by the EU's type-approval regime. Design protection, by its very nature, cannot provide overall safety and – again so ruled by the Court – industrial property rights are not allowed to be used (say: abused) as safety instruments.

    Presentation at European Parliamentary hearing, <www.europarl.europa.eu/comparl/juri/hearings/20050421/riehle_en.pdf>, (13 Jul. 2007).

6. H.L. MacQueen, *Copyright, Competition and Industrial Design*, 1st edn (1989); 2nd edn (1995). Competition law has been particularly concerned to prevent the use of intellectual property to stifle innovation in secondary markets, see the following chapter by V. Korah.

7. W.R. Cornish, *Intellectual Property: Omnipresent, Distracting, Irrelevant?* (2004), 113-114. 'Freedom to compete should remain the norm from which any argument for a special case has to be made.'

8. 65 F.3d 941, 36 USPQ 2d 1129 (Fed. Cir. 1995); cf. *King Instrument Corp. v. Otari Corp.*, 814 F.2d 1560, 1564, 2 USPQ 2d (BNA) 1201, 1204 (Fed. Cir. 1987).

9. G.W.G. Karnell, 'Computation of Damages for Patent Infringement in Particular as Related to Extensions Outside the Scope Of Patented Matter: A Comparative Overview', *IPQ* (1997): 92. See, also, Filardi, 'The Adequacy Of Compensation For Patent Infringement-An Analysis Of Monetary Relief Under 35 U.S.C. § 284', *Fordham Ent. Media & Intell. Prop. L.F.* 3 (1992): 57.

damages for loss in the spare parts market consequent on infringement of the main patent. In *Gerber v. Lectra*,[10] damages were awarded for 'secondary losses' consisting of sales of unpatented items that went with the patented item as a commercial matter, including service and spares. This was upheld by the English Court of Appeal.[11]

In *Canon v. Green*,[12] it was recognized that for products with a long useful life, manufacturers and consumers may have a choice as between high capital/initial costs and lower maintenance/repair costs, or vice versa.[13] (Pendleton has argued that *Canon* was just what Hong Kong didn't need at the time.[14]) A view similar to that in *Canon* had been expressed nearly ten years earlier by Advocate-General Mischo in his opinion in *CICRA v. Renault*,[15] a reference to the European Court of Justice concerning the compatibility of spare parts protection with the free movement rules of the European Community (EC):

> As regards the question of the possibility of a 'double return' for that creative effort or amortization in excess of the sums invested in research and development and the perfecting of new models, I do not see in what way a national legislature would be exceeding the limits of the protection of industrial and commercial property if it allowed a car manufacturer to apportion that return or amortization between the price of the vehicle as a whole, on the one hand, and the price of the spare parts, on the other.

---

10. *Gerber Garment Technology Inc. v. Lectra Systems Ltd* (1995) RPC 383 at 402, Patents Court, England & Wales; distinguished in the design case of *Claydon Architectural Metalwork Ltd v. D.J. Higgins & Sons Ltd* (1997) FSR 475 Ch. D.
11. (1997) RPC 443. See comments by Rogers & Moss, 'Damages for Loss of Profits in Intellectual Property Litigation', *EIPR* (1997): 425; Samuel, 'Extended Damages For Patent Infringement', *IPQ* (1997): 384; Karnell, fn. 9 above.
12. *Canon KK v. Green Cartridge Co.* (Hong Kong) Ltd (1997) AC 728 (1997) 3 WLR 13 (1997) FSR 817 PC. G. Wei, Spare parts and copyright (1998) LQR 39; J. Rawkins, 'Copyright – Designs – British Leyland Spare Parts Defence', *EIPR* (1997): 674.
13. As Prof. Valentine Korah remarked at the Macau conference, one advantage of postponing costs to spares/consumables is that the heavy user pays more. All intellectual property rights protect business models of one form or another: Kamiel Koelman, Macau conference.
14. M.D. Pendleton, 'The Danger of Protecting Too Much: A Comparative Analysis of Aspects of Intellectual Property in Hong Kong, Britain and the United States', *EIPR* (2000): 69.
15. *Consorzio Italiano della Componentistica di Ricambio per Autoveicoli and Maxicar v. Regie Nationale des Usines Renault* (case C-53/87) (1988) ECR 6039 at para. 31; (1990) 4 CMLR 265 at 273. Whilst the European Court of Justice did not allude to this point in the same terms, it did state at para. 17 of its judgment:

> With reference more particularly to the difference in prices between components sold by the manufacturer and those sold by the independent producers, it should be noted that the Court has held (case C-24/67, Parke Davis (1968) ECR 55, (1968) CMLR 47) that a higher price for the former than for the latter does not necessarily constitute an abuse, since the proprietor of protective rights in respect of an ornamental design may lawfully call for a return on the amounts which he has invested in order to perfect the protected design.

Postponing the cost of use to be recovered from the supply of consumables is a risky strategy for a manufacturer,[16] although knowledge that spares and consumables are available at low cost may act as an incentive for consumers to buy the product.

The present paper[17] investigates ways in which aspects of design law affect the balance in the aftermarket between the interests of the designer and those of others. Copyright[18] may be available for works of applied art, as envisaged by Article 2 Berne.[19] Likewise, unfair competition may be a potent legal tool in the design arena.[20] Here we shall mainly consider specific laws for the protection of industrial design.

Europe has been grappling with three alternatives for harmonizing design laws in relation to spare parts: 'liberalization', or removal of protection for spare parts; reducing the effective term of protection; or replacing exclusive rights with the right to reasonable remuneration.[21]

However, there is a spectrum of ways of dealing with spare parts, from the substantive – denial of any protection for parts of articles, express exceptions, and limitations on rights – through specific procedural mechanisms, such as limiting the availability of injunctions, or providing redress for unjustified threats, through to extrinsic limits: general defences such as implied license, abuse of rights, non-derogation from grant, or the application of competition (antitrust) law. Some of these later aspects are dealt with more fully in other papers; cross-references to these will be made where apt. The following analysis uses examples drawn from the present and past laws of a number of countries and regions, including strategies considered by EC[22] and Australian[23] legislators.

---

16. For example in the 'Senseo' coffee machine dispute, where the patentee had to pay damages to a wrongly injuncted supplier of consumables; see case comment by F. de Visscher (2004) EIPR N105.
17. Revised as of July 2007. The options canvassed are inspired by the work of Prof. Jim Lahore, especially that with the Australian Law Reform Commission: see Discussion Paper No. 58 Designs, Sydney, 1994 (ALRC DP 58) and Report No. 74, Designs, Sydney, 1995 (ALRC 74).
18. See A. Kur, 'The Green Paper's "Design Approach" – What's Wrong With It?', *EIPR* (1993): 374 for the drawbacks of copyright protection.
19. Article 2(1); see also Art. 2(7) and Art. 7(4). For interplay between copyright and design see D. Llewelyn in the first chapter of this book.
20. For surveys of alternative modes of protection, see Australian Law Reform Commission discussion paper 58 Designs (1994); C. Fellner, 'The Future of Legal Protection for Industrial Design' (1985); A. Firth, 'Aspects Of Design Protection In Europe', *EIPR* (1993):42; U. Suthersanen, *Design Law in Europe* (2000).
21. Impact assessment of possible options to liberalize the aftermarket in spare parts, Final Report to DG Internal Market, <http://oami.europa.eu/en/office/pdf/spare.pdf>, 18 Nov. 2003 (last visited 09 Jul. 2007). This rejected the second and third options.
22. D. Musker, *Community Design Law* (2002) para. 1-138 et seq.; A. Kur, ' "Freeze Plus" Melts the Ice – Observations on the European Design Directive', IIC 620 (1999); J. Lahore, 'The Protection Of Functional Designs: The Amended Proposal For A European Designs Directive', *IPQ* (1997): 128 and books listed at fn. 20.
23. See Australia Law Reform Commission discussion paper 58 Designs 1994; Explanatory Memorandum to the Designs Bill 2002 (Cth).

II.   LACK OF TREATY CONSTRAINTS AND VARIETY
                       OF DESIGN LAWS

A.   Paris, Berne, TRIPs

The requirements of the international intellectual property conventions –
Paris,[24] Berne,[25] and the WTO Trade-Related Aspects of Intellectual Property
(TRIPs) agreement,[26,27] – are remarkably permissive in relation to design

---

24. Article 5quinquies. 'Industrial designs shall be protected in all the countries of the Union.'
         Article 10*bis* does not specifically require protection against unfair competition by
     misappropriation.
25. Article 2: Protected Works:

     1) The expression 'literary and artistic works' shall include every production in the literary,
     scientific and artistic domain, whatever may be the mode or form of its expression, such as . . .
     works of applied art;
         (7) Subject to the provisions of *Article 7(4)* of this Convention, it shall be a matter for
     legislation in the countries of the Union to determine the extent of the application of their laws to
     works of applied art and industrial designs and models, as well as the conditions under which
     such works, designs and models shall be protected. Works protected in the country of origin
     solely as designs and models shall be entitled in another country of the Union only to such
     special protection as is granted in that country to designs and models; however, if no such
     special protection is granted in that country, such works shall be protected as artistic works.

     Article 7 Term of Protection:

     (4) It shall be a matter for legislation in the countries of the Union to determine the term of
     protection of photographic works and that of works of applied art in so far as they are protected
     as artistic works; however, this term shall last at least until the end of a period of twenty-five
     years from the making of such a work.

26. Agreement on Trade Related Aspects of Intellectual Property Rights, 1994, Arts 25-26. Perceived
     losses to US industry caused by the counterfeiting of automotive spares was one of the influences
     leading to inclusion of intellectual property into the GATT Uruguay round and ultimately to
     WTO/TRIPs. See M. Blakeney, 'Intellectual Property In World Trade', *Int TLR* (1995): 76.
     Reichman has argued that by its criteria of 'new and original' in Art. 25(1), TRIPs represents
     'a backhanded attempt to oblige Congress to align the legal protection of industrial designs in this
     country with more protectionist trends abroad.' J.R. Reichman, 'GATT/WTO Universal
     Minimum Standards Of Intellectual Property Protection under the TRIPS Component of the
     WTO Agreement', Int Law 29 (1995): 345. See, generally, D. J. Gervais, 'The Changing Land-
     scape of International Intellectual Property', *JIPLP* (2006): 249.
27. Article 25 Requirements for Protection:

     (1) Members shall provide for the protection of independently created industrial designs that are
     new or original. Members may provide that designs are not new or original if they do not
     significantly differ from known designs or combinations of known design features. Members
     may provide that such protection shall not extend to designs dictated essentially by technical or
     functional considerations.
         (2) Each Member shall ensure that requirements for securing protection for textile designs,
     in particular in regard to any cost, examination or publication, do not unreasonably impair the
     opportunity to seek and obtain such protection. Members shall be free to meet this obligation
     through industrial design law or through copyright law.

protection, so there is considerable scope for variation[28] in national or regional design laws.[29]

B.   DEFENCES

It is also the case that, as with other rights, the international treaties make little reference to defences. Paris Convention defences relating to use of patented devices on ships, etc,[30] are not replicated for designs. TRIPs does impose a 'three-step test' for exceptions from design protection: Article 26.2.[31] Straus has argued that a 'repair clause' allowing for third party manufacture of spares would violate Article 26.2.[32] His elegant argument draws upon World Trade

---

Article 26 Protection:

(1) The owner of a protected industrial design shall have the right to prevent third parties not having the owner's consent from making, selling or importing articles bearing or embodying a design which is a copy, or substantially a copy, of the protected design, when such acts are undertaken for commercial purposes.

(2) Members may provide limited exceptions to the protection of industrial designs, provided that such exceptions do not unreasonably conflict with the normal exploitation of protected industrial designs and do not unreasonably prejudice the legitimate interests of the owner of the protected design, taking account of the legitimate interests of third parties.

(3) The duration of protection available shall amount to at least ten years.

28. Described as 'disturbing' by H. Cohen Jehoram, 'Hybrids on the Borderline Between Copyright and Industrial Property Law', *Aus IPJ* (1991): 190; cited by J. Lahore, 'The Herchel Smith Lecture 1992: Intellectual Property Rights And Unfair Copying: Old Concepts, New Ideas', *EIPR* (1992): 428.
29. C. Fellner, *The Future of Legal Protection for Industrial Design* (1985); U. Suthersanen, *Design Law In Europe* (2000).
30. Article 5*ter*.
31. 'Members may provide limited exceptions to the protection of industrial designs, provided that such exceptions do not unreasonably conflict with the normal exploitation of protected industrial designs and do not unreasonably prejudice the legitimate interests of the owners of the protected design, taking account of the legitimate interests of third parties.' The reference to third-party interests is specific to design protection. For the more familiar three-step test in copyright law, see C. Geiger, 'The Three Step Test, a Threat to a Balanced Copyright Law?', 37 IIC 683 (2006); M. Senftleben, 'Towards a Horizontal Standard for Limiting Intellectual Property Rights? – WTO Panel Reports Shed Light on the Three Step Test in Copyright Law and Related Tests in Patent and Trade Mark Law', 37 IIC 407 (2006); M. Senftleben, *Copyright, Limitations and the Three Step Test* (2004).
32. J Straus, 'Design Protection for Spare Parts gone in Europe? Proposed Changes to the EC Directive: The Commission's Mandate and its Doubtful Execution' *EIPR* (2005): 391, relying upon WTO panel decisions on the three-step test in patents and copyright: *Canada – patent protection of pharmaceutical products WT/DS 114/R* and *United States – Section 110(5) of the US Copyright Act WT/L/160/Rev1* and citing D.J. Gervais, *The TRIPS Agreement: Drafting History and Analyses* (2nd edn, 2003), para. 2.250; A. Kur, 'Provisions of the TRIPS Agreement Relevant to Design Law', in *From GATT to TRIPS*, ed. F.-K. Beier & G. Schricker (1996). As Musker has pointed out, the fact that Straus' article was based on research for the motor industry (and says so) should not be seen as undermining the force of his opinions: D. Musker,

Organization (WTO) panel decisions on the three-step test in patents and copyright: *Canada – patent protection of pharmaceutical products* WT/DS 114/R and *United States – Section 110(5) of the US Copyright Act* WT/L/160/Rev1. Unlike the 'three-step tests' for copyright[33] and patents,[34] however, Article 26.2 contains the additional reference to 'taking account of the legitimate interests of third parties'. Straus argues from European case law that this would not take a repair clause outside Article 26.2. However, it is submitted that, given the wide variety of views and laws on the design protection of spare parts, it is doubtful whether any international consensus could be reached on what is or is not 'normal exploitation' or the balance of 'legitimate interests' as between rights owners and third parties.

C.   HAGUE

The Hague System[35] for the International Registration of Industrial Designs, being a filing treaty and mechanism, does not address substantive issues, apart from the obligation of contracting Parties to comply with the provisions of the Paris Convention on industrial designs: Article 2(2).

D.   LOCARNO

The Locarno Agreement Establishing an International Classification for Industrial Designs[36] implicitly recognizes the protection of component parts for motor

---

Community Design Law: Principles and Practice (2002), at 72, fn. 53. On arguments somewhat different from Straus' opinion, A. Gerdau de Borja argues that the European spare parts exception fails to satisfy TRIPS Art. 26(2): 'Exceptions to Design Rights: the Potential Impact of Art. 26(2) TRIPs' (2008) *EIPR* 500.

33. TRIPs Art. 13.
34. TRIPs Art. 30.
35. Hague Agreement (1925), revised at London (1934) and The Hague (1960) (supplemented by the Additional Act of Monaco (1961), the Complementary Act of Stockholm (1967) and the Protocol of Geneva (1975), and amended in 1979) and at Geneva (1999). As of 13 Apr. 2007, the Hague Union comprised forty-seven States. L. von Gerlach has summarized the position of key non-members: Japan as having an interest to join the Hague Agreement, but no date yet; People's Republic of China also interested, having in 2005/2006 hosted a number of seminars on the topic, the US having signed the Geneva Act in 1999 but awaiting ratification; the European Union estimated for accession with effect from Jan. 2008, the EC Council having approved accession to the Geneva Act on 18 Dec. 2006. L. von Gerlach, 'Design Protection – Where Do We Stand? ECTA 26th Annual Conference', Deauville, 20-23 Jun. 2007; presentation available at <www.ecta.org/Deauville/CD-Rom/Speeches.htm> (13 Jul. 2007).
36. Signed at Locarno on 8 Oct. 1968, as amended on 28 Sep. 1979. As of 1 Jan. 2004, the 8th edition of the International Classification for Industrial Designs is in force: see <www.wipo.int/classifications/nivilo/locarno/index.htm#>.

vehicles and other products. The notes to Class 12: 'Means of transport' or hoisting state:

(1) Including all vehicles: land, sea, air, space and others.
(2) Including parts, components and accessories which exist only in connection with a vehicle and cannot be placed in another class; these parts, components and accessories of vehicles are to be placed in the subclass of the vehicle in question, or in Class 12-16 if they are common to several vehicles included in different subclasses.
(3) Not including, in principle, parts, components and accessories of vehicles which can be placed in another class; these parts, components and accessories are to be placed in the same class as articles of the same type, in other words, having the same function. Thus, carpets or mats for automobiles are to be placed with carpets (Cl. 6-11); electric motors for vehicles are to be placed in Class 13-01, and non-electric motors for vehicles in Class 15-01 (the same applies to the components of such motors); automobile headlamps are to be placed with lighting apparatus (Cl. 26-06).
(4) Not including scale models of vehicles (Cl. 21-01).

Other sections of the Locarno classification deal with components of what in EC law have come to be termed 'modular products': scaffoldings and their components, composite furniture, and so forth.

Adherence to the Locarno Agreement is not mandatory for members of the Paris Union or WTO. Furthermore, it is perfectly possible for a country or region to use the Locarno classification or a variant of Locarno[37] to structure its register of protected designs without signing up to the Agreement.

E.   SCOPE FOR EXPERIMENT

Lack of constraint in the treaties leaves wide freedom for experimentation. As David Llewelyn points out in Chapter 1 of this book, Australia[38] has been very adventurous in reforming its design laws time and again.[39] Business often seems to

---

37. The Office for Harmonization in the Internal Market, responsible for registering Community Designs under Council Regulation (EC) No. 6/2002 of 12 Dec. 2001 on Community Designs, operates a version called 'Eurolocarno' – see <http://oami.europa.eu/en/design/eurolocarno.htm>.

38. Although it has been overtaken by several waves of legislative reform, the Australian Law Reform Commission's discussion paper 58 Designs (1994) remains a classic analysis of the principles of design protection. See also J. Lahore, 'The Herchel Smith Lecture 1992: Intellectual Property Rights and Unfair Copying: Old Concepts', New Ideas', *EIPR* (1992): 428.

39. Design law could perhaps be regarded as a playground for scholars and legislators, despite often being described as the Cinderella of intellectual property, e.g. J. Phillips, 'International Design Protection: Who Needs It?', *EIPR* 12 (1993): 431; H. Cohen Jehoram, 'Cumulation Of

prefer legal certainty over the search for optimal solutions,[40] but at the international level, legal certainty in the field of design law is far from being achieved. In many jurisdictions,[41] design law uncomfortably straddles the divides between the aesthetic and the functional, between intellectual and industrial property. Suthersanen[42] has argued for 'reassessment of the traditional science/culture/market-source led trichotomy in intellectual property rights, based on the centrality of the notion of the design process to all intellectual property subject matter', but design laws remain fixated on the end product, usually a tangible good.[43]

III.   CUMULATION

The trend in Europe[44] is to allow cumulation of protection, as between specific design laws,[45] copyright/author's right, arguably patents[46] and unfair

---

Protection In The EC Design Proposals', *EIPR* (1994): 514; C.-H. Massa & A. Strowel, 'Community Design: Cinderella Revamped', *EIPR* (2003): 68.

40. For a similar argument in relation to collective copyright licensing, see M. Frabboni, 'Online Music Licensing: The Calm After the Storm', *Ent LR* (2006): 65; see also the remarks of E. Micheler, 'English and German Securities Law: A Thesis in Doctrinal Path Dependence', *LQR* (2007): 251:

Market participants may be happy to take commercial risks but they put a high premium on achieving legal certainty. The result is that the lawyers advising them apply existing legal concepts to accommodate new developments rather then adopt new solutions that may create more efficient, but less well-tested, results. Legal practice needs to deliver predictable results. This discourages experiments with new techniques. [citation omitted].

41. P. Ganea, Th. Pattloch & C. Heath, *Intellectual Property Law In China* (2005); K.A. Levin & M.B. Richman, 'A Survey of Industrial Design Protection in the European Union and the United States', *EIPR* (2003): 111; C. Heath (ed.), *Intellectual Property Law in Asia* (2002).

42. U. Suthersanen, 'Breaking Down the Intellectual Property Barriers', *IPQ* (1998): 267. See also H. Cohen Jehoram, 'Hybrids on the Borderline between Copyright and Industrial Property Law', *Aus IPJ* (1991): 190; J.R. Reichmann, 'Legal Hybrids Between the Patent and Copyright Paradigms', *Colum. L. Rev.* 94 (1994): 2432.

43. The definition of 'product' in EC design law embraces such subject matter as graphic symbols and typographic typefaces, though not computer programs: Art. 1(b) Directive 98/71/EC of the European Parliament and of the Council of 13 Oct. 1998 on the legal protection of designs; Art. 3(b) Council Regulation (EC) No. 6/2002 of 12 Dec. 2001 on Community Designs. See D. Musker, *Community Design Law: Principles and Practice* (2002).

44. U. Suthersanen, 'Harmonising Design Law in a Free Trade Area', in *Intellectual Property Harmonisation with ASEAN and APEC*, eds C. Antons, M. Blakeney & C. Heath (2004); D. Musker, *Community Design Law: Principles and Practice* (2002); U. Suthersanen, *Design Law In Europe* (2000); M. Franzosi (ed.), *European Design Protection: Commentary to Directive and Regulation Proposals* (1997).

45. On the difficulties, see e.g. A. Carboni, 'The Overlap between Registered Community Designs and Community Trade Marks', *JIPLP* (2006): 256.

46. M. Schlotelburg, 'Design Protection for Technical Products', *JIPLP* (2006): 675 argues that as patents protect principle and design law the specific appearance, provided there is design freedom (see below), there is nothing contradictory about a patent and a design over the same embodiment. In the US, courts are reluctant to confer trade dress protection following

competition,[47] although European trademark law seeks to keep functional and aesthetic design out of the trademark registration system[48] (and vice versa[49]). This is achieved by refusing registration to 'signs which consist exclusively of':

- the shape which results from the nature of the goods themselves; or
- the shape of goods which is necessary to obtain a technical result; or
- the shape which gives substantial value to the goods.[50]

These provisions have been interpreted in a manner restrictive to trademark protection/registration in cases such as *Koninklijke Philips Electronics NV v. Remington Consumer Products Ltd*[51] and Dualit Ltd's (Toaster Shapes) Trade Mark Applications.[52] In Dyson,[53] trademark registration was refused to what in design terms might be regarded as a principle of construction – the transparency of the dust collection chamber in the applicant's vacuum cleaners. The European Court of Justice held that it was not a 'sign' within the meaning of trademark legislation. Despite eloquent arguments advanced by Dinwoodie[54] in favour of an approach

---

an expired utility patent, but are said to be more generous after expiry of a design patent: D.A. Valenzuela, 'Can an Inventor Continue Protecting an Expired Patented Product Via Trade Dress Protection?', *N.D.L. Rev.* 81 (2005): 145.

47. See, e.g., *Jeans I* and *Jeans II* German Federal Supreme Court, 15 Sep. 2005 and 19 Jan. 2006, 38 IIC 128 and 137 (2007).

48. By contrast, an intriguing decision of the Dutch Supreme Court appears to have imported trademark concepts into the protection of design by copyright. *G-Star v. Benetton* Hoge Raad (Elwood jeans), 8 Sep. 2006, (2006) NJ 492; and BIE 2007/1, 41. See criticism by H. Cohen Jehoram, 'The Dutch Supreme Court Recognises "Dilution of Copyright" by Degeneration of a Copyright Design into Unprotected Style: The Flying Dutchman: All Sails, No Anchor', *EIPR* (2007): 205-8.

49. Article 25(1)(e) of Reg. (EC) No. 6/2002 on Community Designs. See *Zellweger Analytics Limited's designs* OHIM, noted by D. Smyth, 'Community Registered Design Invalidated by Prior Registered Trade Mark', *JIPLP* (2006): 509.

50. Article 7(1)(e) of Council Regulation (EC) No. 40/94 of 20 Dec. 1993 on the Community trademark; Art. 3(1)(e) of First Directive 89/104/EEC of the Council, of 21 Dec. 1988, to Approximate the Laws of the Member States Relating to Trade Marks. See A. Firth, E. Gredley & S. Maniatis, 'Shapes as Trade Marks: Public Policy, Functional Considerations and Consumer Perception', *EIPR* (2001): 86; P. Ströbele, 'The Registration of New Trademark Forms', IIC 161 (2001).

51. (C299/99) (2002) ECR I-5475; (2002) ETMR 81 (non-registrability of the configuration of a three-headed electric shaver) (ECJ); see U. Suthersanen, 'The European Court of Justice in *Philips v. Remington* : Trade Marks and Market Freedom', *IPQ* (2003): 257; J. Clark, 'Adorning Shavers with Clover Leaves: *Koninklijke Philips Electronics NV v. Remington Consumer Products Ltd*', *EIPR* (2006): 352. In *Three Headed Rotary Shaver* noted at 38 IIC 499 (2007), the German Federal Supreme Court considered the same subject matter and gave useful guidance on the application of Art. 6 quinquies of the Paris Convention in the context of international trademark registrations.

52. (1999) RPC 890 Ch. D (on equivalent provision of the UK Trade Marks Act 1994).

53. *Dyson Ltd v. Registrar of Trade Marks* (2007) 2 CMLR. 14; (2007) ETMR. 34; (2007) RPC 27 ECJ (3rd Chamber); M. Walmsley, 'Too Transparent? ECJ Rules Dyson Cannot Register Transparent Collection Chamber As A Trade Mark', *EIPR* (2007): 298.

54. G. Dinwoodie, 'Death of Ontology', *Iowa LR* 84 (1999): 611; see also G. Dinwoodie, 'Reconceptualizing the Inherent Distinctiveness of Product Design Trade Dress', *North Carolina Law Review* 75 (1997): 471.

based upon factual distinctiveness, the US seems to be taking a similarly restrictive attitude to trademark protection of 'trade dress'. Japan appears to require an especially high degree of uniqueness and lack of functionality for three-dimensional shapes to be registered as trademarks.[55]

The trend to cumulation in EC law, coupled with the fact that EC design law has attempted a liberal approach to subject matter,[56] has made the issue of spare parts particularly problematic in Europe.[57]

IV.   THE SPARE PART NON-PROBLEM

The spare parts scenario does *not* usually engage one of the most difficult areas of intellectual property law, that of inexact infringement.[58] No one wants to buy a gasket that does not fit, or a car panel that does not match, although the importance of match may vary.[59] Across the world, there is a wide range of tests, based on substantial similarities or significant differences. Until recently, Australian design law retained the fascinating concept of 'fraudulent imitation', whereby differences caused by a wish to disguise copying or, because of a 'conscious desire to come as close as possible to the registered design while avoiding infringement' would not prevent infringement.[60] This was replaced by a new test for infringement under the Australian Designs Act 2003,[61] that of 'identical to, or substantially similar in overall impression' to the registered design. The same test is used in assessing the registrability of a design and is premised on similarities rather than differences.[62]

---

55. J.A. Tessensohn & S. Yamamoto, 'Trade Marks: Registrability of Three Dimensional Trade Marks in Japan', *EIPR* (2004): fn. 65, commenting on *Suntory Co Ltd v. Commissioner of the Japanese Patent Office* (2003).
56. Under Directive 98/71/EC of the European Parliament and of the Council of 13 Oct. 1998 on the legal protection of designs and Council Regulation (EC) No. 6/2002 of 12 Dec. 2001 on Community Designs.
57. Admirably discussed by A. Horton, 'European Design Law and the Spare Parts Dilemma: The Proposed Regulation and Directive', *EIPR* (1994): 51; not much has changed – J. Straus, 'Design Protection for Spare Parts Gone in Europe? Proposed Changes to the EC Directive: The Commission's Mandate and its Doubtful Execution', *EIPR* (2005): 391 and citations.
58. As opposed to indirect infringement, see Ch. 4 of this book.
59. *Dyson Ltd v. Qualtex* (UK) Ltd (2005) RPC 19 (2004) EWHC 2981 (Ch) Ch. D; (2006) RPC 31; (2006) EWCA Civ 166 CA (Civ Div) – less important for vacuum cleaners than for motor vehicles.
60. *Polyaire Pty Ltd v. K-Aire Pty Ltd* (2005) 216 A.L.R. 205 (HC (Aus)); noted by A. Monotti at *EIPR* (2005): fn. 220; and by W. Rothnie at *EIPR* (2005): fn. 245. See, also, *Koninklijke Philips Electronics NV v. Remington Products Australia Pty Ltd* (1999) 91 FCR 167 at 200.
61. In force from 17 Jun. 2004, with accompanying Designs Regulations 2004.
62. A. Monotti, 'Australia: Design Right: Changes to the Designs Law', *EIPR* (2005): fn. 31; *EIPR* (2005): fn. 101; See also Sep. 2000 Final report by the Intellectual Property and Competition Review Committee <www.austlii.edu.au/cgi-bin/disp.pl/au/other/clrc/1.html?query="design%20law"%20and%20"spare%20parts"#disp12>.

V.   IN, OUT, OR HALFWAY HOUSE: DESIGN LAW
          STRATEGIES AND THEIR IMPACT ON THE
          PROTECTION OR NON-PROTECTION OF SPARE PARTS

The following strategies include those considered by EU[63] and Australian[64] legislators. Not all of the strategies are calculated specifically to deal with 'spare
parts'. However, a common problem is that of throwing the baby out with the
bath water: adopting a design law strategy with a view to controlling the level of
protection of spare parts and adversely affecting the laws' coherence and application to other types of product.

A.   REQUIRE ORNAMENTAL ASPECT AS A PRE-REQUISITE FOR
          PROTECTION AND SET HIGH THRESHOLD

Some countries and regions, including EU countries and Australia, have aban-
doned ornamental quality, aesthetic features, or 'eye-appeal' as a pre-requisite
for protection. However, many other countries do have an aesthetic requirement.[65]
Although it does not affect the problem of 'must-match' spares for components
with visual appeal, it ensures that functional design is not protected by design
registration.

For example, the People's Republic of China's Patent Law 1984[66] provides
that an industrial design may be protected by applying for a patent. The Patent Act
Implementing Rules, r.2(3) (aesthetic), stipulate that 'the term "design" refers to
any new *aesthetic* and practically applicable design of shape, pattern or combination of shape and pattern, or their combination with a colour, of a product'.[67]

Another jurisdiction using the patent system for the grant of rights in designs is
the United States of America, under 35 USC 171. US design patents[68] have to meet

---

63. D. Musker, *Community Design Law* (2002) para. 1-138 et seq.; A. Kur, ' "Freeze Plus" Melts
    the Ice – Observations on the European Design Directive', 30 IIC 620 (1999); J. Lahore, 'The
    Protection of Functional Designs: The Amended Proposal for a European Designs Directive',
    IPQ (1997): 128.
64. See Australia Law Reform Commission discussion paper 58 Designs 1994; Explanatory Mem-
    orandum to the Designs Bill 2002 (Cth).
65. E.g. Brazil's Industrial Property Code, 14/05/1996, s95; <www.wipo.int/clea/docs_new/en/br/
    br003en.html> (22 Jul. 2007); Republic of Korea's Design Act 1961, as amended: <www.
    wipo.int/clea/docs_new/en/kr/kr037en.html> (22 Jul. 2007); for a persuasive opinion in favour
    of an aesthetic requirement, see M. Franzosi, 'Design Protection Italian Style' *JIPLP* (2006): 599.
66. Patent Law (amended 1992, 2000).
67. P. Ganea, 'Patents, Utility Models and Designs' Part A in *Intellectual Property Law in China*,
    eds P. Ganea, Th. Pattloch & C. Heath (2005), at 9.
68. J. Hudis & P. Signore, 'Protection Of Industrial Designs in the United States', *EIPR* (2005): 256.
    For comparison of design protection in the US with that in the EU, see U. Suthersanen, 'Har-
    monising Design Law in a Free Trade Area: Jurisprudential Lessons from the EU and the US',
    Ch. 5 in *Intellectual Property Harmonisation within ASEAN and APEC*, ed. C. Antons,
    M. Blakeney & C. Heath (Kluwer: 2004). Other countries having a design patent approach

the main criteria for 'utility' patents;[69] the high threshold for registration, examination,[70] limitation to a single claim,[71] and cost of prosecution[72] have probably kept aesthetic as well as functional spare parts relatively free of exclusive claims in the USA.[73] Furthermore, the infringement rights under a design patent are narrow:[74] 'design patents are entitled to almost no scope beyond the precise content of the patent drawings'.[75] The defensive arguments and findings in the *Jazz Photo* case[76] would apply to design patents as to utility patents.

Fryer[77] in particular has criticized this system for its focus on registration (and therefore shortcomings at the market entry stage) but also its failure to protect functional aspects of design. Citing the sector-by-sector move away from the classic US position – first semiconductor chip protection, then the Vessel Hull Design Protection Act 1998 – Fryer states:

> Most U.S. attorneys would prefer the E.U. approach to subject-matter. The problem is how to convince Congress that additional design protection is

---

include United Arab Emirates, Thailand (although the Thai Patent Act 1979 as amended does not have an ornamental criterion). See <www.wipo.int/clea/docs_new/en/th/th007en.html> (22 Jul. 2007), as amended by the Patent Act (No. 2) B.E 2535 (1992) and the Patent Act (No. 3) B.E. 2542 (1999).

69. The similarities and differences between utility and design patents are discussed by S. D. Locke, 'Fifth Avenue and the Patent Lawyer: Strategies for Using Design Patents to Increase the Value of Fashion and Luxury Goods Companies', *J. Marshall Rev. Intell. Prop. L.* 5 (2005): 40.

70. This is in contrast to the UK or European community design system, where applications are examined as to form but are not subject to substantive examination. Article 47 of Reg. (EC) No. 6/2002 on Community designs provides that if the Office notices that the design does not correspond to the definition under Art. 3(a) or is contrary to morality or public policy, it shall refuse the design after giving the applicant the opportunity to be heard. See, also, Art. 11 of Commission Regulation (EC) No. 2245/2002 of 21 Oct. 2002, implementing Council Regulation (EC) No. 6/2002 on Community Designs. Texts are available online at <http://oami.europa.eu/en/design/legalaspects.htm>.

71. By contrast the Community Design Regulation allows multiple applications Art. 37(1) Reg. 6/2002; Art. 2(1) CDIR Regulation (EC) No. 2245/2002. The number of designs contained in a multiple application is not limited, but higher fees are payable.

72. G.N. Magliocca, 'Ornamental Design and Incremental Innovation', *Marq L Rev* 86 (2003): 845.

73. For support of the status quo in the US, see G.N. Magliocca, 'Ornamental Design and Incremental Innovation', *Marq L Rev* 86 (2003): 845.

74. The notion of deceptive similarity is present, see e.g. *Elmer v. ICC Fabricating, Inc.* 67 F.3d 1571 C.A.Fed. (Fla.), 1995, citing *Gorham Co. v. White*, 81 U.S. (14 Wall.) 511, 528, 20 L.Ed. 731 (1871). However, the 'ordinary observer' test established in Gorham appears to have been superseded by the judicial construction exercise required by the utility patent case of *Markman v. Westview Instruments, Inc.*, 517 U.S. 370 (1996): *Minka Lighting, Inc. v. Craftmade International, Inc.* 93 Fed.Appx. 214; Petition for writ of certiorari to the United States Court of Appeals for the Federal Circuit denied 543 U.S. 814, 125 S.Ct. 50 (Mem) (2004).

75. *Durdin v. Kuryakyn Holdings, Inc.* 440 F.Supp.2d 921 W.D.Wis., 2006, citing *Brooks Furniture Manufacturing, Inc. v. Dutailier International, Inc.*, 393 F.3d 1378, 1383 (Fed. Cir. 2005); *Elmer v. ICC Fabricating, Inc.* 67 F.3d 1571 C.A.Fed. (Fla.), 1995.

76. See below, fn. 145

77. W.T.Fryer, 'The Evolution of Market Entry Industrial Design Protection: An International Comparative Analysis', *EIPR* (1999): 618

needed for a broad range of products. Overall the E.U. Regulation has a very effective approach to market entry design protection.

South Africa has an interestingly 'branched' design law, explicitly providing for both aesthetic design and functional design, with different criteria for protection.[78]

B.   EXCLUDE FUNCTIONAL DESIGN FROM PROTECTION

A slightly different approach omits a positive requirement of aesthetic appeal but denies protection to functional design to some degree. The effect of this exclusion will depend upon the legislative text and its interpretation. Sri Lanka's Code of Intellectual Property Act No. 52 of 1979 (as amended) takes this approach in section 27 and its proviso: 'Provided that anything in an industrial design which serves solely to obtain a technical result shall not be protected under this Part.'[79] Section 113(2) of the Philippines' Intellectual Property Code 1997[80] excludes from protection: 'Industrial designs dictated essentially by technical or functional considerations to obtain a technical result.'

A 'belt and braces' approach can be found in the former registered design laws of the United Kingdom.[81] For a long time UK law not only required eye-appeal but also excluded functional design in the abstract – methods and principles of construction – and denied protection to specific designs 'solely dictated by function'. In *Amp v. Utilux*[82] this was held to exclude not only those cases where only one design would do the job – hence no design freedom – but also those cases where function was the primary consideration, although the designer was not constrained to a particular design. This broad and enthusiastic exclusion of functional design from the registration system, coupled with other provisions, produced the anomalous result that unregistrable, functional design was protected under copyright in design drawings for a term far beyond that of any design laws.[83] Pendleton[84] has succinctly charted the judicial decisions that led to this result, which was reversed for the UK in 1988 by the Copyright, Designs and Patents Act 1988, section 51, but remained effective in Hong Kong. As in Malaysia, where the case of *Peko Wallsend Operations Ltd v. Linatex Process Rubber Bhd*, took the copyright protection for industrial artefacts a step further by holding that a slurry pump was itself a copyright work, as well as the design drawings.[85]

---

78. Designs Act No. 195 of Dec. 22, 1993, s. 1. <www.wipo.int/clea/docs_new/en/za/za007en.html> (22 Jul. 2007). See, also, <www.saiipl.org.za/>.
79. <www.wipo.int/clea/en/fiche.jsp?uid=lk001> (22 Jul. 2007).
80. <www.wipo.int/clea/en/fiche.jsp?uid=ph001> (22 Jul. 2007).
81. Registered Designs Act 1949, as amended.
82. (1972) RPC 103.
83. See the first chapter of this book by D. Llewelyn and V. Barresi.
84. M.D.Pendleton, 'The Danger of Protecting Too Much: A Comparative Analysis of Aspects of Intellectual Property in Hong Kong, Britain and the United States', *EIPR* (2000): 69.
85. Ida Slurry Pumps And The Obscurity Of Artistic Copyright Works (1994) *EIPR* 123.

Article 8 of the EC Design Regulation[86] uses a similar turn of phrase to that in the former UK statute: '[A] Community design shall not subsist in features of appearance of a product which are dictated solely by function'. Article 7 of Directive 98/71/EC on the legal protection of designs harmonizes the national design laws of EU Member States to the same effect.[87]

However the explanatory recitals[88] to these European legal instruments state 'this does not entail that the design must have an aesthetic quality'. Furthermore, it has been held that this exclusion should be restrictively construed,[89] even in the UK where identical wording had previously been given broad interpretation. In *Landor & Hawa International v. Azure Designs*,[90] HH Judge Fysh held that the exclusion bites where the design is the only one by which the product could perform its function. In coming to this conclusion, he associated himself with the thinking of Advocate-General Colomer in *Philips v. Remington*.[91] This approach was upheld on appeal[92] and endorsed by the English High Court in *Procter & Gamble Co v. Reckitt Benckiser (UK) Ltd:*[93]

> Next, the court noted that a Community design does not subsist in features of appearance of a product which are solely dictated by its technical function. The notion of a feature whose appearance is 'solely dictated' by function is narrowly interpreted. The exclusion only applies where the part of the design in question was the only way to achieve the particular function.[94]

Article 5.3 of Japan's Design Law takes a similar line in prohibiting the registration of shapes that are 'indispensable' to function.[95] Other countries use the litmus test of design freedom. Belize's Industrial Designs Act 2000 excludes from design protection anything that 'leaves no freedom as regards arbitrary features of appearance'.[96]

---

86. Regulation 6/2002.
87. Dinwoodie, 'Federalized Functionalism: The future of Design Protection in the European Union', *AIPLA QJ* 24 (1996): 611.
88. Regulation recital; Dir Recital 14.
89. M. Schlötelburg, 'Design Protection for Technical Products', *JIPLP* (2006): 675.
90. (2006) FSR 22: the exclusion did not apply to a zipped suitcase expansion panel.
91. (2001) RPC 38 AGO; (2003) RPC 2 ECJ, a trademark case in which the A-G distinguished EU trademark legislation, precluding registration of a three-dimensional mark where 'necessary to obtain a technical result', from the narrower exclusion under EU design law.
92. (2006) EWCA Civ 1285.
93. (2007) FSR 13; (2007) ECDR 4; (2006) EWHC 3154 Ch. D (Patents Ct).
94. *Ibid.*, citing *Landor & Hawa International Ltd v. Azure Designs Ltd* (2006) EWCA Civ 1285. The decision on validity was upheld on appeal in Procter & Gamble *v.* Reckitt Benckiser, although that on infringement was reversed: (2007) EWCA Civ 936; (2008) FSR 8.
95. See J. A. Tessensohn & S. Yamamoto, 'Japan: Trade Marks: Changes to Law', *EIPR* (2006): N 236.
96. Section 2. see <www.wipo.int/clea/docs_new/en/bz/bz002en.html> (22 Jul. 2007). There is also a requirement of eye-appeal.

C.   ALLOW FUNCTIONAL DESIGN TO BE PROTECTED, AT LEAST
                     WHERE THERE IS DESIGN FREEDOM, BUT STILL FOCUS ON THE
                     PRODUCT'S APPEARANCE

EC law, for example, does this, but it may have the effect of giving extremely narrow protection to functional design. This may be illustrated by the Australian case of *Firmagroup v. Byrne & Davidson Doors*,[97] where the defendants had made deliberate use of the plaintiff's registered design for garage door handles and taken novel features, the elongation of the handle and recessing of the handle and lock. Nonetheless, it was held that the defendants had not infringed. It has been argued that this result will always be a consequence of using designs registration to protect functional design.[98] Such narrow protection may be entirely appropriate if there is another 'second-tier' route to protection of functional principle, such as petty patents or utility models.[99] In the absence of such alternatives, however, design protection may be too 'thin'.

The 'under-the-bonnet' exclusion of EU design law,[100] whereby a component part of a complex product may be protected only where visible in normal use[101] – and not only during maintenance, servicing, and repair – may be considered an extension of this strategy. Despite this, a number of Community Design registrations for motor engines appear to have been filed.[102]

---

97. *Firmagroup v. Byrne & Davidson Doors (Vic) Pty Ltd* (1987) 180 CLR 483.
98. J. Lahore, 'The Herchel Smith Lecture 1992: Intellectual Property Rights and Unfair Copying: Old Concepts, New Ideas', *EIPR* (1992): 428; see also comments of S. Macchi & M. Richardson, 'Intellectual Property Cases in the Australian High Court: An Economic Reappraisal', *EIPR* (1997): 128.
99. Lahore criticizes the EU's failure to integrate thinking on design protection with proposals on utility models: 'What is surprising in the European context is how the development of designs and utility models is proceeding without any such analysis and any critique of the role of these systems in the overall Intellectual Property spectrum, or indeed their justification at all.' J. Lahore, 'The Protection of Functional Designs: The Amended Proposal for a European Designs Directive', *IPQ* (1997): 128. See also J. Lahore, 'Designs and Petty Patents: A Broader Reform Issue', *Aus IPJ* 7 (1996): 5; S.L. Moritz & A.F. Christie, 'Second-Tier Patent Systems: The Australian Experience', *EIPR* (2006): 230; M. Janis, 'Second Tier Patent Protection', *Harv Int L. J.* 40 (1999): 151; U. Suthersanen, 'A Brief Tour of "Utility Model" Law', *EIPR* (1998): 44; U. Suthersanen, 'Incremental Inventions in Europe: A Legal and Economic Appraisal of Second Tier Patents', *JBL* (2001): 319.
100. Regulation (EC) No. 6/2002, Art. 4(2)-(3); Dir 98/71/EC, Art. 3(3)-(4).
101. I.e. use by the end user and not during maintenance, servicing or repair: Reg. Art. 3.4; Dir Art. 3.4; D. Musker, 'Hidden Meaning? UK Perspectives on Invisible in Use Designs', *EIPR* (2003): 450.
102. See for example the unsuccessful attempts by Honda Motor Co. Ltd to invalidate Community Registered designs held by *Kwang Yang Motor Co Ltd* at <http://oami.europa.eu/pdf/design/invaldec/ICD-000000990-decision-(EN).pdf> and <http://oami.europa.eu/pdf/design/invaldec/ICD_000001006_decision_(EN).pdf>.

Denmark's Design Act 2000,[103] section 4(2) is to similar effect.[104]

The requirement of visibility in normal use can be distinguished from the concept of visibility at point of sale. A 'Ferrero Rocher' spherical chocolate has concentric layers which are invisible at point of sale, but are visible in normal use, namely consumption by the consumer.[105]

However, these last exclusions still do not deal with the question of aesthetic match, so a broader strategy might be required to prevent the protection of spare parts.

D.   PROTECT ONLY WHOLE ARTICLES (CARS, VACUUM CLEANERS)

This strategy should take all spare parts outside the scope of protection, except perhaps where a kit of parts is used to make a whole new article.[106] The problem here is how to define the concept of a 'whole' article. One approach would be to take an economic approach: if there is a distinct market for something, it should be regarded as an article or product in its own right. Automotive parts are 'made and sold separately', so may qualify as 'articles' for design law purposes under this argument, at least where they are optional parts rather than replacement parts: *Ford*.[107]

Australia's Commonwealth Designs Act 2003 section 6(2) uses separate manufacture as the criterion for protection: 'A component part of a complex product may be a product for the purposes of this Act, if it is made separately from the product.' Japanese design law formerly required parts to be made and sold separately. However, this requirement was relaxed in 1999:

> The new law expands the definition of registrable design to include the design of parts of articles whether or not they can be marketed separately. A partial design of this kind will be infringed when copied by only part of the defendant's article. It will no longer be necessary to compare the whole design of the defendant's article with the plaintiff's registered design in order to show infringement.[108]

This quotation demonstrates a perennial problem: where part of an article has been designed and infringed,[109] the whole-article approach requires a whole-article

---

103. P.G. Olson, 'Denmark: Design Right', *EIPR* (2001): fns 42-43; <www.wipo.int/clea/docs_new/en/dk/dk128en.html> (23 Jul. 2007).
104. 'Normal use' shall mean use of the complex product by the end user excluding maintenance, servicing, or repair work.
105. *Ferrero's Application* (1978) RPC 473.
106. See L. Gimeno, 'Spare Parts in Spain and from a European Perspective', *EIPR* (1997): 537.
107. *Motor Co. Ltd.'s Design Applications* (1993) RPC 399; (1994) RPC 545 (Div Ct); (1995) RPC 167 HL.
108. P. Melson, 'Japan: Registered Designs: Changes to the Law', *EIPR* (1999): fn. 7.
109. S. Clark, 'Intellectual Property Infringement of Design Right in the Design of Part of an Article', *Copyright World* 92 (1999): 20.

comparison for infringement purposes. Features that have no bearing on the designer's achievement may be taken into account by the courts.[110] This would lessen the likelihood of over-effective protection for spare parts but also reduce the level of protection generally.

Against this objection may be set the approach of Office for Harmonisation in the Internal Market (OHIM), the EC trademark and designs office in *Erredu v. Arrmet*.[111] Considering whether the design of the bar stool in question made the same overall impression on the informed user as the prior art,[112] the invalidity panel compared both the various features of the two designs taken individually and the overall effect, giving particular weight to visually significant, allegedly novel features.

The EC has tried to get around this conceptual difficulty by introducing the notion of the 'complex product' made up of multiple components that can be disassembled and reassembled.[113] A further distinction is made between complex products and modular products, the design of whose interconnections may be innovative and deserving of full protection.[114]

E.   EXCLUDE CERTAIN INDUSTRIAL SECTORS FROM DESIGN PROTECTION

Despite Beier's criticism of this potential approach,[115] it is perfectly in keeping with Paris, Berne, and TRIPs.[116] This is in stark contrast to the position for patents[117] and trademarks.[118]

---

110. See, e.g., *Clipsal Australia (Pty) Ltd v. Trust Electrical Wholesalers* (2007) SCA 24 (RSA), where the design registration showed the whole of an article and the 'definitive statement' did not indicate any particular aspect in which protection was claimed. The South African Supreme Court of Appeal held that infringement had been established, upholding the claimant's appeal on validity and infringement.

111. Ref ICD 000000024; Decision Of The Invalidity Division 27/04/04; English version available online at <http://oami.europa.eu/PDF/design/invaldec/3595-0001-en.pdf> (24 Jul. 2007).

112. The same test is used for infringement; a similar approach to infringement has been taken by the English courts in *Woodhouse UK v. Architectural Lighting Systems* (2006) RPC 1, PCC (UK registered design), see D. Byrne, 'An Illuminating Case on the Law of Registered Designs', *JIPLP* (2006): 758; (2006) *JIPLP* 442; and *Proctor & Gamble v. Reckitt Benkiser* (2006) EWHC 3154, CA (registered Community Design); see I. O'Connor, 'The Design Trigger: Proctor & Gamble v Reckitt Benkiser', *EIPR* (2007): 293; S. Clark, 'Fresh Air or Thick Fog?', *Copyright World* 169 (2007): 11.

113. Regulation (EC) No. 6/2002, Art. 3(c); Dir 98/71/EC, Art. 1(c).

114. Regulation (EC) No. 6/2002, Recital 11; Art. 8(3); Dir 98/71/EC, Recital 15, Art. 7(3).

115. F.-K. Beier, 'Protection for Spare Parts in the Proposals for a European Design Law', 25 IIC 840 (1994).

116. Apart from the requirement in Art. 27.2 to protect textile designs.

117. E.g. TRIPs Art. 27.1.

      Article 27 Patentable Subject Matter: '(1) Subject to the provisions of paragraphs 2 and 3, patents shall be available for any inventions, whether products or processes, in all fields of technology' (emphasis added).

118. Paris Art. 7; imported by TRIPs Art. 2.1; TRIPs Art.

One problem with this approach would be to define the relevant sector for exclusion. As industrial practices change, the boundaries between different sectors tend to dissolve. For example, many parts of automotive engines are now controlled electronically rather than by mechanical systems. Excluding the entire automotive sector from design protection altogether would be an excessive response to the spare parts dilemma.

F.   PROTECT DESIGNS ONLY FOR SPECIFIC ARTICLES AND
           EXCLUDE SPARE PARTS FROM THE LIST OF ARTICLES
           THAT MAY BE PROTECTED

Although the extremely useful Locarno Agreement Establishing an International Classification for Industrial Designs[119] contemplates design protection of spare parts, as mentioned above, it is non-mandatory and may be used without adherence to the treaty in standard or modified form. However, this approach would reverse a significant trend in design law, which has been to remove the rule of specialization so that design protection is not limited to the article for which the design is registered[120] (a trend that may also be observed in the field of trademarks).[121] One reason for this may be illustrated by the English case of *Bourjois v. British Home Stores,*[122] decided when registration only protected a design for specific articles. The claimant had registered a fancy design for a toiletries container, modelled on a champagne bottle in a cooling basket. The defendant marketed a close imitation, but with basket and bottle separate. Given the 'difference' test for infringement, the claim to an injunction failed. The defendant had escaped liability by splitting the 'article' into two parts. Thus, in order to protect a design across a range of articles, it was necessary to file a number of registrations for the same design to cover different types of article. This 'often proved prohibitively expensive'[123] and was probably an important factor in the low rate of design registration observed in the UK and many other countries with a similar system.[124] Again, this approach would probably be an excessive response to the issue of spare parts.

---

119. Signed at Locarno on 8 Oct. 1968, as amended on 28 Sep. 1979.
120. The European Community Design system shows this feature – A registered design is protected for all products and classification is used only for administrative purposes. See D. Musker, *Community Design Law* (2002) at 2-226.
121. Advocated in the 1920s by Schechter, 'Rational Basis of Trademark Protection', *Harv LR* 40 (1927): 813. See also, S. Maniatis & A. Kamperman Sanders, 'A Consumer Trade Mark: Protection Based on Origin and Quality', *EIPR* (1993): 406; F.-K. Beier, 'The Development of Trademark Law in the Last Twenty-Five Years', 26 IIC 769 (1995). Extension of trademark protection has not been universally welcomed. See, e.g., J. Davis, 'To Protect or Serve? European Trade Mark Law and the Decline of the Public Interest', *EIPR* (2003): 180.
122. (1951) 68 RPC 280 CA.
123. I. O'Connor, 'The Design Trigger: *Proctor & Gamble v Reckitt Benkiser*', *EIPR* (2007): 293.
124. Gerald Dworkin, 'Why are registered designs so unpopular? (1963) 16(2) IP Newsletter, Supp IF, i-11.

G.   Reduce the Duration of Protection for Spare Parts

Denmark's Design Act 2000 extended the maximum duration of registered design protection to twenty-five years for designs in general, in accordance with Directive 98/71/EC on the legal protection of designs, but maintained fifteen years as the maximum term of protection for spare parts.[125]

This option, with a minimum period of ten years' protection, was considered as one of the alternatives for reform of European Design law.[126] The Report to the European Commission[127] rejected this approach as providing no advantage to consumers over the status quo, except in the event that vehicle manufacturers were prepared to sell tooling to new entrants to the spares market after expiry of the term of protection.

Note that the duration of EC *unregistered* design is limited to three years from publication.[128]

H.   Specifically Exclude Spare Parts from Protection by
                      Reference to Their Desiderata: Fitting, Matching,
                      Permitting Re-assembly

This strategy may be seen in action in UK unregistered design right; under the Copyright Designs and Patents Act 1988, section 213(3) excludes certain features of shape or configuration from protection,[129] viz:

(a) a method or principle of construction;
(b) (i) features enabling the article to be connected, placed in, around, against another article so that either may perform its function [often dubbed[130] 'must-fit'];[131] and
(c) (ii) features dependent upon the appearance of another article of which the article is intended by the designer to form an integral part [often dubbed[132] 'must-match'].

---

125. P.G. Olson, 'Denmark: Design Right', *EIPR* (2001): N 42-43.
126. See Impact assessment of possible options to liberalize the aftermarket in spare parts: Report to DG internal market, Nov. 2003, available online at <http://oami.europa.eu/en/office/pdf/spare.pdf>. (23 Jul. 2007)
127. See above, fn. 93.
128. Council Regulation (EC) No. 6/2002 of 12 Dec. 2001 on Community Designs, Art. 11(1).
129. S. Clark, 'A Good Match or a Bad Fit? The "Must Fit" and "Must Match" Exclusions', *Copyright World* 95 (1999): 20.
130. Although the importance of using the statutory language and not shorthand was stressed in *Dyson Ltd v. Qualtex (UK) Ltd* (2005) RPC 19 at para. 27.
131. *Farmers Build Ltd v. Carier Bulk Materials Handling Ltd* (2000) ECDR 42 CA: removes protection from copying completely by express provision.
132. See above, fn. 129.

Surface decoration is also excluded by section 213(c); this is left to be protected (if at all) under copyright.

In *Dyson v. Qualtex,*[133] the English Court of Appeal had to consider whether an independent manufacturer's replacement parts infringed Dyson's unregistered design rights. In delivering the Court of Appeal's leading judgment, Jacob LJ remarked upon the large number of spare parts involved. This had implications for case management and had led to an extremely lengthy enquiry at first instance. On the substantive issues, Jacob LJ approved the comments of Mann J that unregistered design right had been drafted with spare parts in mind but rejecting the notion that they should be excluded from protection or given a special regime. Rather, they were to be dealt with like all other functional articles, although 'one or two provisions had particular application to spare parts'.[134] It was not possible to give the provisions a purposive construction, since the intention of section 213 was not clear.[135] Jacob LJ confirmed Mann J's approach to construction of the provisions 'without any particular leaning towards the suppliers of original parts, the suppliers of replica parts or consumers.'[136] The 'must-fit' exclusion was widely construed as embracing not only cases where there was no design freedom, but any situations where fit was involved. Jacob LJ clarified that 'must-fit' does not require the interconnecting elements to touch.[137] On the application of 'must-match' he held that the public's preference for an exact copy is not necessarily conclusive.[138] He expressed scepticism as to need for match with vacuum cleaners.[139]

Singapore introduced equivalent provisions in its Registered Designs Act 2000.[140]

Provisions such as these not only permit the manufacture and supply of spare parts, but also accessories not envisaged by the original designer. This is illustrated by the case of *Parker v. Tidball,*[141] where features of mobile telephone cases that were necessary to permit a case to be used with a particular phone, for example the shape of the transparent window through which the screen is viewed, were held to be excluded from UK unregistered design right.

---

133. *Dyson Ltd v. Qualtex* (UK) Ltd (2005) RPC 19 (2004) EWHC 2981 (Ch) Ch. D; (2006) EWCA Civ 166 CA (Civ Div). J. Smith & S. Burke, 'Design Rights: Original Manufacturers Maintain Control of Unregistered Design Rights', *EIPR* (2006): fn. 110; J. Sykes, 'The Unregistered Design Right: Interpretation and Practical Application of the Must-Match Exemption', *JIPLP* (2006): 442.
134. At paras 8-9, citing Mann J.
135. Paragraph 11.
136. Paragraph 10.
137. At paras 36 and 38.
138. At para. 64.
139. At para. 68.
140. Act No. 25 of 2000; S.H.S. Leong, 'Protection of Industrial Designs as Intellectual Property Rights: New Laws in Singapore' *JBL* (2003): 239.
141. *Parker (t/a PJ International Exclusive Leathercrafts) v. Tidball (t/a Satchel)* (1997) FSR 680. Interestingly, in this case the defendant was a former manufacturer and supplier of cases to the claimant. The defendant's claim to joint authorship of the designs failed.

I.   CREATE DEFENCES FOR SPARES AND REPAIRS

The EC Design Regulation has a transitional spare parts defence[142] in Article 110:

> 1. Until such time as amendments to this Regulation enter into force on a proposal from the Commission on this subject, protection as a Community design shall not exist for a design which constitutes a component part of a complex product used within the meaning of Article 19(1) for the purpose of the repair of that complex product so as to restore its original appearance.

This ensures that 'must-match' spares do not infringe. Note that the wording is broad enough to exclude the manufacture and sale of the part as well as its use by the repairer.

Ireland's Industrial Designs Act, 2001 contains a similar defence in section 42(5): 'The design right shall not apply to the use of a component part of a complex product for the purpose of repair of that product so as to restore its original appearance.' This form of words clearly exempts the repairer from infringement; it less clearly exempts the independent spare parts manufacturer or supplier.

The Japanese patent decision in *Canon v. Recycle Assist*[143] is considered in the chapter by Mineko Mohri.[144]

Australia's Commonwealth Designs Act 2003 takes this approach to the ultimate extreme. The 2003 Act contains an extraordinarily elaborate cascade of defence and definition that is worth setting out in full:

> Section 72 Certain repairs do not infringe registered design
>
> (1) Despite subsection 71(1), a person does not infringe a registered design if . . .
>   (b) the product is a component part of a complex product; and
>   (c) the use or authorisation is for the purpose of the repair of the complex product so as to restore its overall appearance in whole or part . . .
> (3) For the purposes of subsection (1):
>   (a) a repair is taken to be so as to restore the overall appearance of a complex product in whole if the overall appearance of the complex

---

142. Council Regulation (EC) No. 6/2002 of 12 Dec. 2001 on Community Designs, Art. 110 (1) 'Until such time as amendments to this regulation enter into force on a proposal from the Commission on this subject, protection as a Community Design shall not exist for a design which constitutes a component part of a complex product used within the meaning of Article 19(1) for the purpose of the repair of that complex product so as to restore its original appearance.'

143. IP High Court, 31 Jan. 2006 37 IIC 867 (2006), overturning the first instance that refilling constitutes permissible repair; in consequence, patent infringed. The decision of the IP High court was confirmed (although on different grounds) by Supreme Court, 8 Nov. 2007, 39 IIC 982 (2008).

144. See Ch. 3 of this book. See, also, C Heath & M. Mori, Ending Is Better Than Mending : Recent Japanese Case Law on Repair, Refill and Recycling', 37 IIC 856 (2006).

product immediately after the repair is not materially different from its original overall appearance; and

(b) a repair is taken to be so as to restore the overall appearance of a complex product in part if any material difference between:

 (i) the original overall appearance of the complex product; and

 (ii) the overall appearance of the complex product immediately after the repair; is solely attributable to the fact that only part of the complex product has been repaired.

(4) In applying subsection (3), a court must apply the standard of the informed user.

(5) In this section: repair, in relation to a complex product, includes the following:

(a) restoring a decayed or damaged component part of the complex product to a good or sound condition;

(b) replacing a decayed or damaged component part of the complex product with a component part in good or sound condition;

(c) necessarily replacing incidental items when restoring or replacing a decayed or damaged component part of the complex product;

(d) carrying out maintenance on the complex product.

In this section: standard of the informed user, in relation to the overall appearance of a complex product, means the standard of a person who is familiar with the complex product, or with products similar to that product use, in relation to a product, means:

(a) to make or offer to make the product; or

(b) to import the product into Australia for sale, or for use for the purposes of any trade or business; or

(c) to sell, hire or otherwise dispose of, or offer to sell, hire or otherwise dispose of, the product; or

(d) to use the product in any other way for the purposes of any trade or business; or

(e) to keep the product for the purpose of doing any of the things mentioned in paragraph (c) or (d).

The question as to whether a distinction between repair and reconstruction can be sustained was considered in the US case *Jazz Photo*,[145] involving disposable cameras:

Permissible repair is limited, as discussed herein, to the steps of removing the cardboard cover, cutting open the casing, inserting new film and film container, resetting the film counter, resealing the casing, and placing the device in a new cardboard cover. Included in permissible repair is replacement of the battery in flash cameras and the winding wheel in the cameras that so require.

---

145. *Jazz Photo Corp. v. ITC* 264 F.3d 1094, 59 USPQ2d 1907; *Sandvik Aktiebolag* 121 F.3d at 673, 43 USPQ2d at 1623 and cross-references.

J.   COMPULSORY LICENSING/LICENSES OF RIGHT

Article 31 TRIPs provides detailed conditions for involuntary patent licenses, but again there is no specific provision in TRIPs relating to design rights. Is this omission significant, suggesting that TRIPs does not permit compulsory licensing? Or does it mean that TRIPs is as permissive about this as it is about other aspects of design law? It is submitted that the second view is to be preferred.[146] Meinberg[147] has remarked:

> There are hardly any provisions – none in existing design Acts and only very limited in copyright Acts – which provide for a compulsory license of the respective intellectual property right. Compulsory licensing is not a familiar feature of the copyright terrain.[148]

This suggests that the failure of TRIPs to deal with the issue stems from a lack of concern amongst negotiators rather than a deliberate attempt to exclude compulsory licensing under design laws. In the same way, the Paris Convention has fairly detailed provisions on the compulsory licensing of patents in Article 5A(2) and (4). Article 5(3) states that patents may only be forfeit where the grant of a compulsory license would not be sufficient to prevent abuse, for example by failure to work the patent. This shows that the concept of forfeiture does not include compulsory licensing. As regards designs, however, Article 5B has only brief provision:

> The protection of industrial designs shall not, under any circumstances, be subject to any forfeiture, either by reason of failure to work or by reason of the importation of articles corresponding to those which are protected.

This provision makes no mention whatsoever of compulsory licensing. It is submitted that compulsory licensing of designs is not prohibited by Paris or TRIPs.

Meinberg's assertion that no existing design Acts contain compulsory licensing provisions is slightly wide of the mark as regards UK design law. A general provision for compulsory licensing of registered designs was repealed in 2001.[149] However, sections 11A-12 of the UK's Registered Designs Act 1949, as amended, make provision for Crown use of registered designs and for compulsory licensing in the public interest where the competition authorities have made certain findings. Sections 238-243[150] of the UK Copyright, Designs and Patents Act 1988 make similar provision for unregistered design right, whilst section 237 makes unregistered design right subject to license of right for the last five years of its term.

---

146. Especially in the light of Art. 8(2), see below, p. 176.
147. H. Meinberg, 'From Magill to IMS Health: The New Product Requirement and the Diversity of Intellectual Property Rights', *EIPR* (2006): 398.
148. Citing B. Ong, 'Anti-competitive Refusals to Grant Copyright Licences: Reflections on the IMS Saga', (2004) *EIPR* 505-514 at 512.
149. Section 10 of the Registered Designs Act 1949 (as amended) was repealed by Reg. 6 of the Registered Designs Regulations 2001. See G. Scanlan & S. Gale, 'Industrial Design and the Design Directive', *JBL* (2005): 91.
150. For the effect of s. 239, see below, fn. 155.

In *Azrak-Hamway,*[151] Mr Sean Dennehey gave a detailed preliminary decision on the question whether the license of right provisions were compatible with TRIPs. While concluding that TRIPs could not be applied directly, he went on to state that since unregistered design right was in addition to the requirements of TRIPs,[152] licenses of right could not be in breach of the requirements that TRIPs prescribes. The case had been argued on the basis that the license of right provisions of section 237 took the duration of protection below the TRIPs minimum of ten years.

Licenses of right under industrial copyright were available under the transitional provisions of the Copyright, Designs and Patents Act 1988. Royalties were awarded to compensate the rights owner for use of the designs, including royalties on spares: *Bance.*[153]

K.   LIMIT THE REMEDIES AVAILABLE FOR INFRINGEMENT

This is the effect of a number of general doctrines, such as the US misuse doctrine.[154] A specific statutory example can be seen in s.239 of the UK's Copyright, Designs and Patents Act 1988. This applies to unregistered designs in the final five years of their term of protection and ensures that injunctions will not be awarded against defendants who undertake to take a license of right.[155] Von Mühlendahl[156] has questioned whether injunctive relief must be available as of right once infringement of an intellectual property right has been established. Referring to the 'weak language' of TRIPs Article 44, the EC's enforcement directive,[157] the decision of the European Court of Justice in *Nokia v. Wardell*[158] and the US Supreme Court decision in *eBay v. MercExchange,*[159] he concludes not, except where legislative language gives an 'almost absolute' right to an injunction.[160]

---

151.   *Azrak-Hamway International Inc.'s Licence of Right (Design Right and Copyright) Application* (1997) RPC 134 PO.

152.   Which were satisfied by the availability of design registration for up to twenty-five years.

153.   *Bance and R. Bance & Co. Ltd's Application* (1996) RPC 667: copyright license of right under transitional provisions: 6.75% royalty for spares: *Stafford Engineering Services Ltd's Licence of Right (Copyright) Application* (2000) RPC 797 PO.

154.   See below, fn. 184.

155.   *Ultraframe (UK) Ltd v. Eurocell Building Pastics Ltd* (2005) EWCA(civ) 761; noted at 37 IIC 360 (2006).

156.   A. von Mühlendahl, 'Enforcement of Intellectual Property Rights: Is Injunctive Relief Mandatory?', 38 IIC 377 (2007).

157.   Directive 2004/48/EC of 29 Apr. 2004 on the enforcement of intellectual property rights (2004) OJ EU L195/16, Art. 11.

158.   Case C-316/05 *Nokia Corp. v. Wärdell* (2007) 1 CMLR 37; (2007) ETMR 20 ECJ (1st Chamber).

159.   *eBay Inc. v. MercExchange LLC* 126 S.Ct. 1837, noted at 37 IIC 751 (2006).

160.   Specifically, Art. 98(1) of Council Regulation (EC) No. 40/94 of 20 Dec. 1993 on the Community trademark.

L.   MAKE AVAILABLE A 'THREATS' ACTION TO DETER
                         OVERWEENING USE OF RIGHTS

In the UK and certain other Commonwealth jurisdictions,[161] laws relating to
registered rights[162] contain provisions to protect against groundless threats of
infringement proceedings being made against non-primary infringers. The rationale for this is that, whilst manufacturers and importers may be in a position to
stand up to a threat of infringement proceedings, retailers (or repairers) will shy
away from litigation. Thus, the person issuing the threats can erode the market for
the products quite effectively without ever issuing a direct challenge to the manufacturer or importer.[163] A person aggrieved by the threats, who may be the
recipient of the threat but can also be the manufacturer or importer whose market
is being eroded, may sue for a restraining injunction and damages. This will be
awarded unless the person making the threats can show that they were justified.
This reversed burden of proof makes the threats action a potent tool,[164] forcing
right-owners to choose between rushing into litigation, making bland notifications
of the existence of the rights, or making what have been called 'Delphic utter-
ances':[165]

> The Letter is the work of a master of Delphic utterances who uses all his skills
> to say everything and nothing and to convey an enigmatic message which has
> the same effect on the recipient as a threat or adverse claim whilst disclaiming
> to be either.

---

161.   Including Australia: A. Dufty, 'Australia: Trade Marks: False Threats', *EIPR* (1998): fn. 183;
       Hong Kong: H. Wheare, 'The Foundations of Hong Kong Patent Law', *EIPR* (1997): 29;
       C. Carnabuci, G. Pratt & J. Davidson, 'Under Threat: Obligation and Liability in the UK and
       Hong Kong', *Patent World* 156 (2003): 18; New Zealand: B. Brown & D.C. Calhoun, 'New
       Zealand: Interface Between Misuse of a Dominant Position and the Exercise Of IP Rights',
       EIPR (1990): 437; Singapore: *Aztech Systems Pte Ltd v. Creative Technology Ltd* (1996) FSR
       54 HC (Sing) started as a threats action.
162.   In the UK the threats action is also available in relation to unregistered design right: Copyright
       Designs and Patents Act 1988, s. 253. In *Quads 4 Kids v. Colin Campbell* (2006) EWHC 2482
       (CD) Ch. D notification to eBay was held to be a threat in relation to an unpublished Community
       registered design. In relation to copyright, see R. Taylor & J. McDonnell, 'Focus Point: A Threats
       Action for Copyright?', *JIPLP* (2007): 364, commenting upon *Point Solutions Ltd v. Focus
       Business Solutions Ltd* (2007) EWCA Civ 14. For a history of the common law position, see
       H.G. Lim, 'The "Threats" Section in the UK Trade Marks Act 1994: Can A Person Still Wound
       Without Striking', *EIPR* (1995): 138.
163.   The history and spread of the threats action is summarized in H.G. Lim, 'The "Threats"
       Section in the UK Trade Marks Act 1994: Can a Person Still Wound without Striking',
       EIPR (1995): 138.
164.   An attempt to strike out a threats action as an abuse of process was rejected in *Reckitt Benkiser
       UK v. Home Pairfum Ltd* (2004) FSR 37.
165.   *L'Oreal (UK) Ltd v. Johnson & Johnson* (2000) FSR 686 Ch. D: the 'utterance' was held to be
       a threat.

In the UK, though not in all other jurisdictions[166] with 'threats' provisions, lawyers may be liable as well as the client for whom they act.[167] In jurisdictions without the statutory threats action, issuing unjustified threats to sue may be regarded as a form of unfair competition, or abuse of right,[168] or contrary to general civil law principles on harm. In Germany, a letter containing a threat of infringement proceedings relating to trademarks that proved invalid was held contrary to section 823(1) of the German Civil code, despite the fact that the claimant did in due course institute proceedings.[169] The availability of threats actions in the UK and Ireland in particular may create a distortion in the enforcement of design rights across the EU, undermine the principle of disclosure in litigation,[170] discourage settlement,[171] and run counter to the aims of the EC enforcement directive.[172] It has been argued that the current regime is no longer justified.[173] However, it can be regarded as protecting the small repairer against improper bullying by rights owners; it is always open to the design right owner to issue proceedings or to justify the threats.

M.   'INTERNAL' OR 'EXTERNAL' LIMITS TO DESIGN LAW PROTECTION?

The discussion so far has centred on internal limits to protection, whereby the design laws themselves are adapted to deal with the balance of interests between the suppliers of original parts, the suppliers of replica parts, and consumers. The notion that the design laws should contain the entire code is an attractive one, and has support from competition lawyers[174] as well as intellectual property

---

166. For Australia, see J. Stuckey-Clarke, 'Copyright, Publication, Indirect Infringement and Unjustified Threats', *EIPR* (1991): 385.
167. D. Bainbridge, 'Solicitors: Beware Groundless Threats Actions', *IP & IT* 11 (2006): 7; I. Davies & T. Scourfield, 'Threats: Is the Current Regime Still Justified?', *EIPR* (2007): 259; an attempt to join solicitors after judgment failed in *Kooltrade Ltd v. XTS Ltd* (2002) FSR 49 Ch. D.
168. See below and I. Davies & T. Scourfield, 'Threats: Is The Current Regime Still Justified?', *EIPR* (2007): 259.
169. *Warning letter* Case GSZ 1/04, 15 Jul. 2005, Grand Civil Panel of the Federal Supreme Court, noted at 37 IIC 94 (2006). See S Steininger, 'German Supreme Court Stands Firm on Liability for Unjustified Warning Letters', *JIPLP* (2006): 247. The aggrieved party was not limited to suing under unfair competition law.
170. R. Ashmead, 'Threats and Woolf/CPR', *CIPAJ* 29 (2000): 62; Lambert, 'IP Litigation after Woolf Revisited', *EIPR* (2003): 406; N. Minogue & V. Salmon, 'You and Whose Army? Problems with Threats Provisions and the Patents Act 2004', *EIPR* (2005): 294.
171. See above, fn. 130, and R. Willoughby, 'Without Prejudice Discussions, Patents Threats and the Right to Intervene in Opposition Proceedings', *EIPR* (2000): 373; they may also lead to interesting conflict of laws issues in enforcing settlements: *Kenburn Waste Management Ltd v. Heinz Bergmann* (2002) FSR 45.
172. Directive 2004/48/EC of 29 Apr. 2004 on the enforcement of intellectual property rights (2004) OJ EU L195/16
173. I. Davies & T. Scourfield, 'Threats: Is the Current Regime Still Justified?', *EIPR* (2007): 259.
174. According to Korah in the following chapter, internal limits to intellectual property protection are to be preferred over the external limit of competition law, applied ex post.

law scholars.[175] However, no code can be complete, and principles from general law, substantive and procedural, may be pressed into service. Some of the main contenders are set out below.

N.   'NON-DEROGATION FROM GRANT'

In *British Leyland v. Armstrong*, a Common Law override[176] to copyright protection for car exhausts was imported from land law. The effect of *British Leyland* in the UK has now been replaced for copyright by Copyright Designs and Patents Act 1988 sections 51 and 213, but the defence is still available otherwise: *Mars v. Teknowledge.*[177] *British Leyland* was distinguished by the Privy Council in an appeal from Hong Kong in *Canon v. Green* and is likely to be of limited application in the future.

O.   SUBJECT THE EXERCISE OF DESIGN RIGHTS TO THE DOCTRINE OF *ABUS DE DROIT*, OR 'PATENT MISUSE', WHERE THIS IS AVAILABLE[178]

Perillo,[179] surveying the English language literature on *abus de droit* in civil law jurisdictions, takes the Civil Code of the Netherlands, 1992 as an exemplar and starting point:[180]

1. The holder of a right may not exercise it to the extent that it is abused.

2. Instances of abuse of right are the exercise of a right with the sole intention of harming another or for a purpose other than for which it was granted; or the exercise of a right where its holder could not reasonably have decided to exercise it, given the disproportion between the interest to exercise the right and the harm caused thereby.

3. The nature of the right can be such that it cannot be abused.

---

175. Non-legislative solutions, especially competition law, increase the cost of litigation. This will be especially so in Europe where private enforcement of competition law by way of actions for damages is being encouraged: see R. Lane, 'Current Development European Union Law II Competition Law', *ICLQ* 56 (2007): 422. See also the arguments of J. Drexl, R.M. Hilty & A. Kur, 'Design Protection for Spare Parts and the Commission's Proposal for a Repairs Clause', 36 IIC 448 (2005).
176. See chapter one of this book by Llewelyn and Barresi.
177. *Mars UK Ltd v. Teknowledge Ltd* (2000) FSR 138 Ch. D cf. *Canon v. Green*, below.
178. The Scots concept of aemulation is said to be similar to the French concept of the *abus de droit*: P. Forbes Scott Computer Hacking – The Scottish Dimension, Fifth BILETA conference <www.bileta.ac.uk/Document%20Library/1/Computer%20Hacking%20-%20The%20 Scottish%20Dimension.pdf> (9 Jul. 2007).
179. J.M. Perillo, 'Abuse of Rights: A Pervasive Legal Concept', *Pacific L. J.* 27 (1995): 37.
180. P.P.C. Haanappel & E. Mackaay, transl., *New Netherlands Civil Code Patrimonial Law: Property Obligations And Special Contracts* (1990).

The French doctrine of *abus de droit* has been summed up by Netanel[181] in the context of moral rights:

> An author may not exercise the right 'abusively to the detriment of third parties, nor unnecessarily impair interests he has granted to others in his works.

The problem with using this principle to free spare parts from intellectual property rights generally is that, given the range of opinion on the spare parts issue, it is difficult to argue conclusively that protection of spare parts is unreasonable or disproportionate. French commentators have pointed out that the courts will generally not interfere[182] with intellectual property exercise,[183] save in extreme cases.

The US doctrine of patent misuse is exemplified by the classic case of *Morton Salt v. Suppiger*,[184] in which it was held:

> It is a principle of general application that courts, and especially courts of equity, may appropriately withhold their aid where the plaintiff is using the right asserted contrary to the public interest.

In the instant case, the patentee's use of its patent to restrain competition in the sale of an unpatented article resulted in its being denied an injunction to restrain alleged infringement by a competitor. This is said to be a specific case of the general doctrine that he who seeks Equity must come with clean hands.[185] The doctrine of patent/copyright[186] misuse in the US is said to be equivalent to *abus de droit* in civil law systems,[187] but the cases also display interesting parallels with cases on breach of competition law by abuse of dominant position, in the next of our

---

181. N. Netanel, 'Alienability Restrictions and the Enhancement of Author Autonomy in United States and Continental Copyright Law', 12 *Cardozo Arts & Ent L. J.* 12, no. 1 (1994) at 55, citing Colombet, *Propriete Litteraire Et Artistique* (6th edn 1992), 109.

182. E.g. A. Bertrand, 'Multimedia: Stretching The Limits Of Author's Rights In Europe', *Beverly Hills B Ass'n J* 28 (1994): 113, citing F. Pollaud-Dulian Abus de Droit et Droit Moral, D. Jur. 1993 Ch. XXI.

183. See, also, *Chiavarino v. Sté SPE*, Cass. Civ 1, May 14 note by P. Sirinelli (1991) RIDA 272; D. Weiller, Abus de droit et propriété littéraire et artistique, Strasbourg, 1962, cited by N. Dalton, 'Will Remakes or Television Adaptations of Motion Pictures Give Rise to Moral Rights Claims by the Original Screenwriter and/or the Director under French Law?', *Ent L. R.* (2002): 75; R. Burrell & A. Coleman, *Copyright Exceptions: The Digital Impact* (2005) at 108, 207, 287.

184. 314 US 488, 62 SC 402 SC (1942) para. 5.

185. *Ibid.*

186. E.g., *Lasercomb America Inc. v. Reynolds* 911 F2d 970 (4th Cir. 1990).

187. J.M. Perillo, 'Abuse of Rights: A Pervasive Legal Concept', *Pacific L. J.* 27 (1995): 37. cf. P. Millett, 'Ramsay Comes to Hong Kong', *Hong Kong L. J.* 31 (2001): 20. Perillo makes a distinction between English and American law. See also J. Dufaux, 'Equity and French Private Law', in *Equity In The World's Legal Systems: A Comparative Study*, ed. R. Newman (1973), cited by N. Netanel 'Alienability Restrictions and the Enhancement of Author Autonomy in United States and Continental Copyright Law', *Cardozo Arts & Ent. L. J.* 12 (1994): 1.

strategic categories. At this point we may recall that Article 8.2 of the TRIPs Agreement states, as a 'Basic Principle':

> Appropriate measures, provided that they are consistent with the provisions of this Agreement, may be needed to prevent the abuse of intellectual property rights by right holders or the resort to practices which unreasonably restrain trade or adversely affect the international transfer of technology.

This suggests that abuse of right doctrines, and competition law remedies in these circumstances, are consistent with TRIPs.

P.   LEAVE SPARE PARTS PROTECTED, WITH COMPETITION LAWS
                             PROVIDING A BACKSTOP AGAINST ABUSE

Competition law control of abusive licensing practices is explicitly permitted by TRIPs Article 40. However, in the context of design rights over spare parts, refusals to license, at all or on reasonable terms, have been more troublesome. Law relating to abuses of dominance are called into play rather than law relating to restrictive agreements.[188]

MacQueen[189] argued for the application of competition law principles in the wake of *British Leyland* and Korah's chapter deals with the issues in detail.[190] In EC competition law, the classic case on spare parts was *Volvo v. Veng*.[191] The European Court of Justice confirmed that the essence of exclusive intellectual property rights gave their owner the right to refuse to license, unless further special circumstances prevailed, such as clearly excessive pricing, discriminatory conditions of sale (refusal to supply spare parts to independent repairers, for instance), or refusal to continue to manufacture spare parts for a vehicle no longer in production even though many vehicles of that type were still in use.[192]

As may be seen in Korah's analysis, in subsequent cases much emphasis was placed on the use of power in one market (conferred by the intellectual property

---

188. For the interplay of competition law and intellectual property under TRIPs generally, see H. Ullrich, 'Expansionist Intellectual Property Protection and Reductionist Competition Rules: A TRIPs Perspective', *J. Int'l Econ. L.* 7 (2004): 401.

189. H.L. MacQueen, *Copyright, Competition and Industrial Design* (1989; 1995); see also H.L. MacQueen, *Towards Utopia or Irreconcilable Tensions? Thoughts on Intellectual Property, Human Rights and Competition Law* (2005) 2:4 SCRIPT-ed 486 @: <www.law.ed.ac.uk/ ahrb/script-ed/vol2-4/hlm.asp>.

190. See the following chapter by Valentine Korah.

191. Case C-238/87 (1988) ECR 6211.

192. A. La Chimia, 'Steps to Untie Aid: the DAC/OECD Recommendation on Untying Official Development Assistance to the Least Developed Countries', *PPLR* (2004): 1 at fn. 22 (at p. 4 of the article) cites the problem of non-availability of spare parts for machines supplied under development aid programmes.

right) to prevent the emergence of (or competition in) a second market. Henrik Meinberg[193] notes:

> [T]he requirement of two distinctive markets which has been developed in the line of case law developing the 'exceptional circumstances' test might serve as a decent tool in this respect. Yet the ECJ gave up on this requirement more or less explicitly. In any case, to use this requirement would serve a similar purpose as to use the requirement of the prevention of a new product, namely to promote innovation instead of imitation.

At the time of writing, Hong Kong is introducing a new general competition law.[194]

At the legislative and judicial level, the US has the intriguing Noerr-Pennington[195] antitrust immunity doctrine,[196] whereby lobbying or combining to present an amicus brief does not infringe antitrust laws.

Q.   THE CONTEXT OF OTHER RELEVANT LAWS

In the final analysis, few of these strategies will be effective to free up the supply of spares if the specific design laws overlap significantly with other intellectual property laws, especially with laws of unfair competition.[197]

------

193. H. Meinberg, 'From Magill to IMS Health: The New Product Requirement and the Diversity of Intellectual Property Rights', *EIPR* (2006): 398, citing case C-418/01 *IMS Health GmbH & Co OHG v. NDC Health GmbH & Co KG* (2004) ECR I-5039 at para. 44. For comprehensive overviews of the IMS decision see *inter alia*: B. Ong, 'Anti-competitive Refusals to Grant Copyright Licences: Reflections on the IMS Saga', *EIPR* (2004): 505-514, and Stothers, 'IMS Health and Its Implications for Compulsory Licensing in Europe', *EIPR* (2004): 467-472.

194. See, e.g., C. Carnabuci, 'Competition Law the Beginning of a New Era: A General Competition Law for Hong Kong', G.C.R. 2007, Jun Supp (The Asia-Pacific Antitrust Review 2007), 45.

195. From *Eastern R. R. Presidents Conference v. Noerr Motor Freight, Inc.*, 365 U.S. 127, 81 S. Ct. 523, 5 L. Ed. 2d 464 (1961) and *United Mine Workers of America v. Pennington*, 381 U.S. 657, 85 S. Ct. 1585, 14 L. Ed. 2d 626 (1965).

196. See, e.g., Ann K. Wooster ' "Sham" Exception to Application of Noerr-Pennington Doctrine, Exempting from Federal Antitrust Laws Joint Efforts to Influence Governmental Action Based on Petitioning Administrative or Judicial Body', 193 A.L.R. Fed. 139 (2004).

197. For a comparative survey of species of unfair competition law, see A. Kamperman Sanders, *Unfair Competition Law: The Protection Of Intellectual Property And Industrial Creativity* (Oxford University Press, 1997). See also C. Galli, 'Italy: Unfair Competition: The Shape of a Good May Be Protected Even Though It Is Not Registered as a Trade Mark or Design', *EIPR* (2006): fn. 173; A. Horton & A. Robertson, 'Does the United Kingdom or the European Community Need an Unfair Competition Law?', *EIPR* (1995): 568; L.T.C. Harms, 'The Role of the Judiciary in the Enforcement of Intellectual Property Rights: Intellectual Property Litigation under the Common Law System with Special Emphasis on the Experience in South Africa', *EIPR* (2004): 483; S. Heim, 'Protection of competitors, consumers and the general public: The New German Law against Unfair competition', *JIPLP* (2006): 524; G. Schricker, 'Twenty-five Years of Protection Against Unfair Competition', 26 IIC 782 (1995); G. Schricker & F. Henning-Bodewig, 'New Initiatives for the Harmonisation of Unfair

Lahore[198] concluded that attempting to protect functional design within the design registration system was misguided and that, if unfair copying is the real issue, then that should be addressed directly. This suggests an unfair competition approach. However, Gimeno[199] has surveyed the application of Spanish unfair competition law to a dispute over spares. He points out that misappropriation, rather than misrepresentation, is a difficult area of unfair competition law.[200] Furthermore, when slavish imitation is necessary to compete at all, it is difficult conclusively to categorize it as unfair. In any event there will be a time lag before independent manufacturers 'reverse-engineer' the parts and tool up.

This natural limit on market entry by competitors may be sufficient protection for vehicle manufacturers. As regards the position of vehicle manufacturers at the point of their own market entry, Fryer[201] refers to Japan's law of unfair competition providing good market entry protection:

> Another example of improved industrial design market entry protection was in Japan, with its new unfair competition law that prevented,[202] slavish, almost identical copying of a product for three years from product introduction.

However, comment from Japan suggests that the law is being used in a manner favourable to the competitive process rather than to a particular market player.[203]

A legislative solution is to be preferred; if a balanced regime can be attained within design laws, at the very least it may act as a guide to the interpretation and the application of other laws to the spare parts issue. EC law is striving for a solution within design law. If this is achieved, it will apply in twenty-seven states and may be considered elsewhere, especially in civil law countries where Australia's legislative style may not be appropriate.

Competition Law in Europe', *EIPR* (2002): 271; C. Wadlow, 'Unfair Competition in Community Law: Part 1: the Age of the "Classical Model" ', *EIPR* (2006): 433; C. Wadlow, 'Unfair Competition in Community Law: Part 2: Harmonisation Becomes Gridlocked', *EIPR* (2006): 469.

198. J. Lahore, 'The Herchel Smith Lecture 1992:Intellectual Property Rights and Unfair Copying: Old Concepts, New Ideas', *EIPR* (1992): 428.

199. L. Gimeno, 'Spare Parts in Spain and from a European Perspective', *EIPR* (1997): 537, commenting on *Ford Werke AG v. Construcciones Metalicas Arregui SA*.

200. Article 10*bis* of the Paris Convention does not expressly require protection against misappropriation.

201. W.T. Fryer, 'The Evolution of Market Entry Industrial Design Protection: An International Comparative Analysis', *EIPR* (1999): 618.

202. An important innovation in this area of Japanese unfair competition law was the introduction of the injunction to restrain unfair trade practices at the suit of competitors. See C. Heath, 'YuPack', 38 IIC 363 (2007), commenting on *Yamamoto Holdings KK v. Japan Post*, Tokyo DC 19 Jan. 2006. The right of a sole importer to sue to restrain slavish imitation was confirmed in the Nu-Bra case: *Goldflag v. C'est La Vie*, Osaka DC 26 Jul. 2004, noted at 37 IIC 480 (2006).

203. J.A. Tessensohn & S. Yamamoto, 'Japan: Unfair Competition: Pharmaceuticals – Trade Dress', *EIPR* (2007): fn. 43.

VI.   REVIEW IN EUROPE: WHAT HAVE THE EUROPEAN
                    COMMISSION AND THE EUROPEAN PARLIAMENT
                    PROPOSED?

The existence in EC design law of a temporary compromise on the spare parts issue has been mentioned above at various points. Article 14 of Directive 98/71/EC on Legal Protection of Designs permitted Member States to retain protection of spare parts under design law or to amend their design laws in such a way as to liberalize the market for spare parts. A committee of the UK House of Lords[204] summed up the position as at 2004 thus (citations omitted):

> A number of Member States, including the UK, have provision in their laws relating to design rights to permit the use of 'must match' spare parts in repair or replacement in the after-market. Such so-called 'repair clauses' exist in the laws of Belgium, Hungary, Ireland, Italy, Latvia, Luxembourg, the Netherlands, Spain and the United Kingdom. Other Member States, including such substantial motor vehicle producers as the Czech Republic, France, Germany,[205] and Sweden still effectively retain design right protection for spare parts.

Article 18 required the European Commission to analyse the spare parts market and submit proposals for change to the European Parliament. Article 110 of Regulation (EC) No. 2/2002 on Community designs permits repair pending review of the Directive.

A report was commissioned[206] and in September 2004[207] the Commission proposed a directive to amend Directive 98/71/EC. Of the options set out in the report – maintaining the status quo, full liberalization of the parts market (no design protection of spare parts), shorter term of protection for spares, or providing the right to remuneration but not exclusivity of rights over spares – the Commission favoured the full 'liberalization' option,[208] with a proposed replacement text for Article 14:

> 1. Protection as a design shall not exist for a design which constitutes a component part of a complex product used within the meaning of

---

204. HL Select Committee on European Scrutiny Thirty-Fourth Report, 23 Sep. 2004.
205. Von Gerlach summarized a decision of the German Higher Court of Munich, 12 May 2005, as establishing that German law protected car body parts and conferred protection against distribution of unauthorized car body parts and that 'infringement claims based on current national design laws were neither excluded by current European Design law nor by a declaration of the car industry (lobby) to tolerate the free trade of car body parts'. L. von Gerlach, 'Design Protection – Where Do We Stand?', ECTA 26th annual conference, Deauville, 20-23 Jun. 2007.
206. See Impact assessment of possible options to liberalize the aftermarket in spare parts Final Report to DG Internal Market, <http://oami.europa.eu/en/office/pdf/spare.pdf>, 18 Nov. 2003 (last visited 9 Jul. 2007).
207. Press release IP/04/1101; COM(2004) 582 final 2004/0203 (COD) Proposal for a Directive Of The European Parliament And Of The Council Amending Directive 98/71/EC on the legal protection of designs.
208. <http://eur-lex.europa.eu/LexUriServ/site/en/com/2004/com2004_0582en01.pdf>.

Article 12(1) of this Directive, for the purpose of the repair of that complex product so as to restore its original appearance.

2. Member States shall ensure that consumers are duly informed about the origin of spare parts so that they can make an informed choice between competing spare parts.

A consultation was launched in EU Member States and the European Parliament's Economic and Social Committee published its views on 8 and 9 June 2005,[209] stating:

4.6 The Commission is right to say that design protection is meant to reward the intellectual effort of the creator of a design, and not to safeguard its technical functions or quality (see Explanatory Memorandum, page 9 of the proposal). It follows that it is right to describe design protection and safety as being on two different conceptual levels. However, it is evident that in practice, the liberalisation proposed by the Commission could lead to more components on the market which have not been properly tested[210] under the procedures mentioned in point 4.3 above and which do not meet the requirements of the ELV Directive. Consequently, the advantages to consumers which the Commission claims will flow from liberalisation should be balanced against the greater risks which the same consumers may possibly run...

5.6 The Committee supports the Commission's proposal, which comes in the wake of earlier legislative initiatives welcomed by the Committee and which may contribute to greater competition, lower prices and the creation of new jobs, particularly in SMEs.

5.7 However, the Committee considers that the proposal would benefit from being better grounded in terms of a clear demonstration of its compatibility with the TRIPS Agreement, from more illustration of its effects on employment and, in particular, from a guarantee that consumers – quite apart from the right to information which seems to have been secured – will not be affected in their choices, either directly in terms of the safety and reliability of products used by independent suppliers, or indirectly by the consequences of the use of such parts in the repair of complex products for which they are intended (basically, motor vehicles) on either their residual market value or on indirect costs (e.g. insurance).

---

209. 2005/C 286/03. J. Drexl, R.M. Hilty & A. Kur, 'Design Protection for Spare Parts and the Commission's Proposal for a Repairs Clause', 36 IIC 448 (2005).

210. Note the estimate that counterfeit and pirated goods are said to account for 5%-10% of vehicle spares: <http://europa.eu.int/comm/internal market/en/indprop/piracy/piracyen.pdf>.

Part 5

Issues under Competition Law

Chapter 8

Antitrust Considerations: Refusal to License Intellectual Property in the U.S. and EC

Valentine Korah

I.   INTRODUCTION

In both jurisdictions the courts have held that a firm with significant market power may be under a duty to supply goods or services to its competitors in exceptional circumstances, but in the U.S. recently this duty has been minimized generally by the Supreme Court.[1] The DC Circuit Court of Appeals, which hears all federal IP appeals, has held that there is an almost absolute right not to license intellectual property rights (IPRs).[2] The extent of a duty to license under EC law is less clear, and there may well be a duty on dominant firms to grant licenses. The amount of market power that is required for dominance under Article 82 of the EC Treaty[3] is

---

1. See, e.g., *Verizon Communications IC. v. Trinco LLP*, 540 U.S. 398, 124, S Ct. 872, 157 L Ed 2d 823 (2004), and fn. 7, below.
2. *Independent Service Organizations Antitrust Litigation (CSU v. Xerox) 203 F.3rd 1322 (Fed Cir 2000)*, cert. denied, 531 U.S. 1143 (2001) and *Intergraph Corp. v. Intel Corp.*, 195 F.3d 1346 (Fed Cir 1999).
3. Article 82 of the EC Treaty forbids as incompatible with the common market the abuse of a dominant position within the common market or a substantial part of it. It gives four examples, including:

   (b) limit or control production, markets, technical development, or investment to the detriment of consumers . . .

Christopher Heath, Anselm Kamperman Sanders (eds.), *Spares, Repairs and Intellectual Property Rights*, pp. 183-205.
© 2009 Kluwer Law International BV, The Netherlands.

considerably less than the threshold for monopolization contrary to section 2 of the Sherman Act in the U.S.[4]

Perceived ex post facto, after the investment has proved successful, a duty to supply may enable more firms to compete in a neighboring market, more to be produced and supplied at a lower price. Moreover, where the holder of a break-through patent refuses to license, it may have little incentive to invest in improving its invention. So, a license may enable a firm with such an incentive to invest in improvements even before the original patent expires. All this sounds pro-competitive, perceived ex post, after the investment in innovation has succeeded.

Nevertheless, the prospect of being required to share its invention with competitors reduces the incentive of the originator to invest in creating the invention and its incentive to improve it, and will require the appropriate amount of compensation to be determined and continually reassessed between unwilling parties. There is tension between the rationale of intellectual property (IP) and competition in the short term, although competition policy relates also to the long term and to incentives to investment. The basic rationales are similar.

In both jurisdictions a doctrine of essential facilities was developed in relation to goods or facilities, and the question is how far it extends to exploiting IPRs.

II.   U.S. LAW

Monopolization is a felony by virtue of section 2 of the Sherman Act. The crime presupposes that the perpetrator has significant market power. Conditions of entry are highly relevant and sufficient market power is seldom found unless a firm supplies over 70% of the market. Even an attempt to monopolize is seldom alleged against a firm without more than 50% of the market.

The U.S. Supreme Court created a doctrine of essential facilities, according to which the owner of facilities that were essential for others to enter a market was required to make access available to competitors downstream to avoid being guilty of monopolization. The origins of the doctrine lie in the Supreme Court case, *US v. Terminal Railroad Association*.[5]

Six of the railroads that converged near St. Louis, some on one side of the Mississippi, and some on the other, formed the Terminal Railroad Association. It acquired the St. Louis Union Station and the St. Louis Bridge. Later, it acquired the Wiggins Ferry Company and the Merchants' Bridge, giving it control over every way by which rail traffic could cross the river at that point. Over time, some

---

(d) apply dissimilar conditions to equivalent transactions with other trading parties, thereby placing them at a competitive disadvantage.

4.   'Every person who shall monopolise, or attempt to monopolise . . . any part of the trade or com-merce among the several States . . . shall be guilty of a felony. . . .'
5.   224. U.S. 383, 32 S.Ct. 507, 56 L.Ed. 810 (1912).

other railroads were admitted to membership, but the association never included all the railroads that terminated at St. Louis.

The government sought dissolution of the Association under section 2 of the Sherman Act. The Supreme Court held that the combination of all terminal facilities in a single system would be illegal unless it accorded equal treatment to all railroads. But the Association would not be dissolved, provided access were given to all terminal facilities on reasonable term. The Supreme Court held that normally the members of a joint venture may exclude third parties:

> But the situation at St. Louis *is most extraordinary* and we base our conclusion in this case, in a large measure upon that fact. It would be wasteful and impractical for each company to build its own bridge across the river [emphasis added].

The Court would not permit some railroads to acquire the only means of crossing the river and exclude competitors. The case was extreme in that there was nowhere within a hundred miles north or south where a third bridge could be built. The usual incentives to create the original bridge were not involved; the bridges already existed and they, and other means of crossing the huge river, were bought by a joint venture. Moreover, there was no need for the Court to decide what compensation was reasonable. Some new members had already been admitted to the Association and the newcomers could be admitted on similar terms. This was an extreme case, and the obvious problems of fixing compensation that arise when requiring access were not acute.

Lower courts, however, applied the doctrine of essential facilities in cases where the need for access was far less. A generalized obligation by a dominant firm to give access might reduce not only the incentive to make the original investment in the facility, but also further investments to improve it, and often there is no fair or simple way to determine the amount of reasonable compensation.

This expansive development was, however, ended by the seminal article by Philip Areeda, 'Essential facilities: an epithet in need of limiting principles'.[6]

The most recent judgment of the Supreme Court was in *Trinko*,[7] not an IP case, where the application of the essential facilities doctrine was so reduced as hardly to exist.[8] Verizon owned the local telephone loop for a large swath of the Northeastern United States, and was not required to provide its local telecommunications competitors with full access to the local loop. There was such a duty under a regulatory statute, but it expressly did not preempt application of the antitrust laws, so the Supreme Court was drawn into a full discussion of what antitrust law requires in the absence of a regulatory duty.

---

6. *Antitrust L.J. 841*, 54 (1989).
7. *Verizon Communications IC. v. Trinco LLP*, 540 U.S. 398, 124, S Ct. 872, 157 L Ed 2d 823 (2004). See *The Antitrust Bulletin* (Winter 2005); the whole issue is devoted to the case.
8. E. Fox, 'Is There Still Life in *Aspen* after *Trinko*? The Silent Revolution of Section 2 of the Sherman Act', *Antitrust L. J.* 73, no. 1 (2005): 153.

The discussion started (*Trinko*, paragraph 3) with a strong principle that even firms in a dominant position have no antitrust duty to deal save in narrowly drawn situations that did not fit the case. It linked this to the importance of not undermining incentives for investment and innovation by an incumbent and its rivals. It added that Courts are ill suited to identify the proper price, quantity, and other terms of dealing. Moreover requiring parties to negotiate supply 'may facilitate the supreme evil of antitrust: collusion'. It went on to consider (paragraph 4) how far the high value it placed on the right to refuse to deal was qualified. It read the closest precedent, *Aspen Skiing Co. v. Aspen Highlands Skiing Corp.*,[9] very narrowly.

Aspen may stand for the proposition that there is a duty to deal when a refusal would significantly exclude rivals, unless the defendant proves an efficiency justification. Indeed Professor Eleanor Fox[10] considers that *Trinko* did fit into the limited exceptions in *Aspen* and that the Supreme Court was altering the law by stealth. The owner of three mountains in Aspen had previously collaborated with the owner of the fourth mountain, Highlands, in selling a ticket that gave access to all four mountains. One year it terminated the arrangement and was not prepared to sell even its ticket to three mountains at the usual retail price, to enable Highland to sell a four-mountain ticket that had been popular. In *Trinko*, the Court distinguished *Aspen* on the ground that Aspen had dealt with Highlands previously. Such dealing must have been profitable, so terminating the arrangement gave rise to an inference that Aspen was sacrificing profits that flowed from a pro-competitive relationship for an anticompetitive reason.

That reasoning should not be extended too widely. Often supply is broken off because the market has changed dramatically, although that may not have been true in Aspen. In *Trinko*, the Supreme Court distinguished *Aspen*, as it had chosen to incur short-term losses for longer-term gain, and implied that this reflected anticompetitive malice. This is the second basis of liability for refusing to supply under U.S. law. The *Trinko* judgment, however, did not state that giving up short term profits for future gains amounts to monopolization, let alone work out the scope of such an offence. Most long-term investment amounts to relinquishing current profits for future gain. The Court merely distinguished the facts in *Aspen* from those in *Trinko*.

Cases in lower courts since *Trinko* have narrowed the essential facilities doctrine even further.

III.   EC LAW

Article 82 of the EC Treaty forbids, as incompatible with the aim of a common market, the abuse by one or more undertakings of a dominant position that may

---

9.   472 U.S. 585, 105 S.Ct. 2847, L.Ed.2d 467 (1985).
10. 'Monopolization, Abuse of Dominance, and Refusals to License IP to Competitors, Do Antitrust Duties Help or Hurt Competition and Innovation? How Do We Know?', European University Institute, Competition Law Workshop, 3-4 Jun. 2005.

affect trade between Member States in a substantial part of the Common Market. The EC Commission, which enforces Article 82, started in the 1970s to condemn as contrary to Article 82 refusals to sell goods to former customers when supply was indispensable to a customer's business. These decisions were confirmed by the European Court of Justice (ECJ).[11]

A.   COMMERCIAL SOLVENTS

In *Commercial Solvents*,[12] patent rights had expired, but considerable know-how was needed to produce the raw materials required to make ethambutol, a medicine for treating tuberculosis. The ECJ confirmed that Commercial Solvents enjoyed a de facto monopoly over the raw materials. Refusal to supply them created a stranglehold downstream, and it was abusive not to renew the contract. The medicine was being made by Commercial Solvents' joint venture and by Cyanamid Italia. The raw materials were indispensable for making ethambutol.

The early cases related to goods and services rather than to IPRs and to the supply of former customers, after the contract had expired or become frustrated. The first case concerned with the refusal to license IPRs was *Volvo*[13] in 1988.

B.   VOLVO

Volvo held a registered design for front wing panels for a specific model of car. It sued successfully when multiple items were imported for resale to repairers from a Member State that granted no IPR for spare parts. The importer stated that it was prepared to pay a reasonable price, but did not suggest any specific figure or method of reaching one. The ECJ said:

> 8. It must also be emphasized that the right of the proprietor of a protected design to prevent third parties from manufacturing and selling or importing, without its consent, products incorporating the design constitutes the very subject-matter of his exclusive right. It follows that an obligation imposed upon the proprietor of a protected design to grant to third parties, even in return for a reasonable royalty, a licence for the supply of products incorporating the design would lead to the proprietor thereof being deprived of the substance of his exclusive right, and that a refusal to grant such a licence cannot in itself constitute an abuse of a dominant position.

---

11. *United Brands Company and United Brands Continental BV v. Commission* (27/76), 14 Feb. 1978 (1978) ECR 207, (1978) 1 CMLR 429, CMR 8429.

12. *Istituto Chemioterapico Italiano SpA and Commercial Solvents Corp v. Commission* (6 & 7/73), 6 Mar. 1974 (1974) ECR 223, (1974) 1 CMLR 309, CMR 8209. See the opinion of AG Warner.

13. *Volvo AB v. Erik Veng (UK) Ltd* (238/87), 5 Oct. 1988, (1988) ECR 6211, (1989) 4 CMLR 122, CMR 14498.

9. It must however be noted that the exercise of an exclusive right by the proprietor of a registered design in respect of car body panels may be prohibited by Article 82 if it involves, on the part of an undertaking holding a dominant position, certain abusive conduct such as the arbitrary refusal to supply spare parts to independent repairers, the fixing of prices for spare parts at an unfair level or a decision no longer to produce spare parts for a particular model even though many cars of that model are still in circulation, provided that such conduct is liable to affect trade between Member States.

10. In the present case no instance of any such conduct has been mentioned by the national court. Accordingly, and having regard to the answer given to the second question, it is unnecessary to give an answer to the first and third questions.

11. It must therefore be stated in reply to the second question submitted by the national court that the refusal by the proprietor of a registered design in respect of body panels to grant to third parties, even in return for reasonable royalties, a licence for the supply of parts incorporating the design cannot in itself be regarded as an abuse of a dominant position within the meaning of Article 82.

Paragraph 8 contains strong language against a duty to license, but the qualifications in paragraph 9 have caused trouble in later cases. Since it was not suggested that any of those things had happened, no one had any interest in arguing that they were not abusive. Nevertheless, it has been assumed that in those circumstances a refusal by a dominant firm to supply or license might be abusive.

C.   Magill

Magill[14] Is probably the best-known EC case on refusal to license. The Commission and courts limited intellectual property rights. The three television stations transmitting programs that could be received in Ireland and Northern Ireland, separate Member States, each published its own weekly guide of programs in advance. When Magill started to publish a comprehensive guide to the three stations, each sued it successfully for copyright infringement. The Commission adopted a decision finding that this amounted to an abuse of their dominant positions and, in effect, required each to grant Magill a copyright license. This was confirmed by the Court of First Instance and the ECJ because of the exceptional circumstances of the case.

Article 82 applies to an abuse only if by a dominant firm. The ECJ confirmed that mere ownership of an intellectual property right does not confer a dominant position (paragraph 46),[15] but that since each station was the only source of

---

14. *Radio Telefis Eireann and Others v. Commission* (C-241 & 242/91 P), 6 Apr. 1995, (1995) ECR I-743, (1995) 4 CMLR 718, (1995) 1 CEC 400 (ECJ).

15. The U.S. Supreme Court came to this view late, only after the conference leading to this book: *Polygram Holdings Inc v. Federal Trade Commission*. At that time, the ECJ had long taken this view, *Parke, Davis & Co v. Probel* (24/67), (1968) ECR 55.

program information for a company publishing a comprehensive guide to television programs, they each enjoyed a dominant position over that information.

The ECJ also confirmed (paragraph 49 of the IMS decision) its established case law that in the absence of standardization or harmonization, the scope of intellectual property rights was a matter for national law, but added that 'the exercise of an exclusive right by the proprietor may, in exceptional circumstances, involve abusive conduct'.

The reference to exceptional circumstances may suggest that IPRs are to be treated differently from goods and other services. For a duty to license IPRs the circumstances must be special. On the other hand, there may be a duty to license those who were not customers previously. Neither Volvo nor the TV stations had ever granted licenses.

The ECJ then went through the various criteria mentioned by CFI in the judgment under appeal[16] and found that the exercise of copyright in *Magill* was abusive. There were no substitutes for the information, the CFI had found that the weekly highlights and daily programmes or the individual guides published by the stations were not sufficient substitutes. The producer of a comprehensive weekly guide was dependent on the stations:

> 54. The appellants' refusal to provide basic information by relying on national copyright provisions thus prevented the appearance of a new product, a comprehensive weekly guide to television programmes, which the appellants did not offer and for which there was a potential demand. Such refusal constitutes an abuse under heading (b) of the second paragraph of Article 82 of the Treaty.

The refusal was not justified, and enabled the stations to reserve the market for weekly television guides to themselves. In the light of all these circumstances, the ECJ held that the CFI had not erred in law.

How far the judgment went remains controversial. What was exceptional? Were the three conditions of paragraph 54 Magill decision cumulative – as indicated by the conjunction 'and' – or alternative? Were they exhaustive, or could other circumstances be special?

Few Member States grant copyright in information. Such copyright gives too broad an exclusive right. The stations needed consumers to be aware of their programs and needed no copyright protection to induce them to publish their own guides.[17] The United Kingdom law of copyright was changed in 1988 to require a statutory license.

---

16. The jurisdiction of the ECJ is limited to judicial review. It does not decide whether the Commission got the answer right, but whether the CFI on appeal committed a manifest error or failed to provide sufficient reasoning. The CFI is the final arbiter of the facts. Both courts allow the Commission considerable discretion in appraising complex economic facts.

17. Hugh Hansen's comment on Ian Forrester's speech on *Magill* in H. Hansen (ed.), *International Intellectual Property Law and Policy*, vol. II (New Jersey: Juris Publishing and London: Sweet & Maxwell, 1998) at 36-41. See also Jacobs AG in *Oscar Bronner GmbH & Co. KG v. Mediaprint Zeitungs-und Zeitschriftenverlag GmbH & Co. KG and others* (C-7/97) (1998) ECR I-7817, para. 63.

Nevertheless, it is questionable whether competition law should limit intellectual property law on grounds of policy. Do judges and competition authorities have the right background for the task? It would lead to great uncertainty, and intellectual property rights might not induce enough investment were their validity subject to so vague a test.

In *Magill*, it might have been argued that there was no market downstream, since no one could legally produce a comprehensive television guide to the three stations. The ECJ did not address the point, which it is thought is bad. It is worse for consumers if there is no one producing than if there are only a few. What matters should be whether the dominant firm controls an input needed to satisfy potential demand downstream. This has been accepted by the High Court of Australia, its Supreme Court, in *Queensland Wire Industries Pty Ltd. v. Broken Hill Pty Ltd.*[18] and by the ECJ in *IMS*.[19]

On the facts I have no objection to the result. The television stations must have enjoyed special or exclusive rights because they must have had a government franchise to transmit and use part of the frequency spectrum. Such licenses usually provide for universal access. This, however, was not the reasoning of the ECJ.

D.   OSCAR BRONNER

The duty to supply under Community law was not referred to by the judges as the essential facilities doctrine until *Oscar Bronner v. Mediaprint*,[20] where the ECJ in principle narrowed the duty to give access to an essential facility. After considering the U.S. case law on a requirement to give to competitors access to an essential facility, Advocate General Jacobs gave several classic reasons why any duty to provide access should be narrowly construed.

First, even when it is possible for two undertakings to use a facility satisfactorily, an obligation to supply reduces the incentive to make the original investment (paragraph 57). Second, it reduces the incentive of the newcomer to duplicate the facility when this is practicable (paragraph 57). And, third, since the holder does not want to grant access, someone will have to establish the amount of compensation and continually reassess it (paragraph 69 of the Sylfait decision). This is difficult for a regulator who is likely to have a great deal of information about the regulated market. It would be even more difficult for a court or general competition authority.

---

18. *Queensland Wire Industries Pty Ltd v. Broken Hill Pty Ltd* (1988) 83 ALR 577, comment Korah (2000) 32 Victoria University of Wellington Law Rev 231, 233 et seq., Hanks & Williams (1990) 17 Melbourne ULR 437. The court of appeal had held that there was no duty to supply because there was no market downstream: no transactions could take place because the monopolist refused to supply. In a famous judgment, this was reversed by the High Court.
19. *IMS Health GmbH & Co KG v. NDC Health* (C-418/01), 29 Apr. 2004, (2004) 4 CMLR1543 (preliminary ruling).
20. (C-7/97) (1998) ECR I-7817.

The Advocate General suggested that it was only when there is a serious bottleneck and no competition downstream (paragraph 58) that there should be a duty to supply. At paragraph 58 of the Bronner decision he said:

[T]he primary purpose of Article 82 is to prevent distortion of competition – and in particular to safeguard the interests of consumers – rather than to protect the position of particular competitors. It may therefore, for example, be unsatisfactory, in a case in which a competitor demands access to a raw material in order to be able to compete with the dominant undertaking on a downstream market in a final product, to focus solely on the latter's market power on the upstream market and conclude that its conduct in reserving to itself the downstream market is automatically an abuse. Such conduct will not have an adverse impact on consumers unless the dominant undertaking's final product is sufficiently insulated from competition to give it market power.

Like Advocate General Fennelly in *Compagnie Maritime Belge*,[21] Advocate General Jacobs suggested that where the dominant position is particularly strong, there may be wider duties to help its competitors.

Oscar Bronner wanted access to Mediaprint's national home delivery service for its paper, *Der Standard*, the circulation of which would not warrant the cost of such a service, but its case was particularly weak. The ECJ held it is not enough to show that use of the facility would be desirable; it must be necessary. *Der Standard*, the newcomer's paper, was enjoying spectacular growth and could be sold in kiosks, by mail, and other methods. The facility for home delivery might be desirable but was not necessary.

The ECJ suggested that where the facility was essential, there was a duty to supply unless the refusal was justified. This is disputed; it would result in patents for important inventions being of little value, as licenses would have to be given. The Court also suggested that once two undertakings enjoyed the facility, further supply would not be required. This is contrary to the implicit view in *Commercial Solvents*, above, where the monopolist's joint venture and Cyanamid Italiano were already making the medicine, yet supply was required.

E.   Microsoft

1.   **Dominant Position**

In *Microsoft*,[22] the Commission imposed the highest fine ever at that time, nearly EUR 500 million, partly for refusing to provide interface information to its competitors for operating systems for workgroup servers. Microsoft did not contest that it was dominant over operating systems for PCs. Not only had Microsoft supplied

---

21.   (C-395/96 P), 16 Mar. 2000, (2000) ECR I-1365, (2000) 4 CMLR 1076.
22.   OJ 2004, L (5.7 below).

over 90% of such licenses for several years,[23] it enjoyed direct and indirect network effects. Customers want an operating system used by as many people as possible (direct network effect) independent firms write application programmes for the system most widely used, so as to increase the demand (indirect network effect, paragraph 459). This in turn increased the height of the direct network effect barrier to entry. It was expensive to adapt a program working on windows to work on other platforms. Moreover, customers wanting to switch to other systems may have learning costs. These barriers to entry are not illegal; they result from the technology; but they help to establish the dominant position.

2.   Extending Dominant Position to Server Market

The Commission alleged, inter alia, that Microsoft had extended its dominant (quasi-monopoly) position over operating systems for client personal computers (PCs) to the adjacent markets in operating systems for work group servers (paragraphs 533, 779-781, 1065).[24] The Commission decided that withholding the information necessary to design competing programmes for work group servers that were fully compatible with Windows was an abuse (paragraphs 779-784) and risked eliminating competition from the server market (paragraphs 585-589 and 692), stifling innovation and reducing consumers' choice by locking them in.[25] At paragraphs 548-559, the Commission briefly considered several of the judgments on refusals to license in exceptional circumstances. It decided that the special circumstances mentioned in *Magill*[26] were not exhaustive (paragraph 555), contrary to the ruling of the ECJ, in *IMS* the following month, that they were exhaustive.

3.   Microsoft's Alleged Justification

Microsoft's justification for refusing to share the interface information was that the information was the result of massive research and development, much of it protected by intellectual property rights (paragraphs 709 and 783). In rejecting this defense, the Commission adopted a concept of the function of intellectual property rights that had not been greatly developed in the EC case law:

> 711. The central function of intellectual property rights is to protect the moral rights in a right-holder's work and ensure a reward for the creative effort. But

---

23. Paragraphs 431-435 give various measures, all over 90%.
24. Earlier the U.S. Department of Justice had attacked Microsoft for extending its market power over Windows PC operating systems to the complementary market for Internet browsers. This prevented Netscape from attracting enough applications software to become satisfactory middleware that might have removed the applications barrier to entry into the market for client PCs.
25. Francois Leveque, 'Innovation, Leveraging and Essential Facilities: Interoperability Licensing in the EU Microsoft Case', *World Competition Law and Economics Review* 28 (2005): 71.
26. The ECJ's preliminary ruling in *IMS* (Section III.F, below), was decided a month after the Commission's decision and did not mention the Commission's view of what circumstances are special.

it is also an essential objective of intellectual property law that creativity should be stimulated for the public good. A refusal by an undertaking to grant a licence may, under exceptional circumstances, be contrary to the general public good by constituting an abuse of a dominant position with harmful effects on innovation and on consumers.

The focus on moral rights is not in the common law tradition, but is widely accepted in civil law systems. The idea of a reward for creative effort may come from the early cases on exhaustion and the civil law justification for intellectual property rights, the essential objective of stimulating creativity for the general good; but it begs the question as to how this should be done. The decision merely asserts that copyright will not prevail in exceptional circumstances, and this had already been decided in *Magill* (see above, fn. 18). The exceptional circumstances in this case, however, were different from those in *Magill* and *IMS* or *Volvo*.

4.   Remedy

The remedy is far reaching and goes far beyond those imposed in the U.S. The decision is based on the concept that Microsoft has the opportunity to spread its near-monopoly in PC client operating systems to adjacent markets. If it be allowed to continue, it may become impossible for a new entrant to compete for the next generation of information technology (IT).

a.   To Supply Whom

The interface information is required to be given to anyone prepared to pay a reasonable and nondiscriminatory price for it in order to provide operating systems for work group servers. The facility must be essential, but how many firms must be given access? Under the early case law, access was required to more than one undertaking that had had previous dealings with the dominant firm. In *Oscar Bronner v. Mediaprint*,[27] the ECJ implied that once two undertakings operated a national delivery service, compulsory access would not be justified. Once the essential facility is being made available to one competitor, there ceases to be a complete monopoly.[28]

On the other hand, the Commission would like to make the dominant firm's resources available to everyone. The problem of setting a reasonable price for access is easier when the essential facility was created by a joint venture,[29] as the original formula may not need much alteration[30] when providing for newcomers.

---

27. (C-7/97), 26 Nov. 1998, (1998) ECR I-7817, (1999) 4 CMLR 112, (1999) CEC 53, see Section III.D, above.
28. Discrimination might be abusive under Art. 82(c) if the transactions are equivalent (see above, fn. 2).
29. As in the first American case, *US v. Terminal Railroad of St. Louis Association*, 224 U.S. 383, 32 S.Ct. 507, 56 L Ed 810 (1912), see above, fn. 5.
30. It may be necessary to raise the amount to take inflation and risk into account.

Would access to interface information have been required had Microsoft been less dominant over PC operating systems, or if it had not already achieved a dominant position in the work group server market? No one knows.

b.   *FRAND Prices*

Requiring Microsoft to charge no higher price than that charged within Microsoft's group of wholly-owned companies or divisions is not a long term solution. Microsoft could raise that price too. It is unlikely to care which department makes profits.

No one knows what is a fair, reasonable, and nondiscriminatory (FRAND) return for a risky, innovative investment, or even the criteria for deciding. Yet if requiring access to an essential facility is ever sensible, this may be the case.[31] Would domination of the entire industry make entry into any part of it virtually impossible? The Commission requires that a trustee be appointed to monitor compliance and he will have to take many decisions that will be criticized as arbitrary.

On appeal the CFI upheld the Commission's decision.[32] It is widely thought that judgment of the CFI was less convincing than the Commission's decision. The Court was a full court of thirteen judges, whose ideas clearly differed. The CFI focused its remarks narrowly on various findings of fact made by the Commission and found no manifest error of appraisal.

F.   IMS[33]

A German court of first instance granted an interim injunction against NDC Health for infringement of copyright in a set of maps that *IMS* had prepared with the help of its customers to organize the trading information that it collected for them commercially. IMS claimed that the use of these maps was essential for its competing business because customers wanted the information prepared in a way that made it easy to compare with earlier periods. Transmitting it on a different basis would not be acceptable to its clients. The German trial court requested a preliminary ruling from the ECJ,[34] which followed *Magill* closely and with no reference to policy.

1.   Conditions in *Magill* Cumulative: Novelty

At paragraph 38 the ECJ stated that the conditions set out above were cumulative. There is an abuse only if

---

31. Another may be where there are legal or de facto standards, Section III.H, below.
32. *Microsoft v. Commission*, T-201/04, (2007) ECR 3601, (2007) 5 CMLR 846.
33. *IMS Health v. Commission II* (T-184/01 R II), 26 Oct. 2001, OJ 2002, C144/45, (2002) 4 CMLR 58 (order of the President of the CFI suspending the duty to license).
34. *IMS Health GmbH & Co KG v. NDC Health* (C-418/01), 29 Apr. 2004, (2004) 4 CMLR 1543, paras 48-50. See also Opinion of AG Tizzano at paras 60-61. The AG merely cites earlier judgments and the Court's judgment is even shorter.

49. . . . The undertaking which requested the licence does not intend to limit itself essentially to duplicating the goods or service already offered on the secondary market by the owner of the copyright but intends to produce new goods or services not offered by the owner of the right and for which there is a potential consumer demand.

This confirms the narrow view of *Magill*. Presumably, case law will have to work out how different and superior the product demanded is from that already supplied. The question may arise when a dispute is before an National Competition Authority (NCA) or a national court, so the level of novelty may not be the same throughout the Community. There is considerable controversy about the requirement of novelty.[35] Not only is the concept imprecise; 'intention' is a slippery word. Perhaps, a minor change to an existing product is not enough, but there must be a new kind of product.[36] Moreover novelty is not always desirable. A novel front wing panel for an existing model of car might not fit.

2.   Conditions in *Magill* Exhaustive

In *Volvo*, the ECJ had indicated other circumstances that might give rise to a duty to license or supply, such as refusing to license a repairer to make spare parts, coupled with a refusal to supply them on reasonable terms. In *Microsoft*, a decision adopted just before judgment in *IMS* and confirmed on appeal,[37] the Commission relied on there being other possible exceptional circumstances.

3.   Access Must Be Essential To Prevent All Competition Being Eliminated

Following constant case law, in *IMS* (paragraphs 40-45) the ECJ repeated that for the refusal of access to amount to an abuse, access must be essential. Whether it was essential is a matter for the national court (paragraphs 46 & 47). AG Tizzano went a little further and stated (paragraphs 84-86) that if there were exceptional

---

35. Contrast D. Ridyard, 'Compulsory Access Under EC Competition Law – A New Doctrine of Convenient Facilities and the Case for Price Regulation', *ECLR* 11 (2004): 669 – who fears that even minor changes intended by the newcomer would create a duty to give access – with C. Ahlborn, D. S. Evans & A. J. Padilla, 'The Logic & Limits of the Exceptional Circumstances Test in *Magill* and *IMS Health*', *Fordham ILJ* 28 (2005): 1109, 1147:

We say that a *new product* is 'new' for the purpose of the implementation of this test is one that satisfies potential demand by meeting the needs of consumers in ways that existing products do not. That is, a new product *expands* the market by bringing in at current prices consumers who were not satisfied before (emphasis original).

36. At a conference organized by the University of Antwerp and LECG, on 10 Jun. 2005, John Temple Lang suggested that that para. 54 in *Magill* related to a new kind of product and not just a new product. I find the distinction difficult to draw. How different must the new product be to be different in kind?

37. *Microsoft v. Commission*, T-201/04, (2007) ECR II-1491. There will be no further appeal.

switching costs for the customers of the firms wanting access, access would be necessary. This might depend on the extent to which the customers had helped *IMS* to create a standard and adapted their organization to the standard. Again, different NCAs and courts may use different standards.

AG Tizzano (paragraph 61) said that not only must access be essential to the complainant; the refusal must eliminate all competition on the secondary market,[38] a phrase used also in the judgment (paragraph 52). Until the judgment in *IMS* was delivered, many judgments referred to eliminating all competition on the part of the person requesting the service or license. That is true in the early cases on refusal to supply goods,[39] also in *Bronner*. In *Magill* (paragraph 56), the Court referred to the dominant firm reserving the market to itself or its subsidiary, but in *Télémarketing*,[40] it referred to this as meaning eliminating all competition on the part of the person requesting the service (paragraphs 26-27).

If the judgment in *IMS* has settled whether all competition or only competition from the complainant has been eliminated, a duty to supply may be reduced by supplying an undertaking that is not likely to act very aggressively. There is always a risk, however, that if the price for supply remains high, or the court is of the view that access is only theoretical (to avoid a duty to supply) the court might refer back to other cases, such as *Bronner*.

4.   Secondary Market May Be Potential or Hypothetical

The ECJ accepted that the duty to supply arises only if there are two separate markets, one upstream and the other down, but it followed AG Tizzano (paragraphs 56-59) and added that 'it is sufficient that a potential market or even a hypothetical market can be identified' (paragraph 44): a question for the national court to answer. This view delights me (see above, fn. 8): requiring only a potential or hypothetical market seems to me to be a polite way of rejecting the doctrine that for a duty-to-supply to arise there must be two markets where transactions are being concluded. It does, however, enable the holder of the essential asset to exploit the primary market.

5.   No Justification

No specific observations were made to the Court about whether the refusal was justified. As in many earlier cases, the ECJ said that there is abuse if the refusal is not justified by objective considerations (paragraph 52).

---

38. In *Magill* (para. 56, [Section 8.1.2, above]) the ECJ referred to the dominant firms reserving the secondary market to themselves, which amounts to the same thing.
39. *Istituto Chemioterapico Italiano SpA and Commercial Solvents Corp v. Commission* (6 & 7/73), Mar. 6,1974, (1974) ECR 223, (1974) 1 CMLR 309, CMR 8209, para. 25.
40. *Centre Belge d'Etudes du Marché-Télémarketing SA (CBEM) v. Compagnie Luxembourgeoise de Télédiffusion* (311/84), 3 Oct. 1985, (1985) ECR 3261, (1986) 2 CMLR 558, CMR 14246.

6. Level of Compensation

Should the compensation be set at a level that enables the newcomer downstream to make a profit? This would act as an umbrella protecting the newcomer even if inefficient. If it be set on the basis of the costs of the incumbent including a normal profit, multiplied by a premium for successful risk-taking, the incumbent would have a perverse incentive to increase its costs! In *Microsoft*, the Commission stated that a reasonable price would not include a monopoly profit. This is controversial. IPRs are granted to encourage firms to invest by enabling them to benefit from their investment. If the monopoly value in the present use can be charged, access would be sought only when the newcomer had added value to contribute.

7. Conclusion on *IMS*

For the reasons given by AG Jacobs in *Oscar Bronner*, I hope that refusals to license rarely amount to an abuse, but there seems to be no good reason for limiting the doctrine to cases where the newcomer wants to make a new product. In cases dealing with an open exclusive license, the Commission never found that a product was new, even if it was the best available, but this was rejected by the ECJ in the *Maize Seed* case, a case on the meaning of an 'open exclusive license',[41] where the Commission had found that the improved varieties were not new. In my view, it is unfortunate that the Court attempted to define the criteria of special circumstances in a short phrase.

G. SYFAIT

In *Syfait*[42] the Greek competition authority asked the ECJ for a preliminary ruling. Greek wholesalers had complained that GlaxoSmithKline (GSK) had ceased in November 2000 to meet in full their orders for three medicines over which it held a dominant position, and that GSK had stated that it would supply hospitals and pharmacies directly. GSK alleged that parallel exports by the wholesalers had led to significant shortages on the Greek market. The Greek authority accepted that GSK enjoyed a dominant position over the three medicines and observed that all the Member States fix the prices of pharmaceutical products within their territories. Prices in Greece were consistently the lowest in any Member State.

Eventually, the ECJ declined jurisdiction on the ground that the Greek authority was subject to ministerial influence and, consequently, was not a court or tribunal entitled to a preliminary ruling. Advocate General Jacobs had, however,

---

41. *Nungesser (LG) KG and Kurt Eisele v. Commission* (258/78), 8 Jun. 1982, OJ 1978 L286/23, (1982) ECR 2015, (1983) 1 CMLR 278, CMR 8805, para. 53.
42. *Synetairismos Farmakopoion Aitolias & Akarnanias (Syfait) and Ors. v. GlaxoSmithKline AEVE* (C-53/03), (2005) 5 CMLR 7. The ECJ declined jurisdiction under Art. 234, so the opinion of the AG will retain some authority.

perceptively analysed the case law and the economic context of the refusal to supply. He accepted (paragraph 66) that on occasion a dominant firm might be under an obligation to supply goods or services, for instance when an interruption would disrupt competition downstream between the incumbent and its customer. He added that, in a narrow range of circumstances, a dominant firm might have to supply a third party for the first time to avoid exceptional harm to competition. He noted the difference between the earlier case law on refusals to supply goods and the later decisions since *Volvo*.

Nevertheless, the ECJ had consistently limited the obligation to supply or license by reference to the possibility of objective justification. Consequently AG Jacobs insisted that a duty to give access does not arise easily or automatically:

> 69. . . . a dominant pharmaceutical undertaking which restricts the supply of its products does not necessarily abuse its dominant position within the meaning of article 82 EC merely because of its intention thereby to limit parallel trade.

He concluded that an intention to limit parallel trade might plausibly be one of the relevant circumstances that would ordinarily render a refusal to supply abusive (paragraph 70). Nevertheless such conduct was capable of objective justification (paragraph 71). The facts of the case were extreme owing to the control over prices and distribution exercised in differing ways by Member States (paragraphs 76-85):

(a) Price differences were imposed by national law: the common market was partitioned not by the dominant firm but by the various kinds of control over price and distribution imposed by Member States (paragraph 84).
(b) If parallel imports were permitted it would be impossible for the pharmaceutical companies to ensure adequate supplies in each Member State, because they would all be sourced from the country where the maximum price was lowest. Moreover, they were subject to regulation by national law that restrained suppliers from withdrawing a medicine once introduced (paragraph 86).
(c) The national regulations were segregated. So, a duty to supply any quantity demanded might lead to the medicines not being supplied at all in the countries where the maximum price was low, or at least to supply being delayed (paragraphs 87 and 91).

These arguments had been raised and dismissed by the ECJ in the early cases on exhaustion, but the Commission and CFI are now looking more to economic arguments. AG Jacobs is well respected and his opinion cogent. He restricted the application of his view strictly, which may make it more acceptable.

In paragraphs 89-91 the Advocate General analysed the economics of the innovative pharmaceutical industry, with substantial investment in high fixed costs – which were mostly sunk (of little use save for developing the particular medicine) – and relatively low variable costs. This made it rational for the pharmaceutical companies to sell wherever they could cover their variable cost. The mere fact that this might be possible does not ensure that a producer could recover its total costs if that price were generalized throughout the Community.

This statement impliedly accepts that unilateral discriminatory pricing does not necessarily infringe Article 82. It is widely accepted by economists, most of whom advocate 'Ramsey pricing'.[43]

Usually parallel trade leads to consumers in the lower-priced countries paying less, but that is not the position for medicines, where the government or insurers normally bears the cost. In some Member States, the government pays as much for medicines subject to parallel trade as for those bought by wholesalers directly from the producer at a higher price.

He concluded, therefore that for a pharmaceutical producer to restrict supplies:

> 100. . . . [T]o limit parallel trade is capable of justification as a reasonable and proportional measure in defence of that undertaking's commercial interests. Such a restriction does not protect price disparities, which are of the under-taking's own making, nor does it directly impede trade, which is rather blocked by public service obligations imposed by the Member States. To require the undertaking to supply all export orders placed with it would in many cases impose a disproportionate burden given the moral and legal obli-gations on it to maintain supplies in all Member States. Given the specific economic characteristics of the pharmaceutical industry a requirement to supply would not necessarily promote either free movement or competition, and might harm the incentive for pharmaceutical undertakings to innovate. Moreover, it cannot be assumed that parallel trade would in fact benefit either the ultimate consumers of pharmaceutical products or the Member States as primary purchasers of such products.

The judgment is clearly limited to markets subject to specific controls such as those exercised by Member States over the pharmaceutical industry. Competition is distorted by the control over prices and distribution. The reasons for desiring 'Ramsey pricing' in this industry are also clearly set out. I hope that this will encourage the institutions to follow the Advocate General. He has not fired a broadside in favor of limiting exports.

On receiving the preliminary ruling of the ECJ, the Greek competition author-ity required GSK to supply one of the medicines. The relevant market was not disputed, but only one of the medicines lacked substitutes. The Greek dealers who had pressed the competition authority to request a reference appealed against the decision and the case reached the administrative court of appeal, which has sought a preliminary ruling from the ECJ. Meanwhile, AG Jacobs has retired and the terms

---

43. F.P. Ramsey, 'A Contribution to the Theory of Taxation', *Economic Journal* 37 (1929): 47-61. Provided that no price is below variable cost, no one is worse off if most of the sunk overhead is recovered from those willing to pay more, and most buyers are better off. In the low-priced market, supplies will be available for those able and willing to pay the variable cost, and this may even provide some contribution to the overhead, which would benefit those who have to pay more. Economists generalize the theory and argue that supply will be most efficient if the sunk overhead is recovered from different markets in inverse proportion to the elasticity of demand.

of many of the judges expired. The judicial work had to be redone, but Mr. Jacobs' opinion was available for study.

H.   SUBSEQUENT DEVELOPMENTS

Much has happened since 2006. Microsoft appealed against the Commission's decision. I must mention, but will not discuss fully, the judgment of the CFI in *Microsoft v. Commission*, the judgment of the ECJ in *Syfait II*, and the Commission's Guidance on its Enforcement Priorities in Applying Article 82 EC Treaty to Abusive Exclusionary Conduct by Dominant Undertakings.

1.   The Judgment of the Full Court of the CFI in *Microsoft*

On appeal,[44] the CFI upheld the Commission's decision. It is widely thought that judgment of the CFI was less convincing than the Commission's decision. The Court was a full court of thirteen judges, whose ideas clearly differed. Separate or dissenting judgments are not delivered. The CFI focused its remarks narrowly on various findings of fact made by the Commission, found no manifest error of appraisal, and confirmed the decision. Microsoft withdrew its appeal to the ECJ.

The CFI's factual focus results in the broader legal significance of its judgment being limited. The CFI confirmed that a refusal to license IPRs may infringe Article 82 when the dominant firm is active in a market downstream, the input is essential for rivals to compete in that market, and the competitor seeking the input wanted to supply an unmet consumer demand.[45] It confirmed the view of the ECJ in *IMS* that a refusal to supply might be abusive even if *all* competition downstream was not eliminated; it is enough if *all effective* competition be eliminated. It added that failing to meet consumer demand included limiting technical progress.

The CFI confirmed that the burden of establishing a justification before the end of the administrative proceeding fell on the dominant firm. It added, however, that it was only an evidentiary burden. The dominant firm should specify and provide evidence of specific kinds of efficiency. It was for the Commission, however, to establish that the justification did not outweigh the consumer harm. This is very important, as neither the consumer harm nor the justification can usually be quantified, and the person on whom the burden rests is likely to lose the case. There has been pressure for some time to limit the burden of proof in this way, and this is a major point for the future.

In October 2007, shortly after the judgment, Microsoft settled the long-going dispute with the Commission about the conditions of supply of the interoperability information by reducing the royalty almost to nothing. Nevertheless, the Commission imposed very heavy fines for failing to comply with its order before the

---

44. *Microsoft v. Commission*, T-201/04, (2007) ECR 3601, (2007) 5 CMLR 846.
45. See John Kallaugher & Andreas Weitbrecht, 'Microsoft and More – Developments Under Articles 81 and 82 EC in 2007', *ECLR* 29 (2008): 418, 424.

settlement was reached. This was greatly criticized because, at the time the information was sought, it was not clear that the refusal to supply it would infringe
Article 82; the terms of supply were uncertain and the Commission repeatedly
refused to define them more precisely. Moreover, the terms of supply also under-
mined the incentive to invest in improving the technology.[46]

There have been many criticisms of the judgment. It was poorly written.
Concepts like 'likely to exclude' and 'of a nature to exclude' were confused
between the French and English versions of the judgment. The Commission
gave no criteria for deciding how viable Microsoft's rivals in producing work
group servers had to be made, how much interaction was required between servers
and the Windows operating system to make other suppliers of servers sufficiently
viable, or how much Microsoft might charge for the technical information. Yet the
decision was confirmed as containing adequate reasoning. Amongst other articles,
see the analysis by the former President of the CFI.[47] – who distanced himself from
the majority opinion – and several articles by Ian Forrester, who represented
Microsoft.[48]

One aspect of the judgment that worries me is that the CFI established the
means of controlling Commission decisions, by requiring that they be adequately
reasoned. It seems to me that the main 'reason' given by the CFI was a reference to
the unknowable: how viable must competitors downstream be made? How much
information is needed for that and at what price? If the judgment of the CFI is
followed, the CFI will have little control if the Commission goes wrong again. Is
the CFI or the Commission more likely to make a proper appraisal?

2.   *Syfait II*[49] *v. GSK Aeve*

Syfait I did not lead to a conclusion, because the ECJ denied jurisdiction to give a
preliminary ruling as it did not accept that the Greek authority was sufficiently
independent of the Minister to constitute a 'court or tribunal'. We expected to wait
for years to read the views of the ECJ. In fact, however, the Greek competition
authority gave a ruling somewhat on the lines of the opinion of AG Jacobs. This
was appealed eventually to the Greek administrative court of appeal, which asked
the same questions of the ECJ. GSK AEVE is a subsidiary of GSK, and the
plaintiffs were members of Syfait: a trade association of Greek wholesalers of
medicines. For three or four months over Christmas 2000, GSK AEVE stopped
supplying the wholesalers, and supplied the clinics and hospitals directly, but it did

---

46. See Philip Marsden, 'Unfair and Unreasonable – The Commission is Demanding that Microsoft
     License Its Intellectual Property to Its Rivals for Nothing', *Competition Law Insight* 6 (2007): 3.
47. <www.icc.qmul.ac.uk/GAR/Vesterdorf.pdf>.
48. I. Forrester, 'Articles 82: Remedies in Search of Theories?', in *International Antitrust Law and
     Policy*, ed. B. Hawk, Fordham Corporate Law Institute (2005), 167, 177.
49. *Sot.Lelos kai Sia EE and others v. GlaxoSmithKline AEVE (Syfait 2)* 16 Sep. 2008 C468/06 to
     C-478/06.

not supply as much as was wanted. GSK AEVE accepted that its motive in so doing was to limit the parallel trade.

GSK AEVE argued:

(1) Intra brand competition did not function for medicines in Greece because of the national regulations controlling prices and requiring it to supply wherever it was authorised to do so (paragraph 41). GSK AEVE's acceptance of the price negotiated with the authorities did not enable it to recover all its fixed costs.

(2) Parallel trade reduced its profits and the amount it could invest in research and development (paragraph 44).

(3) Parallel trade brought few benefits to consumers, as most of the benefit of the price differences between Member States was taken by the parallel traders (paragraph 45).

The ECJ ruled (paragraph 53) that the parallel trade to the countries where prices were higher must have provided some benefits to consumers there. The imports must have exercised some pressure on prices. In many cases not concerning medicines, the ECJ has confirmed the condemnation of agreements isolating national markets (paragraph 65). The competition rules apply to the sector, but the national regulation is relevant (paragraph 67).

69 . . . A pharmaceutical company in a dominant position must be able to take steps that are reasonable and in proportion to the need to protect its own commercial interests.

This statement has been repeated in virtually every case under Article 82 since *United Brands Company and United Brands Continentaal BV v. Commission.*[50]

To see if the steps are reasonable and proportionate the national court must ascertain whether, in the light of the size of their orders and their previous business relations, the wholesalers were acting out of the ordinary (paragraph 70). The ECJ should not tell the national court what to do, but only rule on the points of law. This leaves the difficult questions to the national court that sought a reference to the ECJ.

3.   The Commission Guidance on Enforcement Priorities[51]

The Commission has been unhappy about the cases in 1970 when the ECJ was concerned about the ability of Community firms to enter a market of their choice,

---

50. (27/76), (1978) ECR 207, (1978) 1 CMLR 429, CMR 8429.
51. Com 2008, 3 Dec. 2008, <http://ec.europa.eu/competition/antitrust/art82/guidance.pdf>, to be published in all Community languages in the OJ, when the language versions have been checked by the jurist linguists. It is likely that the Commission will follow them. It may be expected to encourage national competition authorities to do so, but it is unclear how far national judges will do so. Since most Art. 82 cases are dealt with by the Commission, the guidelines should be important, and may even be followed by ECJ and CFI, although the Courts are clearly not bound by them.

and imposed a special responsibility on dominant firms not to prevent this.[52] The Commission's secretariat published a discussion paper on Article 82, but a judgment of the ECJ in *British Airways*, C-95/04 P, was thought possibly to be inconsistent with the discussion paper. So it was thought wrong to issue guidelines that might be inconsistent with recent case law of the ECJ. The Commission decided, instead, to issue guidance on its enforcement priorities.

From paragraph 74, the guidance treats refusal to supply and margin-squeeze as if they amount to a single practice. Consequently, margin-squeeze will be treated as abusive only if the exceptional circumstances required to condemn a refusal to supply prevail. This I welcome. The Court had defined margin-squeezes only in terms of selling at retail at a price that did not permit an efficient wholesaler to operate profitably. In fact all the cases concerned markets where the incumbent had invested at a time when it had exclusive licenses from the EC or from national governments, which ensured that the market was not competitive. I am delighted that margin-squeeze will be treated as abusive, only in similar circumstances.

At paragraph 74, the Commission states that firms, whether dominant or not, should generally have the right to choose their trading partners and to dispose freely of their property. An obligation to supply or license, even for fair remuneration, may undermine a firm's incentive to invest and innovate and thereby possibly harm consumers.

> 75 Typically competition problems arise when the dominant undertaking competes on the 'downstream' market with the buyer whom it refuses to supply.

This is the only situation dealt with by the guidance.

> 80. The Commission will consider these practices as an enforcement priority if the following circumstances are present:
>
> – the refusal relates to a product or service that is objectively necessary to be able to compete effectively on a downstream market;
> – the refusal is likely to lead to the elimination of effective competition on the downstream market;
> – the refusal is likely to lead to consumer harm.

The tenor of this section of the guidance reassures IPR holders that the Commission will seldom require the firm to supply or license except in very exceptional circumstances.

I.   INDUSTRY STANDARDS

We await case law relating to industry standards. In *IMS*[53] the Commission had referred to the maps that were the subject of copyright as being a de facto industry

---

52. *Nederlandsche Banden-Industrie Michelin v. Commission* (322/81), (1983) ECR 3461, para. 57.
53. See Section III.F, above.

standard. The Commission considers that when an association draws up an industry standard to make it easier for members to connect their products with those of others, there should be a duty to permit access on *fair, reasonable and non-discriminatory* (FRAND) terms. It required access to Microsoft's copyright software on FRAND terms. Often when negotiating a standard, the members certify that they have no IPR in the standard, or that they will grant access on FRAND terms.[54] Sometimes the parties promise to give access and state the level of royalty and other conditions. The law has lagged behind the practice. Suppose that on reading the terms, the members decide to pursue different technology and develop a different standard. I hope this will not be treated as an illegal collective boycott of the first, but as a reasonable and proportionate response to unsatisfactory terms offered by a joint venturer.

It is often impossible to invent around an industry standard, so compulsory access may be particularly important. The dominant firm may be required not to discriminate in favor of its own subsidiary, but this is no long term solution, as it could raise the price paid by a wholly-owned subsidiary and enable the group to charge outsiders more. The most intractable problem is what terms are fair.

If it is the monopoly value of the right, it would give access to newcomers only if they were already more efficient than the incumbent, or expected to be so shortly. Often newcomers have higher costs as they climb up the learning curve and develop a reputation. Unless the terms exceed the cost of negotiating and drafting the terms of access, the holder's incentive to create the facility disappears altogether. In any event it is reduced. Where in between these two limits should the price be considered reasonable. This is the kind of problem that is probably better solved by legislation than trial-and-error in the courts.

J.   CONCLUSION

There are now four situations when a duty for a dominant firm to supply may arise:

(1) when access is required by a former customer to prevent a dominant firm extending its dominance to a neighboring market and is essential if the former customer is to carry on its business (the early cases from *Commercial Solvents*[55] to *Télémarketing*[56] and *Tetrapak II.*[57] Either consumer harm

---

54. There is little case law about FRAND terms, but see the Commission's Guidelines on the applicability of Art. 81 to horizontal cooperation, OJ 2001, C3/2, (2001) 4 CMLR 819.

55. *Istituto Chemioterapico Italiano SpA and Commercial Solvents Corp v. Commission* (6 & 7/73), 6 Mar. 1974, (1974) ECR 223, (1974) 1 CMLR 309, CMR 8209.

56. *Télémarketing Centre Belge d'Etudes du Marché-Télémarketing SA (CBEM) v. Compagnie Luxembourgeoise de Télédiffusion* (311/84), 3 Oct. 1985, (1985) ECR 3261, (1986) 2 CMLR 558, CMR 14246.

57. *Tetra Pak International SA v. EC Commission* (C-333/94 P), 14 Nov. 1996, (1996) ECR I-5951, (1997) 4 CMLR 662, (1997) CEC 186.

within Article 82(b) or discrimination as between equivalent transactions within Article 82(c) would probably have to be established;

(2) when the license is required by an undertaking, not necessarily a former customer, who intends to make a new product for which there is actual or potential demand, provided that the input is essential for producing such a product (*Volvo, Magill, Bronner, IMS*); in this event discrimination is unlikely and consumer harm should be established under Article 82(b);[58]

(3) when it can plausibly be argued that the obligation arises because supply is limited with an intention to limit parallel trade (*Syfait*);

(4) when a legal or de facto industry standard is protected by IPRs. This seems to be the view of the Commission in its decisions in *IMS* and in *Microsoft*.

These categories are probably not closed. From the Commission's decisions in *IMS* and *Microsoft* and from the opinion in *Syfait*, it may also be argued that all four classes of refusal may be objectively justified in the light of the specific circumstances of the industry. The justifications vary depending on the specific facts of the case.

Much remains to be decided about the duty to grant access. The Commission still fails to decide the criteria on the basis of which a charge for access may be made, but provides only a mechanism for someone else to settle the price in case of dispute – a formula that did not work in *IMS* – and the extent of access that was contentious in *Microsoft*.

In other recent cases,[59] the CFI has required the Commission to find that the essential facility is really necessary. It is arguable that, where a facility has been paid for by the state, it would be particularly difficult for a new entrant to duplicate the facility.[60] So, a duty to supply may be greater than for firms in the private sector. Moreover, the need to protect incentives to investment is less important for investment by the government or aided by exclusive rights. This distinction may account for the Commission's use of the doctrine in relation to sea- and airports that have often been developed by the public sector.

---

58. See above, fn. 2.
59. E.g., *European Night Services v. Commission* (T-374, 375, 384 & 388/94) (1998) ECR II-3141.
60. See AG Jacobs in *Oscar Bronner*, para. 66. (See above, fn. 20.)

Subject Index

Case Index

OTHER PUBLICATIONS RESULTING FROM THE IEEM
INTERNATIONAL INTELLECTUAL PROPERTY PROGRAMMES

1. Intellectual Property in the Digital Age – Challenges for Asia *Christopher Heath and Anselm Kamperman Sanders (eds.)* Published by Kluwer Law International 2001 ISBN 90-411-9847-4
2. Intellectual Property in the Bio-Medical Age – Challenges for Asia *Christopher Heath and Anselm Kamperman Sanders (eds.)* Published by Kluwer Law International 2003 ISBN 90-411-9926-8
3. New Frontiers of Intellectual Property Law *Christopher Heath and Anselm Kamperman Sanders (eds.)* Published by Hart Publishing 2005 ISBN 1-84113-538-0
4. Intellectual Property and Free Trade Agreements *Christopher Heath and Anselm Kamperman Sanders (eds.)* Published by Hart Publishing 2007 ISBN 978-1-84113-801-5
5. Spares, Repairs and Intellectual Property Rights *Christopher Heath and Anselm Kamperman Sanders (eds.)* Published by Kluwer Law International 2009 ISBN 978-90-411-3136-2